## ABOUT THE AUTHOR

Christopher Barnatt is a futurist, keynote speaker and freelance academic. For 25 years he lectured in computing and future studies at the University of Nottingham, and now runs ExplainingComputers.com, ExplainingTheFuture.com and their associated YouTube channels. He also works for a range of clients across industries that include the arts, food production, financial services, healthcare and logistics.

By the same author:

## BOOKS

*3D Printing: Third Edition*
*The Next Big Thing: From 3D Printing to Mining the Moon*
*3D Printing: Second Edition*
*3D Printing: The Next Industrial Revolution*
*Seven Ways to Fix the World*
*25 Things You Need to Know About the Future*
*A Brief Guide to Cloud Computing*
*Valueware: Technology, Humanity and Organization*
*Challenging Reality: In Search of the Future Organization*
*Management Strategy & Information Technology*
*Cyber Business: Mindsets for a Wired Age*
*The Computers in Business Blueprint*

## YOUTUBE CHANNELS

YouTube.com/ExplainingComputers
YouTube.com/ExplainingTheFuture

## WEBSITES

ExplainingTheFuture.com
ExplainingComputers.com

# DIGITAL GENESIS

The Future of Computing,
Robots and AI

Christopher Barnatt

ExplainingComputers.com

First published by ExplainingComputers.com

For press, rights, translation and other enquiries,
please e-mail press@explainingcomputers.com

Copyright © Christopher Barnatt 2017.

The right of Christopher Barnatt to be identified as the author of this work has been asserted by him in accordance with the Copyright, Designs and Patents Act 1988.

All rights reserved. This book is sold subject to the condition that it shall not, by way of trade or otherwise, be lent, re-sold, hired out or otherwise circulated in any form of binding or cover other than that in which it is published and without a similar condition including this condition being imposed on the subsequent purchaser.

ISBN-10 : 1-9760-9806-2
ISBN-13 : 978-1-9760-9806-2

Printed and bound on demand.

Typeset in Adobe InDesign by Christopher Barnatt.

### Disclaimer
While every effort has been made to ensure that the content in this book is as accurate as possible, no warranty or fitness is implied. All trademarks included in this book are appropriately capitalized and no attempt is made or implied to supersede the rights of their respective owners.

1 3 5 7 9 10 8 6 4 2

To Mum & Dad

# CONTENTS

| | |
|---|---|
| Acknowledgements | ix |
| Preface: Cyber Business | 1 |
| 1. The Computing Machine | 7 |
| 2. Digital Transformation | 49 |
| 3. The Dawn of AI | 91 |
| 4. Robot Horizons | 135 |
| 5. Quantum & Organic Frontiers | 170 |
| 6. Cyborg Fusion | 199 |
| References | 224 |
| Index | 238 |

# ACKNOWLEDGEMENTS

*Digital Genesis* is my thirteenth and quite possibly my final book. Certainly I have no immediate plans to begin another work of this length, with my future intention being to focus on producing videos and short-form written content. Here I would therefore like to thank those who have supported and influenced not only this particular tome, but all of my books. It has been quite a journey.

Firstly, thanks to Henrik Nilsson for a conversation that fundamentally re-shaped what you are about to read, and to the National Museum of Computing for allowing me to film some of their amazing collection. A great many thanks also to Kathleen Visser for her meticulous proof reading and help with my books over the last four years.

Less specifically, thanks to all of those I once worked with at the University of Nottingham. These individuals include former heads of department Brian Chiplin, Ian Gow and Alistair Bruce, all of whom were very supportive of my rather unusual if productive take on academia. Other former colleagues I would like to particularly thank are Teresa Bee, Tracey Bettinson, Bob Berry, Wendy Chapple, Thomas Chesney, James Devlin, Christine Ennew, Suzana Grubnic, Sally Hopkinson, Sallie Kirk, George Kuk, Andrea O'Mahony, Steve Moore, Gina Rogers, Duncan Shaw, Ken Starkey, Sue Tempest, Steve Upcraft, Tony Watson, Kieran Woodward and Victoria Wrigley.

From the wonderful world of traditional publishing, I would also like to thank Diane Van Bakel, Ingmar Folkmans, Leo Hollis, Diane Taylor and Howard Watson.

As I head toward the end of this list, a massive nod of appreciation to Mark Daintree, Stephen Diacon, Deborah Kong and Nicholas Browne for their support over many years. Finally, thanks to Margaret Hiscox, to my sister Helen, and to my parents for too many things to list.

If I do ever write another book, I guess I may sign it off by also thanking a future robot or AI. But as I am not currently going to acknowledge the assistance of either Google Docs or an Intel processor, it is now time for the *Preface*.

# PREFACE
# CYBER BUSINESS

In 1984 science fiction author William Gibson published his first novel. Entitled *Neuromancer*, this envisaged a future in which people worked and spent leisure time in the virtual reality of 'cyberspace'. Gibson described cyberspace as the electronic 'consensual hallucination experienced daily by billions'. His hero, Case, even had a 'cranial jack' that allowed him to directly connect his brain to the global digital matrix.

*Neuromancer* inspired a lot of people to start thinking about the online realm. One of those individuals was myself, and in the Summer of 1994 I finished writing a book called *The Cyber Business* that predicted a future awash with virtual communities and e-commerce. Manuscript complete, I began ringing up publishers, and quickly discovered two things. Firstly, that few editors understood what I meant by 'doing business in cyberspace'. And secondly, that it would have been far easier to sell a book called *The Cider Business* about the apple-based alcoholic drink.

Fortunately, toward the end of 1994 my luck improved. In fact, following twelve rejections, two publishers actually ended up competing for the rights to my work. In the Spring of 1995, *Cyber Business: Mindsets for a Wired Age* was subsequently released and rode the very start of the Dot Com wave. It even got some coverage in the *Financial Times*.

Eleven books and twenty-two years later, *Digital Genesis* marks my return to writing in depth about the future of computing and the online realm. So far, most of what I predicted in *Cyber Business* has come true, with goods and services regularly purchased online, a wireless computing device in over two billion hands, and social lives orchestrated by what I then termed 'personal virtual networks'. Without doubt, over the past two decades computers and the Internet have dramatically altered many aspects of our lives. Even so, as we shall see across this book, the most radical digital transformations are yet to come.

## SYNTHETIC CITIZENS

So just what are those computational watersheds that lie ahead? Well, for a start, artificial intelligence (AI) is widely expected to be the Next Big Thing. This means that, in as little as five years, a lot of dumb computing interfaces are going to be replaced with chatbots, digital assistants and other smart AIs. These will allow us to communicate with digital technologies by speaking or typing in English or any other human language, with the system able to speak or write back.

Already many people are familiar with first-generation AI interfaces such as Amazon's Alexa, Apple's Siri, Microsoft's Cortana and Google Assistant. Today these are often dismissed as a gimmick. But they really should not be ignored, as by the early 2020s the next generation of AI interfaces is going to be very useful indeed.

As chatbots and digital assistants develop, many organizations will adopt them as their main customer interface. Indeed, according to a March 2017 survey from Accenture, by 2020 most bankers expect AIs to be 'their primary method for interacting with customers'. This will, I expect, prove to be a pretty accurate prediction – and not only in banking. Just as, 20 years ago, the world-wide web was poised to transform organizational interfaces, so today AI is set to do exactly the same thing.

In addition to becoming a common means of accessing business services, over the next decade AIs will start to take on many professional jobs. Until this point in time, accountants, doctors, lawyers and most managers have held positions that could not be automated. But in the 2020s this will no longer be the case.

Future AIs will also take control of many machines that currently require a human operator. By 2025, an increasing number of products are therefore destined to be produced in 'dark factories' manned entirely by robots. Within 15 years, the majority of new automobiles, trucks and tractors are also likely to be equipped with AIs that will allow them to drive themselves. By the early 2030s, I even anticipate that tens of millions of humanoid robots will be labouring at tasks that are no longer considered cost-effective or safe enough to be undertaken by a person.

The implications of the next wave of automation on human employment could be very stark indeed. This said, the data analysis skills of future AIs should help us to optimize our use of increasingly scarce resources. Equally beneficial will be the improvements in engineering and medicine that will arise from the cognitive abilities of future AIs. In fact, to solve challenges such as climate change and mass antibiotic resistance, we may have no choice but to turn to the promise and power of AI.

## QUANTUM & ORGANIC TECHNOLOGY

In addition to the rise of AI and robots, another digital transformation will be the evolution of next generation hardware. Today, computers are based on inorganic microprocessors that contain millions or billions of miniature transistors. These have served us well for many years, and will remain in use for the foreseeable future. Even so, over the coming decades we should expect traditional computers to be complemented by hardware based on quantum and even organic components.

Quantum computers process data not in binary bits, but using quantum mechanical 'qubits'. As we will see in chapter 5, IBM, Google, Microsoft and others are now investing in quantum computing research and development, with commercial systems a realistic possibility in the late 2020s.

Further into the future, developments in organic technology may allow the brains and bodies of some future computers and robots to be fashioned from living 'wetware', rather than semiconductors, metals and plastics. Perhaps by the 2040s, autonomous vehicles may also be organically grown. This is, after all, how autonomous vehicles were manufactured in the past (when we used to call them horses).

Already practitioners of the new science of synthetic biology (SynBio) are learning how to digitally manufacture things from modular DNA components. For at least 200,000 years, the most sophisticated computers on the planet have been the 86-billion-neuron blobs of wetware that we call 'human brains'. As synthetic biology advances, the odds are therefore in favour of at least some of tomorrow's computers being organic.

## HUMANITY 2.0

While AI, robots and next-generation hardware offer incredible possibilities, the ultimate digital transformation will be the fusion of computers with the human body. In April 2017, Tesla and SpaceX CEO Elon Musk announced a new company called Neuralink that is 'developing ultra high bandwidth brain-machine interfaces'. While this venture is in its very early stages, Neuralink is far from alone in its ambition to directly link people with artificial digital technology. By the 2040s, we may therefore have computers installed inside our heads.

In addition to allowing people to enter cyberspace using direct brain interfaces, future 'cyborg fusion' may one day allow the human body to be digitally upgraded. Already extraordinary progress in synthetic biology, genetic medicine and nanotechnology point to a future in which our own physical forms – and all other organic matter – will be able to be digitally programmed. Such programming will lie far beyond the limits of any human individual or team thereof. But it is going to be child's play for some future AIs.

Long before AIs learn how to reprogram human biology, our race looks certain to have irrevocably melded with digital machines. Even today, millions of people find it traumatic to function in the absence of a computer. Not least the smartphone has rapidly evolved into a critical prosthesis, while both our economy and our culture have become reliant on the Internet. To suggest that we will sooner or later physically merge with artificial computing systems is therefore hardly a radical proposition. This book's examination of the future of computing, robots and AI is therefore also an exploration of the future of ourselves.

## BEYOND THE INTERNET

Around 375 million years ago our ancestors dragged themselves out of the oceans. Critical to their success in this venture was the innovation of a new, organic technology called 'lungs' that remains vital to our survival to this day. This said, few people would dispute that the 'Breathing Air Revolution' is now well and truly over. A very long time ago we not only developed lungs, but learnt how to live in a new way while using them, and so moved on to greater innovations.

To embrace the revolutions of the future we need to accept the ending of the revolutions of the past. As I mentioned a few pages back, I got in early on the whole cyberspace thing. But I firmly believe that the Internet Revolution is now over.

Granted, it is over in the same way that the Breathing Air Revolution is over, with both Internet usage and the inhaling of air remaining vital for our survival in the modern world. But just as the development of lungs is no longer a radical innovation in progress, so the continued evolution of the Internet is likely to prove relatively insignificant. This book will therefore not concern itself with the future of social media and the world-wide web.

Instead, and at a far more fundamental level, the following chapters explore the scope and scale of the most radical digital revolutions of the next few decades. Right now, we stand on the brink of a new age of digital genesis that will shake our civilization to its core. And, for better or for worse, it is going to be truly extraordinary.

Christopher Barnatt,
September 2017.

# 1
# THE COMPUTING MACHINE

In May 2017 I visited Bletchley Park in the United Kingdom. Here, during WWII, military codebreakers made pioneering developments in computing. Today, Bletchley Park is maintained as a site of international historic importance. It is also home to the National Museum of Computing, where they have painstakingly rebuilt and restored several very early computers.

Pride of place in the National Museum is taken by a recreation of Colossus. As pictured in figure 1.1, this was one of the world's first electronic computers, and was used to help decipher encrypted radio communications. The original machine was designed and built by a man called Tommy Flowers, and attacked its first scrambled message in February 1944. A Mark 2 Colossus was then developed, and by the end of the war 10 Colossus computers were being used by the codebreakers at Bletchley Park.

As its name implies, Colossus is a large and imposing piece of technology. To my surprise, it is also quite a noisy contraption. In part this is because it has no electronic memory, and hence has to be constantly fed data from a continuous loop of rapidly-circulating paper tape. Each tape contains up to 25,000 5-bit characters, and travels around a set of wheels and pulleys at up to 27 miles per hour.

In addition to the whirr of its paper tape, Colossus emits a deep, repetitive 'clunk' as its relays cycle. The aggregate sound is almost hypnotic. Indeed, when you stand next to the machine, you can almost feel its mechanical pulse resonating out from the past, and deep into our computing future.

## LEARNING FROM PIONEERS

At the end of the *Preface* I stated that the Internet Revolution is over, and that to embrace the future we need to accept its passing. While I absolutely believe this to be the case, it would be strange in a book called *Digital Genesis* not to delve into computing history. As Colossus highlights, WWII codebreakers used early electronic technologies to achieve amazing things that were at the time beyond most people's comprehension. In the decades ahead, we are due for a similar round of digital innovation that many will find hard to believe. An excursion into the history of computing may therefore provide a useful reminder of just how frequently the apparently impossible has already morphed into digital reality.

Many historians and textbooks divide the history of computing into four or five generations, with each of these associated with a specific technology. So, for example, 'first generation' computing is generally accepted to have taken place between the early 1940s and the mid 1950s, and to have involved electronic computers that were based on vacuum tubes.

Computing's 'second generation' then spanned from the mid 1950s to the mid 1960s, and involved systems whose circuits were built from individual transistors. The development of integrated circuit (IC) technology next allowed multiple transistors to be manufactured on a single chip, so giving rise to IC-based 'third generation' computers from the mid 1960s to the early 1970s.

**Figure 1.1: The Reconstructed Colossus at the National Museum of Computing.**

The early 1970s heralded a 'fourth generation' of computing based around microprocessors, and which arguably continues to this day. However, in 1982, the Japanese Ministry of International Trade and Industry proposed a 'fifth generation' focused on AI and natural language systems. Quite when and if this began continues to be debated. Which all means that today, we are either at the end of the fourth generation of computing, or at the start of the fifth.

## THE FIVE AGES OF COMPUTING

Until the early-to-mid 1990s, the four/five generations model of computing history served its purpose as a reasonable analytical tool. Yet since that time, it has become evident that any categorization of the evolution and impact of computing needs to be based on more than a measure of its underlying hardware. Within this book, I have therefore chosen to distinguish five 'ages of computing'. As illustrated in figure 1.2, these inevitably and rightly overlap. It is also important to understand that each of the five ages is distinguished by its focus on *additional* digital capabilities, rather than the replacement of what has gone before.

At the top of the figure we have the Early Computing Age. This began with the invention of the earliest mechanical calculators, was catalyzed by the construction of the first electronic computers in the early 1940s, and began to draw to a close in the mid 1970s. During all of this period computing was a minority, elite activity, with no personal computers in existence, and only large organizations able to invest in non-human computational resources.

From the mid 1970s onwards we had the arrival of the Personal Computing Age. During the following couple of decades most forms of media started to go digital, and computing became a mainstream human activity. The use of mainframes and other large computers did advance considerably during this period. Nevertheless, it was the rise of personal computing that was most significant in the 1980s and 1990s, with over a billion PCs entering commercial and domestic use.

Just before the turn of the millennium, the arrival of the public and business Internet heralded the dawn of the Network Computing Age. This current slice of computing evolution continues to be characterised by mass digital interconnection and widespread interpersonal communication. To this end it has seen a growing addiction to mobile computer hardware, including laptops, tablets and smartphones.

Looking ahead, I predict that the period between about 2020 to 2040 will be the Cognitive Computing Age, with the next two decades characterised by the mass application of AI. In particular, during the Cognitive Computing Age we will witness a transition away from dumb computer systems, and toward smart 'attentive computers' that will anticipate human needs. Almost certainly, many of these attentive computers will be robots that will work and play with us in the physical world.

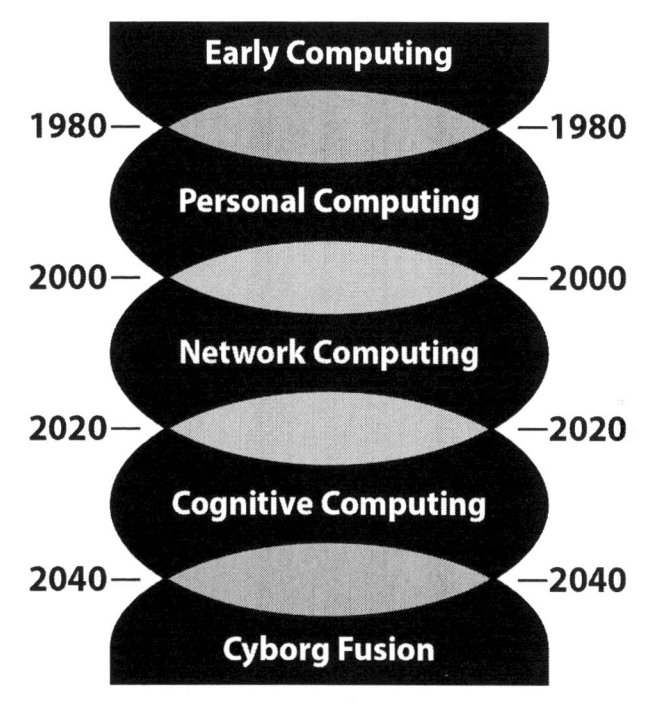

**Figure 1.2: The Five Ages of Computing**

Finally, speculating even further into the future, I predict that around 2040 we will enter the era of Cyborg Fusion. This means that, a little over 20 years from now, it will become increasingly common for human beings to be directly augmented with digital technology. Beyond 2040, it will therefore become difficult to separate some computers from their users.

To provide a foundation for the rest of this book, the remainder of this chapter explores each of the Five Ages of Computing. Along the way it also charts the origins of key players in the computing industry, including IBM, Apple, Microsoft, Amazon, Google and Facebook. All of these companies are likely to play an important role in shaping our digital future, and I will report on their endeavours throughout this book. It is therefore wise for us to gain some understanding of their early beginnings.

## THE EARLY COMPUTING AGE

A 'computer' is technically any device capable of undertaking computation. For thousands of years human beings have sought to make such contraptions, with the abacus in use by the Mesopotamians as early as 3000 BC. However, it was not until 1642 that the first mechanical adding machine was constructed by French scientist and tax collector Blasé Pascal.

The next significant development came in 1823, when Cambridge professor Charles Babbage designed his famous 'Difference Engine'. This was intended to assist in the calculation of astronomical, ballistics and engineering tables to an accuracy of up to twenty decimal places. But unfortunately, due to problems with funding and engineering accuracy, Babbage never managed to construct operational hardware. In fact it took until 1990 for Babbage's vision to be vindicated, when a team of researchers at the London Science Museum used his blueprints to build a working Difference Engine. The completed machine has over 4,000 iron, bronze and steel parts and weighs three tonnes.

By 1837, Babbage had designed an even more ambitious mechanical computing device called the 'Analytic Engine'. This used punched cards for data and program storage – a technique which had been pioneered in 1804 by Joseph-Marie Jacquard in the automation of mechanical weaving looms.

The use of interchangeable punched cards to store instructions for the Analytic Engine resulted in the development of computer programming. In fact Lady Ada Augusta – who worked on the Analytic Engine with Babbage – developed several coding techniques that remain in use today.

Sadly, attempts to build a working Analytic Engine were again frustrated by the accuracy of available fabrication methods. It is also worth keeping this historical fact firmly in mind. Why? Well simply because the world is awash with sceptics who will try and convince you that intelligent humanoid robots, organic biocomputers and many other predicted computing developments will never actually arrive. So please remember Charles Babbage and Ada Augusta as pioneers *whose computing innovations lay ahead of the manufacturing capabilities of their era*. Great ideas in computing often arrive ahead of the requisite technology, and should not be dismissed because hardware and software have yet to catch up.

Following Babbage, in 1887 American inventor Dorr Eugene Felt patented a simple mechanical calculator called the 'Comptometer'. This was commercially developed by William Sears-Burroughs, who added a printing mechanism. The machine was then adopted by the United States Treasury, and became the most widely used accounting machine of the early 20th century.

Another pioneer of mechanical computing was Herman Hollerith, who developed an electromechanical data processing machine that once again stored data on punched cards. By the early 20th century this was being developed and marketed by a consortium known as the Computer Tabulating-Recording Company, or C-T-R. In 1914, C-T-R took on a new General Manager called Thomas John Watson, who ten years later changed the name of the company to International Business Machines or 'IBM'.

By the early 1940s, electromechanical hardware was becoming increasingly sophisticated. Not least, in 1941 German engineer Konrad Zuse started a business that developed and sold a number of electromechanical computers. These included models known as the Z3 and Z4, which used thousands of relays to perform calculations. Meanwhile, a machine called the Bombe was built at Bletchley Park. Devised and constructed by computing pioneers Alan Turing and Harold Keen, this was used to help decode secret German messages encrypted with an Enigma cipher machine.

Across the Atlantic, in 1944 a 3,500 relay electromechanical device known as the Automatic Sequence Controlled Calculator was delivered to Harvard University. This was based on plans initially drawn up in 1937 by graduate student Howard H. Aiken, and was constructed by IBM. Later known as the 'Harvard Mark 1', it remained in service with the United States Navy until 1959.

### *The Electronic Revolution*

All of the aforementioned machines used mechanical mechanisms (like gears and rotating cylinders) and/or electrical components (such as relays) to achieve calculation. Such computing devices may hence seem very primitive today. Nevertheless, they laid the foundations for the first hardware that processed data using electronic components.

The very first electronic computer is generally accepted to be the Atanasoff-Berry Computer (ABC), which was designed and built in Iowa by Professor John Vincent Atanasoff and his student Clifford Berry between 1939 and 1942. The machine was created solely to solve linear equations, and was not a programmable device.

It is fairly broadly agreed that the first electronic computers that were also *programmable* were the Colossus machines used at Bletchley Park in 1944 and 1945. Like the ABC, these were single-application computers, as they were specifically designed to help decrypt German High Command messages that had been encrypted with a Lorenz cipher machine. Yet critically, Colossus operators could set switches to program desired algorithms and other application parameters. In total, over five billion switch and plug settings were available.

Like all of the early electronic computers that followed them, the Colossus machines were based on vacuum tubes (also known as thermionic valves). These control the flow of an electric current between two or more electrodes contained in a sealed glass housing from which the air has been evacuated. The prototype, Mark 1 Colossus had about 1,600 vacuum tubes, and the Mark 2 about 2,500.

Another early programmable, electronic computer was the ENIAC or 'Electronic Numerical Integrator and Computer'. This was completed at the University of Pennsylvania in 1946, and was used to calculate ballistics tables for the US Army. The mighty machine was based on 18,000 vacuum tubes, and was programmed by manually setting the position of about 6,000 switches.

Having to painstakingly reset so many controls to perform a different type of calculation made ENIAC rather inflexible. Consequently, John von Neumann – a collaborator on the project – deduced that if a computer could store its own program in internal memory, it would become far more versatile. This revelation resulted in the creation of the first stored-program computers. These included the EDVAC (Electronic Discrete Variable Automatic Computer), which began construction in the United States in 1946, and the EDSAC (Electronic Delay Storage Automatic Calculator), which started to be built in 1947 in England. Both machines ran their first programs in 1949.

The EDVAC was used in the US Army's Ballistics Research Laboratory, while EDSAC worked in the Cambridge University Mathematical Laboratory. As illustrated in figure 1.3, when I visited the National Museum of Computing they were building a reconstruction of the EDSAC. Like the original, this will have about 140 shelves of vacuum tube electronics supported across 12 racks, and will weigh about two tonnes. This hardware provides an EDSAC with about 1,000 words (or roughly three kilobytes) of memory, and the ability to process about 650 instructions per second. Given that some desktop PCs can now process over 33 billion instructions per second, the EDSAC was not that powerful in modern terms. This said, as a man working on its reconstruction told me, 'this is a computer where you can walk inside the processor'.

The EDVAC and EDSAC catalyzed the development of the first programmable, electronic computers built for business rather than military or scientific purposes. These notably included the UNIVAC 1 (UNIVersal Automatic Computer 1), which in June 1951 was delivered to the US Census Bureau, and LEO (or the 'Lyons Electronic Office'). The latter was built for Lyons in the United Kingdom, where it ran the payroll for a chain of tea houses. Lyons had provided support for the building of EDSAC, and were rewarded with the first computer to run a commercial data processing application.

### *The Power of the Transistor*

LEO, UNIVAC and similar computers were, like their forebears, based on vacuum tubes. This kept the machines large and power hungry, with significant downtime required to replace broken components. But then, in the 1950s, computing started to change dramatically with the introduction of the transistor as a small, low-power and far more reliable replacement for the vacuum tube.

The initial prototype transistor was built at the Bell Labs in the United States in 1947. It then took several years to commercialize, with the first products that included transistors released in the early 1950s. By 1958, the first all-transistor computer (the TX-0) was completed in the Lincoln Labs of the Massachusetts Institute of Technology (MIT) in the United States. The TX-0 was also one of the first computers to be equipped with a monitor screen, and remained in use until 1975.

Figure 1.3: The Reconstruction of the EDSAC at the National Museum of Computing.

In October 1959, IBM announced its '1401 Data Processing System'. This all-transistor, mainframe computer was marketed as the 'first affordable general-purpose computer'. The advertising strap line also proved to be correct, with IBM receiving 5,200 orders in the first five weeks, and eventually supplying over 10,000 1401 systems. The cost was a $2,500 a month rental fee, and by the mid-1960s almost half of the world's computers were IBM 1401 models.

Alongside hardware developments, the late 1950s and early 1960s saw the introduction of 'assembly languages'. These made computers easier to program, as they used abbreviations to represent computer instructions, rather than reams of numbers. In 1959, the first 'high level language' (HLL) was also introduced. Known as COBOL (the COmmon Business Orientated Language), this allowed programmers to write software using English-style instructions that were then 'compiled' into the final application. Today most computer programming continues to take place in similar high-level languages, such as C++.

Following the transistor, the next major hardware milestone was the introduction of the integrated circuit (IC). This was invented by Jack Kilby at Texas Instruments, who was searching for a method that would allow complex circuits to be created without the hassle of having to solder each individual component together.

Kilby's breakthrough was to realize that all of the transistors, resistors, capacitors and wiring required in many circuits could be made from the same material, and manufactured in situ to form a complete, interconnected circuit. This is achieved using ultraviolet light to project images of circuit layers onto a plastic film atop a silicon wafer. Chemical vapours, heat, ion beams and various other materials and methods are then used to develop the exposed images into tiny electronic components and conductive wiring.

Kilby demonstrated the first working IC in September 1958. As with many previous computing innovations, the earliest adopters were the military, with the first computers that used 'silicon chips' being supplied to the United States Air Force in 1961. Texas Instruments then capitalized on integrated circuits to make the first pocket calculators, so opening up a mass market.

As IC technology developed, 'large scale integration' (LSI) allowed large arrays of electronic components to be included on a single chip. Such large arrays of transistors allowed the development of random access memory (RAM) chips, with each transistor able to store a value of '1' or '0'.

Before RAM chips existed, computers had relied on magnetic 'core' storage, with hundreds or thousands of tiny ferrous rings laced on a matrix of thin wires. Each of these cores could be magnetized or demagnetized to store either a '1' or a '0'. This worked, but core storage was bulky, heavy and very expensive. So it was not until the invention of IC

RAM chips that large amounts of memory became a realistic possibility.

You may not be surprised to learn that IBM was quick to market with a computer based on IC technology. Specifically, in April 1964, the company introduced a mainframe called the System/360 (S/360). This used 'hybrid integrated circuits' that encapsulated many discrete components in glass or plastic. IBM's process for making hybrid ICs became known as 'solid logic technology' (SLT), and resulted in many technological innovations.

At a stroke, the System/360 replaced all five of IBM's existing product lines with one strictly compatible family. The System/360 also pioneered the processing of data in the eight-bit 'bytes' that are still used in computing today.

In addition to capitalizing on IC technology, the System/360 was revolutionary because it allowed customers to purchase a computer that they could upgrade over time. At launch, the machines were available with six different processors, as well as 54 peripherals that included magnetic storage devices, visual display units (monitor screens), printers, card readers and card punches. As IBM later explained, the System/360:

> . . . changed the way customers thought about computer hardware. Companies for the first time could buy a small system and add to it as they grew. Companies other than IBM found they could make peripheral equipment that worked with the S/360. An entire industry was soon created, consisting of companies making and supplying plug-compatible peripheral products . . . . Led by Telex with tape drives in 1967, and Memorex with disk storage units in 1968, this industry enjoyed dramatic growth.

## THE PERSONAL COMPUTING AGE

As the 1970s dawned, 'very large scale integration' (VLSI) permitted tens of thousands of electronic components to be included on a single IC. This was very significant, as it allowed all of the parts required to make a computer's central processing unit (CPU) to be incorporated onto one silicon chip. The first such 'microprocessor' – the 4004 – was released by Intel in 1971, and was followed by more powerful chips known as the 8008 and 8080. The first ever microprocessor-based computer or 'microcomputer' – the 8008-based Micral N – was subsequently created by R2E Corp in France in 1973.

Over in the United States, electronics enthusiasts quickly saw the potential for individuals to build their own personal computers (PCs), with several kits arriving on the market in the mid 1970s. The first of these is often claimed to be the Altair 8800 from Micro Instrumentation and Telemetry Systems (MITS). This was advertised in *Popular Electronics* in December 1974, used an Intel 8080 microprocessor, and was released in January 1975. However, six months earlier a lesser known product – the 'Mark-8 "Do-It-Yourself" kit' designed by graduate student John Titus – had featured on the cover of *Radio-Electronics*.

The first Micral N, Mark-8 and Altair 8800 computers lacked a keyboard or monitor display. Programs and data therefore had to be entered by flipping switches to set binary values in memory, with output constrained to the illumination of LEDs. In time, additional 'teletype' interfaces did allow direct text entry via keyboard, and output via hardcopy printout. With a suitable interface card, an Altair 8800 was also able to read in a program from a paper tape or audio cassette.

Following these humble beginnings, several companies began to sell PCs. One of the first was Apple, which was founded in 1976 by friends Steve Jobs and Steve Wozniak.

Jobs and Wozniak initially sold a computer called the Apple I, which was a bare circuit board to which users needed to add a power supply, keyboard, case and other components before connecting it to a television.

Around 200 hand-built Apple I computers were sold, and laid the foundation for the development of the Apple II. This launched in April 1977, and came fully assembled. It also had a keyboard integrated into its case, colour graphics (with a resolution of 280 x 192 pixels, or 40 x 24 characters), and could be connected to a television or dedicated Apple monitor. The price for a system with 4 kilobytes of RAM started at about $1,300.

Another signature PC that launched in 1977 was the TRS-80. This was produced by the Tandy Corporation and sold through its Radio Shack chain of electronics stores, with about 200,000 'Tandy Radio Shack' PCs with a Z80 microprocessor being sold. The first machine was retrospectively labelled the Model 1, cost $600, came with a cassette deck for program storage, and had a 64 x 16 character monochrome display. Between 1978 and 1985 about a dozen other TRS-80 computers were launched, including portable models. As a teenager I frequently visited Tandy stores, and remember staring intently at TRS-80 computers on many occasions.

Also launched in 1977 were the first personal computers from Commodore Business Machines (CBM), which like Radio Shack was an established American electronics manufacturer. Commodore's original 'Personal Electronic Transactor' or 'PET' range was sold from 1977 to 1982, with the hardware being upgraded several times. Figure 1.4 shows a second generation model 4016. Note that this particular PC is branded 'CBM' rather than PET as it was sold in the United Kingdom.

Following the retirement of the PET range, Commodore achieved great success selling home computers that consumers could plug into a television. These included the VIC-20

**Figure 1.4: Commodore PET / CBM Model 4016.**

(launched in 1980), the Commodore 64 (launched in 1982), and several Amiga models (which initially hit the market in 1985). The latter had better colour graphics than any other PC of the period, and were often used to produce 2D and 3D graphics for TV shows. Commodore Business Machines sadly went out of business in 1994.

By the early 1980s, a great many different personal computers were on the market from a wide range of manufacturers. All of these ran their own operating system (the software that brings the hardware to life when it is turned on), and had their own dedicated applications. Sadly most of these early computers struggled to import data from a rival system. This was hardly an ideal situation and clearly not sustainable. As in previous decades, the innovation to drive things forward came from IBM, who in 1981 launched the IBM PC.

Figure 1.5 shows the first IBM Personal Computer, technically known as the model 5150. The system came with a

**Figure 1.5: The First IBM Personal Computer (Model 5150).**

4.77 MHz Intel 8088 microprocessor, 16 kilobytes of RAM (which could be expanded to 640 kilobytes), and had an 80 x 25 character text display. A basic system, which connected to a television and used a cassette recorder to store data, cost $1,565. Meanwhile a typical office system with a dedicated monitor and floppy disk drive retailed for about $3,000.

Technologically, the IBM PC was no more advanced than its many competitors. But it was a game changer because the 'IBM PC compatible hardware platform' was an open system. This enabled other manufacturers to copy its technology and to sell both compatible peripherals and even entire 'clone' IBM PCs.

While IBM had wanted to establish an open industry standard, its intention had been for other companies to produce IBM PC peripherals, rather than entire, compatible computers. It therefore fought – and lost – a legal battle when its rival Compaq began to make IBM PC clones.

In the wake of the Compaq court case, the IBM PC standard became very popular indeed, and within a few years 'IBM PCs' from many manufacturers dominated the market. The only other company that managed to set a surviving standard was Apple with its Macintosh models, the first of which was launched in 1984. It was therefore in the mid-1980s that the personal computing marketplace came to be divided between users of 'PCs' or 'Macs'.

## *Computers for Everybody*

Today it can be difficult to appreciate how significant the arrival of the IBM PC and other personal computers really was. No longer was the ability to compute limited to those with military, corporate or similar-sized budgets. Instead, for the first time, pretty much any business could own a computer and use it to run a word processor or a spreadsheet. In case you are wondering, the first spreadsheet was called VisiCalc, ran on an Apple II, and was launched in 1979.

Outside of the workplace, in the early 1980s home computing also started to grow very rapidly, with many hobbyists purchasing hardware that they plugged into TV sets and mainly used to learn programming or to play games. As already mentioned, Commodore was a significant player in this market with its VIC-20, and later its Commodore 64 and Amiga range.

Other companies who sold early home computers for a few hundred dollars included Atari from Japan, and Sinclair from the United Kingdom. The latter's ZX80, ZX81 and ZX Spectrum computers were based on the same Z80 processor used in Radio Shack's TRS-80 models, and were manufactured by Timex. In the United States the ZX81 was rebranded as the Timex Sinclair 1000, where it launched in 1982 for $99.95. Figure 1.6 illustrates my very own, British ZX81. The machine has a totally flat, membrane keyboard, and is

# THE COMPUTING MACHINE

**Figure 1.6: The Sinclair ZX81 Personal Computer.**

about 6.5 x 7 x 1.5 inches (165 x 177 x 38 mm) in size. As you may notice, the ZX81's spacebar is the same size as every other key.

As personal computers became more popular and more powerful, so people wanted to use them away from their office or home. In the 1980s this posed a major problem for manufacturers, as desktop PCs used a lot of power and relied on bulky and heavy cathode ray tubes (CRTs) as their display technology. The earliest portable computers were therefore more 'luggable' than portable, and often limited to running on mains power.

Two signature models were the Osborne 1 and the Toshiba T5100. As illustrated in figure 1.7, the Osborne 1 from 1981 was an 11 kilogram computer that included a 5 inch CRT display. Meanwhile, as shown in figure 1.8, the Toshiba 5100 from 1987 had quite a serviceable, 9.5 inch gas plasma display. This said, like the Osborne 1, it still required mains power. A Toshiba 5100 'notebook' also weighed 6.8 kilograms.

Other early portable computers used monochrome liquid crystal displays (LCDs) to allow them to run on batteries. Notable models included the Compaq LTE, as well as

**Figure 1.7: An Osborne 1 Portable PC.**

Apple's Macintosh Portable, both of which launched in 1989. In the same year Zenith Data Systems released a laptop called the Minisport with a colour LCD display. By 1992 IBM was also selling a colour laptop called the Thinkpad 700C, and in 1993 Apple launched its rival PowerBook 165C.

While by the late 1980s many portable computers were laptops, several manufacturers experimented with other form factors, including 'palmtops'. Like today's smartphones and smaller tablets, these were relatively light and portable, and sometimes ran on standard AA batteries. One of the earliest palmtops was the Atari Portfolio, which launched in 1989. As shown in figure 1.9, this 7.5 inch (190 mm) computer had a 40 x 8 character display, and became famous due to its appearance in the movie *Terminator II*.

Around this time, the first tablet computers also entered the market. These included Apple's Newton MessagePads (which launched in 1987), and larger devices called 'Microsoft Tablet PCs', which were released by several manufacturers in 2002. This said, it took several more years for the technology to become available to make a really effective tablet computer, with Apple's first iPad launched in April 2010.

**Figure 1.8: Toshiba 5100 'Notebook' from 1987.**

## *The Rise of Software*

Across the Personal Computing Age, the focus in digital innovation transitioned from the development of hardware to the development of software. Software is, after all, what makes hardware useful, and as computers were increasingly adopted by non-technical people, so the demand rose for sophisticated programs that were easy to use. Many companies were established to meet this challenge, with the most significant being Microsoft.

In 1974, computing enthusiasts Paul Allen and Bill Gates read about the forthcoming release of the Altair 8800 computer kit, and deduced that a mass market for personal computers was about to emerge. They therefore decided to write a version of the high-level programming language BASIC (the Beginner's All-purpose Symbolic Instruction Code) for the machine, and to establish a business to sell it. Altair BASIC subsequently became the first product of a company initially called 'Micro-soft' which they founded in April 1975. Allen and Gates went on to write further versions of BASIC for the Apple II and Radio Shack TRS-80, and by the end of 1978 their company had a turnover in excess of $1 million.

When IBM was developing its PC, it turned to Microsoft to deliver an operating system called PC DOS, or the PC Disk Operating System. This Microsoft developed from a product called 86-DOS, which had initially been created by Seattle Computer Products, and which in turn had been based on an earlier operating system called CP/M. PC DOS was released with the IBM PC in 1981. Microsoft went on to market its own version called MS DOS (Microsoft DOS), which it developed in parallel with IBM's PC DOS for another 12 years. While the differences between PC DOS and MS DOS did become greater over time, the two operating systems remained highly compatible, with the computer industry usually referring to either as just 'DOS'.

While DOS gave the world a standard PC operating system (at least on IBM PCs and compatibles), it was based on a 'command line interface' or 'CLI'. This meant that DOS required users to enter text-based commands in order to manage files and launch applications, which many people found to be a cumbersome and challenging activity. A better kind of user interface was therefore needed to make computing more accessible, and this arrived in the form of the 'graphical user interface' or 'GUI'.

The pioneer of the GUI was Douglas Engelbart, who in the early 1960s ran a project called 'Augmentation of Human Intellect' at the Stanford Research Institute (SRI) in California. Here, in 1963, he devised the first mouse, which was initially termed a 'bug'. The next year Engelbart worked with computer engineer Bill English to create the first mouse prototype. This was used to control a system called the NLS or 'oN-Line System'. The NLS was the first computer system to present information in windows and to feature clickable 'hypertext' navigation.

**Figure 1.9: The Atari Portfolio Palmtop.**

GUIs were further developed at Xerox PARC (the Palo Alto Research Center) in the early 1970s. Here, software was created that used a mouse to control a computer via a 'WIMP' or 'windows, icons, menus and pointer' environment. The system was the first to be based on a desktop metaphor, with files looking like pieces of paper, deleted files moved to an icon of a trash can, and so on. Xerox PARC's GUI first ran on a computer called the Xerox Alto that was introduced in March 1973. This revolutionary machine was largely used for research purposes, with total sales of about 2,000 units.

The GUI went mainstream in 1984 when Apple launched its Macintosh System Software (later renamed macOS) along with the first Macintosh personal computer. Apple had been working on GUIs since 1979, and in 1983 had tested the market with the launch of a GUI-equipped computer called Lisa. However, the Apple Macintosh was the first product to make GUIs a commercial success.

Equally recognising the potential, in 1983 Digital Research demonstrated a GUI called GEM (the Graphical Environment Manager) that could be used with IBM compatible PCs, and which later featured on a range of Atari home computers. Also in 1983, Microsoft announced the initial version of a GUI called 'Windows', although it did not get Windows 1.0 to market until 1985.

Windows 1.0 (and Windows 2.0 which followed it in 1987) were pale competitors to macOS, and ran poorly on most PCs. The migration from DOS to Windows on IBM PCs and compatibles did therefore not really start until version 3.0 was released in 1990. Indeed, as Guy Swarbrick wrote in *Personal Computer World* in July of that year, 'until recently Windows has suffered, not only from being awkward to use, but from having few applications available for it that were capable of luring users away from traditional DOS applications'. However, with the launch of Windows 3.0, Microsoft finally managed to cover all of its bases, with – as Swarbrick noted – no GUI 'ever being launched with so much software'. In 1992 Windows 3.0 was followed by Windows 3.1, which became a classic, and is illustrated in Figure 1.10.

As the 1990s progressed, the latter years of the Personal Computing Age were characterised more by consolidation and increasing computer adoption, than by any great hardware or software innovations. There really was not a lot you could do with a PC by 2000 that you could not have achieved in the early 1990s. Though undoubtedly, between 1990 and 2000 it became *easier* to accomplish most computing tasks, and to a higher level of quality. In particular, opportunities to work with images, audio and video improved tremendously in this period, as did the availability of peripherals for producing high-resolution colour output via either a screen or a printer. As we shall explore in the next chapter, 3D printers capable of turning computer data into physical objects also developed significantly between 1990 and 2000.

## THE NETWORK COMPUTING AGE

While early computing was largely defined by its hardware, and the Personal Computing Age was increasingly domi-

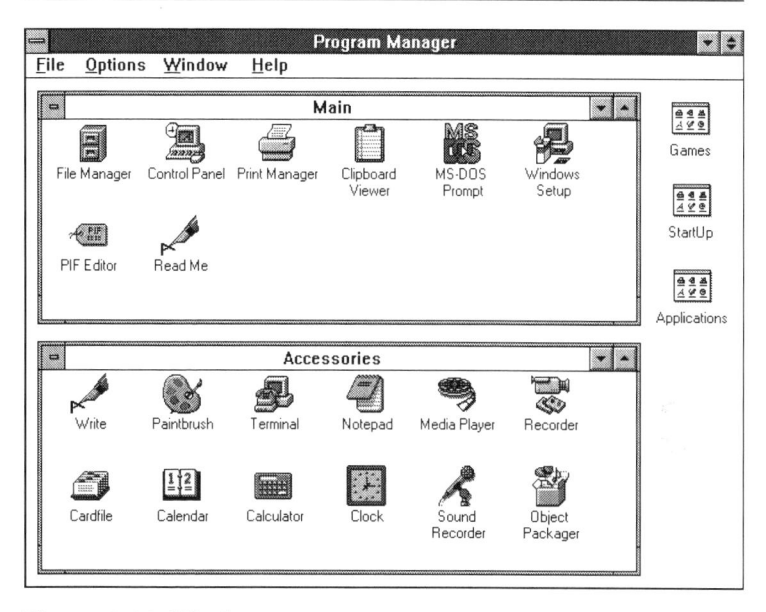

**Figure 1.10: Windows 3.1.**

nated by software, today's Network Computing Age has a core focus on connectivity. The first ever computer-to-computer links were forged in the 1950s, and included a military radar system called the 'Semi-Automatic Ground Environment' or SAGE. However, it was not until the late 1990s that connecting people and things via a computer network started to radically impact human activity.

The seeds of the Network Computing Age were first planted in October 1969, when the 'Advanced Research Projects Agency Network' or ARPANET was switched on. Funded by what is now DARPA (the US Defence Advanced Research Projects Agency), this was initially established to connect computers in different universities and other research establishments. In 1973, ARPANET became a global affair, when University College London, and the Norwegian Seismic Array radar establishment (NORSAR), were connected into the system.

Also around this time, the first local area networks or 'LANs' were created to link computers located in the same building or other confined geographic location. Most significantly, between 1973 and 1975, a networking technology called Ethernet was developed at Xerox PARC by a man called Bob Metcalfe.

A year later, an alternative to Ethernet called ARCNET (or 'Attached Resource Computer NETwork') was invented by the Datapoint Corporation. In 1977 this was installed at the Chase Manhattan Bank in New York to create the first commercial LAN. It was, however, Ethernet that became the more popular, and which was ratified as a standard by committee 802.3 of the Institute for Electrical and Electronic Engineers (IEEE) in June 1983.

In part Ethernet has survived due to the relative ease of upgrading its data transmission speed. While the first Ethernet networks had a speed of just 10 Mbps (megabits per second), today some hardware can transmit data at up to 100 Gbps (gigabits per second), with 400 Gbps Ethernet in development.

As LANs became more common, and as wide area networks (WANs) like the ARPANET grew, so the benefits of being able to create 'internetworks' – or networks of individual networks – became increasingly apparent. In particular, in late 1971, programmer Ray Tomlinson used the ARPANET to send the first e-mail between two computers. In July 1972, Tomlinson subsequently wrote the first e-mail program that was able to list, selectively read, file, forward and respond to messages.

E-mail became ARPANET's first killer application, as it demonstrated the extraordinary possibilities presented by what was then termed computer mediated communication (CMC). This said, the potential was clearly going to be limited unless most computers on the planet could somehow be connected together. Thankfully, the creation of the ARPANET and LAN technologies had laid the foundation for this to occur, with the ARPANET slowly evolving into the Internet.

## *A Global Hardware Platform*

As with the IBM PC, the Internet became successful because it adopted an open approach. Specifically, the creation of Internet technology was based on an idea called 'open architecture networking', which was pioneered by Bob Khan at DARPA in 1972.

Open architecture networking allows different networks to link together into a broader internetwork regardless of their own, internal technology. To make such 'Internetting' possible, Khan and others developed a new communications standard which eventually came to be known as TCP/IP, or the 'Transmission Control Protocol / Internet Protocol'. This remains in use to this day, with every computer on the Internet having its own unique 'IP address' in the same way that every telephone has its own unique number. TCP/IP was adopted as the standard for military network communications in the United States in 1980, and became the sole standard for ARPANET in January 1983.

Khan based the development of the Internet on four key and enduring principles. The first was that each individual network that becomes part of the Internet should continue to operate independently, with no changes required to connect it to the global network.

All data transmitted over the Internet is broken down into small chunks called 'packets' that travel independently before being reassembled on arrival at their destination. As his second design principle, Khan decided that all Internet packets should travel on a 'best effort basis'. This makes it more likely for a 'packet switching network' like the Internet to work reliably, as if a packet of data does not arrive at its destination, it is simply retransmitted, so avoiding the corruption of its parent file.

All of the Internet's constituent networks are interconnected via devices called 'gateways' and 'routers' that direct the flow of data packets. As his third design principle, Bob Khan determined that Internet gateways and routers should not retain a copy of the data that passes through them. This means that Internet gateways and routers simply receive data packets, read the destination addresses contained within their 'headers', and use this information to forward them on toward their intended destination. In effect, this means that Internet gateways and routers function like traditional post offices and delivery depots that work to get our mail to us, but which do not look inside the envelopes they handle or xerox any of the letters.

Bob Khan's final Internet design principle was that the network should not be subject to any form of central control. There has to be some kind of coordinating authority to develop Internet technology standards and to assign IP addresses, and this non-profit body is known as ICANN (the Internet Corporation for Assigned Names and Numbers). Even so, ICANN has no ability to regulate Internet activity, to control its infrastructure, or to access Internet communications.

By the mid 1980s, NSFNET (the National Science Foundation NETwork) in the United States, and JANET (the Joint Academic NETwork) in the United Kingdom, were facilitating Internet access for every person in a higher educational establishment in their respective countries. In September 1988, the first Internet operators trade show (Interop) also brought together those companies who were seeking to commercialize TCP/IP technology. Around this time commercial Internet service providers (ISPs) additionally began to emerge. These facilitated 'dial-up' access to the Internet using a device called a modem that connects a PC to a standard telephone socket.

Surprisingly, it took until 1995 for the Internet to be formally defined. For years it has been debated whether the term refers to the 'global internetwork', 'international network' or a similar term. However, in October 1995, the Federal Networking Council (FNC) in the United States sidestepped such matters to define the word 'Internet' to refer to the 'global information system' that is based on IP addresses, supports communications using TCP/IP, and which makes available public and private services.

As the FNC chose to highlight, the creation of the Internet permitted the development of a 'global hardware platform' comprised of every connected computer in the world. Or as I expressed matters in *Cyber Business* back in 1995, with the development of the Internet it became sensible 'to think of all electronic networks as being sub-components of one single computing infrastructure'. Just as nobody would sanely purchase a telephone and not connect it to the global phone network, so in the Network Computing Age a key reason to invest in a computer is to gain a stake in the global computer system. Today this may sound obvious. But during the Personal Computing Age, most computers had been just that – personal. It therefore really was a turning point when most PCs transitioned into 'ICPs' or 'interpersonal computers'.

### The Growth of the Web

As we have just seen, a lot of critical networking developments took place in the 1970s and 1980s. You may therefore be wondering why I have bounded the Network Computing Age to the period from the mid-to-late 1990s to the early 2020s. The reason is partly because the transition between each of the Five Ages of Computing is inevitably gradual. But mainly, it is because computer networking did not become a mainstream personal and business activity until shortly before the turn of the millennium.

To give you an idea of the growth, figure 1.11 charts the number of Internet users from 1990 to 2020. As you can see, while back in 1990 there were only about 3 million users (or just under 0.06 per cent of the world's population), by 2000 this had reached 415 million (6.8 per cent), and is predicted to be at least 4 billion by 2020. This means that by 2020 we will pass the milestone of over half of humanity being online.

There are two reasons that the Internet took several decades to go mainstream. The first was speed, with Internet communications in the late 1980s and 1990s being slow and often deeply frustrating. Access via a dial-up modem typically provided a connection speed of only 14.4 or 28.8 Kbps (kilobits per second). This compares to a typical modern connection speed of maybe 8 Mbps, and often far more. But even 8 Mbps is 8,000 Kbps, which means that a dial-up Internet user in the 1990s usually had a connection speed roughly 500 times slower than a typical connection speed today.

Fortunately, around the year 2000, the speed issue was overcome when a number of 'broadband' technologies arrived on the market. These offered connection speeds of 512 Kbps, 1 Mbps or even more, as well as 'always-on' Internet connectivity. Across many nations, broadband services subsequently became one of the two major drivers for mass Internet adoption.

The second development that catapulted the Internet into the mainstream was the creation of the world-wide web. Until the late 1980s there was no straightforward means of navigating Internet content, with users reliant on text-based, command line programs. These included e-mail packages, a messaging system called Internet Relay Chat (IRC), and bulletin board systems (BBS) that could be used to exchange messages and files. But in 1990 all of this changed when computer programmer Tim Berners-Lee conceived the world-wide web as a graphical Internet interface. Just as the replacement of DOS with Windows made IBM PCs a lot easier for most people to use, so the web did the same for the Internet.

| Year | Internet Users | Global Population | People Online |
|------|----------------|-------------------|---------------|
| 1990 | 3 million | 5.3 billion | 0.06% |
| 1995 | 45 million | 5.7 billion | 0.79% |
| 2000 | 415 million | 6.1 billion | 6.8% |
| 2005 | 1 billion | 6.5 billion | 15.4% |
| 2010 | 2 billion | 6.8 billion | 29.4% |
| 2015 | 3.2 billion | 7.3 billion | 43.8% |
| 2020 | 4 billion* | 7.6 billion* | 52.6%* |

*predicted*

**Figure 1.11: Global Internet Users 1990 to 2020**

Back in 1989, Berners-Lee was working at CERN (the European Organization for Nuclear Research). His initial proposal to present online content in pages that could be hyperlinked was rejected by his boss with an appraisal of 'vague but exciting'. But fortunately for the human race, Berners-Lee continued to develop his novel project.

By 1990 Berners-Lee had created the 'hypertext markup language' (HTML) in which the first web pages were written, and which some web pages continue to be written in today. He had also invented the 'uniform resource locator' (URL) system that provides each web page with its address, as well as the 'hypertext transfer protocol' (HTTP) standard that remains the bedrock of web communication. For good measure, by the end of 1990 Berners-Lee had additionally coded the first web server and the first web browser (which was also a web page editor and itself called WorldWideWeb). It is difficult to believe that one man so rapidly created so much technology of such significance. But he most certainly did.

By the end of 1990, the first web page was available on the Internet, and in 1991 Internet users outside of CERN were invited to contribute content. As with the IBM-PC and the Internet itself, Berners-Lee recognized that the world-wide web would only be a success if it was totally open, and in April 1993 it was announced that the web's underlying code was being made freely available for anybody to use. The rest, as they say, is history – with programmers and visionaries rapidly piling in to help create the amazing, multimedia content platform that the web has evolved into today. Just one of the web's early pioneers was Jeff Bezos, who in July 1994 founded Amazon.com to sell books online.

In the late 1990s, the web became a phenomenon both culturally and economically. Many in business recognized the opportunity to provide services and to sell products over the Internet, and the stock market invested heavily in almost any e-commerce venture it could find. This created the Dot Com Bubble, which subsequently burst in 2001 when speculators finally recognized that the generation of web traffic did not automatically result in a profitable business.

As sanity returned to the markets, so a more savvy, second-generation of web-centric businesses rose to the fore. In 2004, technology publisher Tim O'Reilly labelled the activities of such companies 'Web 2.0'. As he explained in a seminal article in 2005:

> The bursting of the dot-com bubble in the fall of 2001 marked a turning point for the web. Many people concluded that the web was overhyped, when in fact bubbles and consequent shakeouts appear to be a common feature of all technological revolutions. Shakeouts typically mark the point at which an ascendant technology is ready to take its place at center stage. The pretenders are given the bum's rush, the real success stories show their

strength, and there begins to be an understanding of what separates one from the other.

A poster child of Web 2.0 was Google. Back in 1995, founders Larry Page and Sergey Brin met at Stanford University, and went on to write a web search engine called Backrub. This was subsequently renamed Google, with the company incorporated in September 1998.

Google succeeded where so many other online businesses failed because it viewed the web as an entirely new platform for delivering services. It hence took on the computing industry and won by focusing on connectivity and content, rather than the hardware and software that had defined the previous eras of computing. Or as O'Reilly nicely explains, from the start Google was

> . . . a native web application, never sold or packaged, but delivered as a service, with customers paying, directly or indirectly, for the use of that service. None of the trappings of the old software industry [were] present. No scheduled software releases, just continuous improvement. No licensing or sale, just usage.

In essence, Web 2.0 pioneers built their empires by using computing to forge connections between people, or between people and online content or web-based services. Platforms for social networking and video sharing hence provided the route to success for many Web 2.0 pioneers. Not least Facebook was founded by Harvard University students Mark Zuckerberg and Eduardo Saverin in February 2004. A year later, PayPal employees Chad Hurley, Steve Chen and Jawed Karim founded YouTube, with the first video – *Me at the Zoo* – uploaded in April 2005. A mere 18 months later, Google purchased YouTube for $1.65 billion.

...puting and online content into their ...al lives, people needed access to the ...tty much any location. The three key ... helped deliver such ubiquitous digital a... Fi, digital cellular networks, and smartphones. ...all went mainstream during the Network Computing Age, and in combination now allow a great many people to maintain an almost constant connection to the digital realm.

Short-range wireless data networks created for specific industrial or military purposes date back to the early 1970s. However, mainstream wireless computer networking only came into existence after 1985, when the Federal Communications Commission (FCC) in the United States decided to allocate three regions of the radio spectrum for unlicensed, short-range communications. By 1988, the NCR Corporation had invented a system it called 'WaveLAN' for linking up wireless cash registers, and saw the benefit of establishing a standard. Along with Bell Labs, NCR subsequently approached the IEEE, who formed a committee called 802.11.

Sadly it took many years for members of the 802.11 committee to come to agreement. It was hence not until 1997 that the first version of the '802.11 wireless networking protocol' was released. In 1999 this was updated with a standard called 802.11b, which permitted higher speed data communications (11 Mbps rather 2 Mbps). The latest standards include 802.11 'g', 'n' and 'ac'.

In 1999 the name 'Wi-Fi' was attached to 802.11 technology. This potentially stood for 'wireless fidelity', as it was based on the term 'Hi-Fi' or 'high fidelity' that had long been used in the world of audio. Whatever the name stood for, by the turn of the millennium Wi-Fi entered the mainstream, with laptops from Apple and other manufacturers starting to be sold with the option of an internal Wi-Fi adapter. From around the year 2000, the broadband routers used to provide wired Internet connections over a telephone line also started to be equipped with Wi-Fi. This allowed homes and businesses to create their own 'Wi-Fi hotspots', and to connect mobile computers to the Internet without a cable.

While Wi-Fi allows somebody within range of a wireless router to access the Internet, digital cellular networks provide broader mobile network access. Perhaps surprisingly, military and vehicle-based wireless telephony date back to the 1940s. For example, AT&T launched its 'Mobile Telephone Service' in 1949, although the 'mobile' equipment involved did weigh about 36 kilograms.

Today, mobile telephone and data services are provided by cellular networks. These deliver connectivity from radio masts, each of which connects to devices within range of its own network 'cell'. The initial 'first generation' (1G) cell phone network was set up by NTT in Tokyo in 1979. The United States then started to roll-out the technology in 1983, and the United Kingdom in 1985.

Second generation (2G) mobile networks followed, with the first launched in Finland in 1991. In contrast to 1G, 2G networks were digital rather than analogue, which not only provided better voice quality, but allowed the introduction of text messaging and other data services. In Finland in 1993 the first text message was sent, while in 1999 NTT DoCoMo in Japan launched a service that provided Internet access on a mobile device.

The above early developments noted, it was not until the arrival of third generation (3G) digital cellular networks that mobile Internet really came of age. 3G networks are still in use today in many locations, and involve a fairly broad basket of technologies and standards that offer higher data transmission speeds than 2G. The first commercial 3G network launched in Japan, again from NTT DoCoMo, in October 2001.

Around 2009, 4G mobile technologies started to be introduced. These offer even higher speeds than 3G, again depending on the standards and carrier involved, and are entirely based on Internet protocol (IP) technology. On a 4G network, voice communications hence travel around in data packets that are no different to any other form of data. The arrival of 4G hence signalled the final transition of digital cellular networks from being phone systems with data added, to data networks that can also be used to make voice calls.

At the time of writing, 5G mobile networks are being planned. These will offer data speeds around ten times faster than most people on the planet currently obtain via a wired or Wi-Fi Internet connection. In February 2017, the International Telecommunications Union (ITU) agreed on a set of performance standards for 5G called IMT-2020. By 2020, this is intended to deliver an 'International Mobile Telecommunication' system that will offer peak download and upload data rates of 20 Gbps and 10 Gbps. In practice this means that 5G users should actually experience data upload and download speeds of 100 Mbps and 50 Mbps.

The rollout of 5G will break down the final barriers that separate wired and wireless Internet connectivity. In turn 5G will empower the next generation of connected hardware, including robots, autonomous vehicles and Internet of Things (IoT) devices as we shall explore in future chapters. 5G will also make it possible to deliver very high quality media and AI experiences to smartphones, tablets and other mobile computers.

Talking of smartphones, the first handheld device with telephone functionality and computing capabilities came from IBM. Known as the Simon Personal Communicator, this was launched in 1994, and was able to send and receive e-mails. Between 1996 and 2004, Nokia also introduced a range of 'Communicator' phones that hinged open to reveal a screen and a physical keyboard. These IBM and Nokia devices undoubtedly had what we would now recognize as smartphone functionality. However, it took until 1998 for a pocket computer and communications device actually *called* a smartphone to arrive on the market.

The hardware in question was the 'newpdQ Smartphone' from Qualcomm. This was announced in September 1998, and was described as an 'all-in-one digital phone and pen-based organizer'. In addition to being able to make voice calls, the pdQ was able to keep track of appointments and contacts, send and receive email, and surf the web. As Qualcomm's vice president Mark Bercow very accurately predicted in the pdQ's press release, 'the introduction of Qualcomm's new smartphone [represented] the beginning of a new era of integrated wireless data and voice communications devices'.

Given the potential, it is not surprising that others quickly leapt on the smartphone bandwagon. Perhaps most notably, Apple released its first iPhone in June 2007. Also in 2007, Google unveiled its Android mobile operating system, which now runs on the vast majority of smartphones and tablets (with most of the rest running Apple's iOS). Sometime in the early 2020s it is anticipated that there will be over 3 billion smartphone users.

## THE COGNITIVE COMPUTING AGE

So there we have it – the development of computing from its mechanical and electromechanical roots to the present day. Looking to the future, I believe that we will soon enter the Cognitive Computing Age, and then some decades beyond that the era of Cyborg Fusion.

The technological, economic and cultural innovations that will define these next, great steps in digital technology will not replace what has gone before. But they will change the dominant focus of computer application, and hence the ways in which individuals digitally interact, and the means by which most computing companies generate their profits.

As the Cognitive Computing Age really starts to take hold in the early 2020s, so any digital technology will be able to possess, or remotely access, a cognitive capacity. In terms of value added, this means that hardware, software and connectivity will be relegated to an also-ran status. Absolutely, hardware, software and connectivity will remain important. But their provision will no longer be a competitive differentiator in the computing marketplace. Rather, the ability to deliver an increasingly sophisticated level of artificial intelligence will be what distinguishes the latest digital products and services.

Perhaps most significantly, the Cognitive Computing Age will see the rise of 'attentive computing', and hence a fundamental shift in the relationship that binds a human being to a digital device. Until this point in history, all forms of computing have demanded high levels of human attention, with users required to learn how to program, operate and interact with their hardware and the digital realm. Granted, a modern tablet or smartphone is far easier to use than a Colossus, an Altair 8800, or the first IBM PC. But even so, all modern computing interfaces still require a human being to devote attention to them in order to be of service.

The rise of AI and attentive computing will turn our relationship with the digital realm through 180 degrees. This is because Cognitive Computing Age technology will be able to learn about and attend to its user, rather than the other way around. It will indeed be impossible for robots and autonomous vehicles to operate in most homes and workplaces, and on most highways, without the rise of attentive digital systems. The Cognitive Computing Age will hence be the period of history in which computing devices become self-aware and develop the ability to live in close harmony with other species. Cognitive computers will even learn to anticipate human requirements before they are typed or vocalized.

As digital technology learns to inhabit, interact and excel in the human realm, it is likely to take on more and more 'human' activities. For some this is already a cause of great concern, although I still think that the majority of individuals and businesses remain in a blissful state of 'AI denial'. In the Network Computing Age, a great many human occupations and social processes were transformed, and in the 2020s and 2030s we should expect this to happen again.

## CYBORG FUSION

By the late 2030s I anticipate that it will be unusual for most people to divert their gaze and fleshy digits to a smartphone or other mobile computing device. Indeed, I think we will look back in 20 years and be amazed at how much time we freely devoted to such attention-grabbing blocks of semiconductors and plastic. Due to attentive computing developments, by the late 2030s we will be living *with* rather than *for* computing. We will also be starting to integrate digital technologies into our bodies, with the line between 'artificial' computer systems and the 'natural world' beginning to blur.

Herein I use the term 'cyborg fusion' to refer to the physical convergence of human beings and computer systems. Around 2040, I also anticipate that such a mashup will signal the arrival of the last computing age that we can reasonably predict. As cyborg fusion takes hold, it will be increasingly difficult to separate ourselves from computer hardware, or at least to do so without opting for an invasive medical procedure.

The signature innovation of the Cyborg Fusion era will be the arrival of mainstream brain-computer interfaces (BCIs). These will allow people to connect their minds to digital technology, so reducing the requirement to rely on screens, keyboards, and other intermediate computing peripherals.

As we shall see in chapter 6, very rudimentary BCIs are now in the lab. The foundations for the fifth age of computing are therefore already being laid.

The widespread application of BCIs will have profound implications. For a start, BCI-enhanced individuals will enjoy direct, frictionless access to the whole of artificial digital creation. In addition, those with a BCI should be able to enter the headspace of other cyborg individuals. Just as, in the Network Computing Age, most computers were connected together, so in the era of Cyborg Fusion millions of human brains will be directly linked online.

Surgically implanted BCIs are also likely to be just the tip of the iceberg. For example, later this century, it is conceivable that AIs will learn to reprogram human biology and trigger the body to grow its own organic computing peripherals. This means that people will not need to sign-up for BCI implant surgery to get their brain hooked up to the net. Rather, they will be able to undergo a genetic treatment that will cause them to biologically fabricate the extra brain components necessary to gain direct access to digital technology.

Today, most of us see with biological eyes and hear with biological ears, and these amazing organs provide our main multimedia interface. Yet maybe only 50 years from now, future AIs may have figured out how to provide the human body with an additional biological sense organ. This would function a bit like an organic Wi-Fi chip, and may have direct access to a person's memory, computational and emotional circuits, and optic and auditory cortexes. Willing individuals – and perhaps less willing people too – would simply need to have an injection, take a pill, or breathe in a chemical vapour, in order to take into their bodies the genetic material required to trigger their digital upgrade.

In time it is conceivable that genetic augmentations to provide a human being with digital connectivity will be able to be passed on to their offspring. This means that if two network-enhanced individuals have a child, their baby will be able to be born with a live Internet connection. Their new family member may even be digitally aware in the womb. She or he could therefore be programmed to greet the world with the ability to speak, as much education as an infant brain can upload, and a following on Facebook and Twitter.

\* \* \*

## THE POWER OF THE MACHINE

With the exception of the last few pages, this chapter has focused on the birth and adolescence of computing. Such history is, I think, too easily and too frequently dismissed by those trying to predict and understand the future. I therefore make no apology for including this material in this book, and hope that it has made you think about the incredible digital power that many people already enjoy.

The past is the only yardstick against which we can measure the future. Those cyborg fusion scenarios that I outlined in the last section may initially seem utterly implausible and totally outrageous. Yet they are no more radical and culturally charged than many recent computing developments that we now take for granted, but which would have been unthinkable when the first Colossus was built, or even in the era of the first IBM PC. I remember that, when I published *Cyber Business* in 1995, I was repeatedly told that few people would ever choose to carry a mobile phone, let alone a pocket-sized computer. This, I was assured, was because it would never become socially acceptable to use such a device in public, so constraining any mass-adoption of the technology.

Seven decades ago, computing was a narrow and highly specialist technical discipline. Since that time, it has evolved into a powerful military and scientific tool, a mainstream business infrastructure, and a social and cultural phenomenon. No other development in history has progressed so quickly to impact every aspect of our lives, and none has the potential to change us so deeply in the future. Like it or not, computing in all of its guises has been born and has fruitfully survived its childhood and adolescence. We therefore need to ask ourselves what we are going to do with its extraordinary power.

# 2
## DIGITAL TRANSFORMATION

One of my favourite books is Gregory Stock's *Metaman*. Published in 1993, this examines how the human species is evolving into a single, technologically-interconnected entity. Stock terms this gigantic creature 'Metaman', and suggests that its emergence signals our fourth transition 'to a new level of complexity'.

Stock explains that the first such transition took place 3.5 billion years ago when biochemicals in the oceans became primitive, bacteria-like cells. Next, around 2.1 billion years back in history, these earliest forms of life combined into more complex cells called eukaryotes. About 700 million years ago, eukaryotes then started to form into even more complex, multicellular organisms such as plants, animals, and eventually human beings.

According to Stock, today's interconnection of billions of individual humans into the combined cells of Metaman marks life's latest transition into an even more complex form. Or as he expressed matters in 1993, 'now, with the arrival of modern technology, particularly electronic communications, human society is becoming an organic whole'.

Today, Stock's idea that we are all interconnecting via digital technology has become obvious. Over the past two decades the Internet has evolved into the nervous system of human civilization, with crowdsourcing increasingly regarded as the best mechanism for dealing with challenges beyond the capabilities of any individual or small group thereof. The more we interconnect, and the more we digitally share, so the smarter we collectively become and the more we can achieve. Granted, many politicians and national administrative systems have not got this yet. But individual citizens are increasingly in step with the new internetworking reality, and so too are a growing number of commercial organizations.

## BRAVE NEW WORLD

In business, the latest buzz-term associated with the aforementioned trend is 'digital transformation'. This uses computing and other digital technologies to create interconnection and smartness, and to deliver new manufacturing systems and working methods.

Market analysts IDC predict that, by 2020, annual worldwide spending on 'digital transformation initiatives' will reach $2 trillion. This point noted, exactly what such initiatives may specifically involve remains open to debate. It is therefore worth reporting how some influential organizations define 'digital transformation'.

According to the IBM Institute for Business Value, digital transformation is about 'embracing the digital revolution'. As IBM go on to explain:

> Social networks and digital devices are being used to engage government, businesses and civil society, as well as friends and family. People are using mobile, interactive tools to determine who to trust, where to go and what to buy. At the same time, businesses are undertaking their own digital transformations, rethinking what customers value most and creating operating models that take advantage of what's newly possible for competitive differentiation. The

challenge for business is how fast and how far to go on the path to digital transformation.

Professional services giant Ernst & Young (EY) similarly explain that digital transformation is about 'providing opportunities to grow and become more efficient through social media, mobile, advanced analytics and cloud computing', and in a manner that can 'help streamline operations and reduce costs, increase top-line growth, enhance customer experiences and create innovative business models'. Market analysts Gartner concur, stressing that digital transformation is about employing digital technologies to 'enable the innovation of [an] entire business'. In April 2017, Gartner went on to report that 42 per cent of the companies it had recently surveyed had 'begun digital transformation'.

Surprisingly perhaps, we get one of the most forward-looking definitions of digital transformation from the European Commission. Here they note that it is 'characterised by a fusion of advanced technologies and the integration of physical and digital systems, the predominance of innovative business models and new processes, and the creation of smart products and services'. With this viewpoint I would also agree, and not least because the application of digital technologies in the physical world – for example within robots – is likely to become a critical aspect of future computing application.

In addition to highlighting digital and physical integration, the European Commission is the only organization cited here to include the word 'smart'. Sadly, what is missing from the other definitions quoted – and from many more that I have spared you from reading – is any implicit or explicit mention of AI. Today, you have to be living under a rock to be unaware of the artificial intelligence tsunami that is about to 'digitally transform' many aspects of our lives. It is therefore surprising that many in business still fail to link the two concepts.

In my work as a futurist I frequently come across 'AI denial'. By this I mean that I often discover examples of individuals and organizations who either refuse to recognize the dawning Cognitive Computing Age, or who have somehow convinced themselves that they will be immune to its impact. More broadly, many businesses seem to have decided that 'digital transformation' need involve no more than playing 'digital catch-up'. Their digital ambitions are hence limited to implementing those computing and communications technologies that pioneers like Google, Amazon and others have already put into service. In business terms this may be a reasonable short- or even medium-term goal. But it is also a strategy that ignores a great many future opportunities.

## DRIVERS OF CHANGE

The best way to understand digital transformation is to focus on those technologies and related developments that will actually make it happen. These are brought together in figure 2.1, and comprise cloud computing, Big Data, blockchain, virtual reality, augmented reality, the Internet of Things, artificial intelligence, autonomous vehicles, robots, dark factories, 3D printing, synthetic biology, molecular self-assembly, quantum computing, organic computing and cybernetic interfaces. The first twelve of these are already quite a big deal, and will become very significant in the coming decade. The last four are likely to impact us somewhat further into the future, but should at least be broadly understood.

Exactly what is included or not included in any such list of digital transformation drivers is obviously open to interpretation. Not least, several categories – such as AI – could be expanded to include many further sub-entries, including 'chatbots', 'smart analytics systems' and 'machine learning'.

| | |
|---|---|
| Cloud Computing | Big Data |
| Blockchain | Virtual Reality |
| Augmented Reality | Internet of Things |
| Artificial Intelligence | Autonomous Vehicles |
| Robots | Dark Factories |
| 3D Printing | Synthetic Biology |
| Molecular Self-Assembly | Quantum Computing |
| Organic Computing | Cybernetic Interfaces |

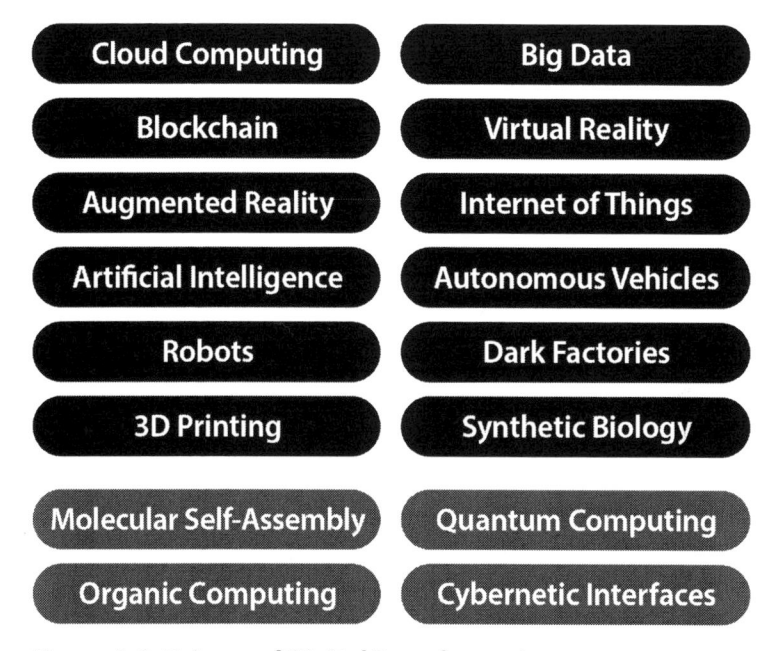

**Figure 2.1: Drivers of Digital Transformation**

I have even reviewed lists of 'top digital transformation developments' that feature entries like 'responsively designed websites with video'. No really, I have. Though if you think this kind of thing should be included as a key aspect of digital *transformation* you are reading the wrong book. As I argued in the *Preface*, while the world-wide web will continue to evolve, the Internet Revolution is over. We therefore need to clear things like 'redesigning websites' from our 'transformation' head and move on. Absolutely, improved and more interactive web design remain the bread-and-butter of marketing departments and media agencies. But they are not where digital transformation is at.

You probably expect the remainder of this chapter to explore each of the digital transformation drivers included in figure 2.1. To a large extent this is also what is going to happen, although we will be focusing the majority of our attention on those technologies that we will not return to in depth later in this book. Even so, once you have read this chapter you will be primed with a knowledge of every fundamental digital trend and technology that is likely to transform the world in the next decade and beyond. So hold on, we are in for quite a journey!

## CLOUD COMPUTING

Since the days of ENIAC and Colossus, most computers have stored data and run programs on their own hardware. Cloud computing challenges this proposition, and is where software applications, processing power, data storage and artificial intelligence are accessed over the Internet. According to Gartner, the global cloud computing market was worth $209 billion in 2016, and is predicted to reach $383 billion by 2020.

Major providers of cloud computing include Amazon, Microsoft, Google and IBM. These companies already operate data centres that collectively contain millions of cloud computing servers. A 'server' is any computer on a network that provides services to another, and is hence the fundamental building block of cloud computing. If you are wondering where the label 'cloud computing' comes from, it is used because the Internet has traditionally been represented on a network diagram by a picture of a cloud.

The potential benefits of cloud computing are considerable. Not least, migrating to the cloud allows the same applications and data to be accessed from any device – and often any *kind* of device – and from any location with Internet access. For those who regularly use a mix of computers (such as a home PC, office PC, laptop, tablet and smartphone), cloud computing subsequently removes the requirement to constantly copy files between devices, and to have the same software installed on every computer.

Keeping data in the cloud also ensures that it is always backed-up, so providing protection from data loss due to hardware failure, theft, fire, flood or other disasters. Opting to cloud compute additionally removes the need to purchase and install application upgrades, as cloud providers incrementally update their service. Cloud computing also allows low-cost, lower-power hardware to deliver sophisticated, processor-intensive applications. This is possible because all of the heavy lifting takes place on the cloud provider's servers, and not on the user's device.

For organizations, cloud computing offers additional benefits, such as facilitating remote and collaborative working. Cloud computing is normally also paid for on a usage basis, and removes the need for companies to invest in their own IT infrastructure. Large organizations that migrate entirely to the cloud can even close down their own data centres, and this is now starting to happen. For example, in 2016 online video provider Netflix completed its migration to Amazon's cloud platform.

Cloud offerings come in a wide range of guises, the most common of which are software as a service (SaaS), platform as a service (PaaS) and infrastructure as a service (IaaS). The first of these, SaaS, offers end-user applications that run in a web browser. So, for example, Google offer an online word processor called Google Docs, which I am using to write this book. Other notable SaaS provision includes business applications from Clarizen, Netsuite, Salesforce and Zoho.

Platform as a service (PaaS) allows users to build their own SaaS applications on a cloud provider's platform. Key players here are Microsoft with an offering called Azure, Google (with Google App Engine), and SalesForce (who run Force.com). Using PaaS to build online applications (including websites) allows a business to avoid the hassle and capital expense involved in hosting them internally, and to offer online services that will scale easily regardless of user demand.

Infrastructure as a service (IaaS) allows companies or individuals to rent online server capacity that may be used for any purpose. This allows a business to move existing, local applications to the cloud in order to save costs and increase flexibility. A major provider of IaaS is Amazon Web Services (AWS), which has a range of offerings that include 'Elastic Compute Cloud' (EC2) and the 'Simple Storage Service' (S3). As you may guess, the latter provides online storage, while the former delivers online processing power.

Both EC2 and S3 are based around 'server instances' that are rented as required. Users create 'Amazon machine images' (AMIs) – effectively a copy of everything they want on a server – and in a matter of minutes this can be made available on a small or large number of cloud servers. At the time of writing, EC2 server instances are priced from $0.012/hour, while S3 starts at $0.023/month per gigabyte.

AWS, and similar IaaS provision from the likes of IBM, empower users to access exactly the level of computing provision they need at a particular point in time. So, for example, a human resources department may require the use of 20 servers for an hour every Friday to run its payroll. This is easy to achieve using IaaS, and far more cost effective than either owning a data centre in which most computers usually sit idle, or having to wait for a task to complete because only limited computing power is available.

As the above example highlights, cloud services are turning computing into a utility that can be switched on and off as required. Today, many individuals and companies are wary of becoming dependent on a cloud provider. Yet it is little different to developing a reliance on the supplier of any other utility, such as electricity. Granted, good Internet connectivity is necessary to cloud compute. But in most locations this is now being delivered, and as we saw in the last chapter, 5G networks will soon provide very high speed mobile Internet links. Good online security is also essential for cloud computing, although this too is perfectly possible to implement. So far there have been no reports of any serious SaaS, PaaS or IaaS provider being hacked.

As I write these words in Google Docs, perhaps 25 per cent of computing is taking place in the cloud. Whether or not the other 75 per cent migrates – and how rapidly – is likely to depend on two factors. The first is the time it takes most companies – and most individuals – to cast off their legacy mindsets and to wrench themselves away from traditional computing practices. This is not to suggest that all computing should be migrated to the cloud. Nevertheless, a great many firms and private individuals could save money and become more flexible by doing more of their computing online.

The second factor that will drive cloud migration is the development of next-generation services. For example, as we shall see in the next chapter, IBM, Amazon, Microsoft, Google and others are starting to deliver cloud AI services that can be easily integrated into all manner of digital devices and software applications. Such AI services have to be cloud-based to capitalize on smart, shared resources. Companies that fail to embrace SaaS, PaaS and IaaS today may therefore be left behind in the adoption of tomorrow's most critical cognitive technologies.

## BIG DATA

Alongside cloud computing, the other well-established computing development that will drive digital transformation is Big Data. This refers to the generation of value from very large quantities of information that cannot be analyzed with traditional computing techniques. Quite what counts as 'Big Data' is open to some interpretation, and will inevitably change across time. Though right now, it is reasonable to assume that we are talking about data sets larger than 100 terabytes (TB), or in other words that contain at least 100 trillion bytes.

Big Data is often characterized by the '3-dimensional data challenge' or '3Vs' framework. This highlights the issues of increased data 'volume', 'velocity' and 'variety', and was devised in 2001 by Doug Laney when he was working at the META Group.

Big Data 'volume' signals the increasing quantity of digital information that is being generated by human civilization. Fifteen years ago, growing data volumes could largely be attributed to the proliferation of e-commerce and related logistics tracking systems, coupled with the rise of digital audio and digital video. But since that time we have additionally seen data volumes rise due to the explosion of social media, digital healthcare, climate and other complex data modelling, and research into data-intensive fields including genetics, AI and nuclear physics. Big Data volumes have also grown due to the arrival of the Internet of Things (IoT), as we will investigate in a few pages time.

One of the ways in which organizations are responding to Big Data volume is by adopting 'tiered storage systems'. These are implemented in data centres, and relegate less frequently accessed data to slower, lower-cost media. AWS S3, for example, offers cloud storage that is 'standard', 'infrequent' or 'glacial'. The last of these resides on media that are only powered-up on a data read request, and can take several hours to access.

Big Data 'velocity' reflects the growing speed at which data is flowing into and out of organizations and homes, and in particular the increasing requirement for real-time information delivery. Only in the past few years has there been a growing demand to stream HD video, to analyze the same with vision recognitions systems, and to track people and objects in real-time. These new types of computing application all present a very significant technical challenge. They are also another driver of cloud computing, as often only large companies like Amazon, Microsoft, Google and IBM have the scale and expertise to implement and maintain the very fastest storage and data processing solutions.

Big Data 'variety' reminds us that the breadth of digital information is increasingly diverse, and in turn harder and harder to process. Twenty years ago, most data was 'structured', which means that it was written in numbers and characters that a computer could easily process. For example, structured data formats include text documents, financial transactions, stock records and personnel files. But fast forward to today, and the vast majority of data is 'unstructured' (at least by volume). Unstructured data includes photographs, video and audio streams, as well as medical and other 2D and 3D scans. Such data is relatively easy to capture and encode into a digital format, but far harder for a machine to 'understand'. Even so, one of the great opportunities presented by Big Data is to apply AI and other analytical tools to extract meaningful knowledge from exceedingly large quantities of unstructured digital content.

We will look more closely at how AI and deep learning are facilitating Big Data analysis in the next chapter. But alongside such cognitive computing developments, other technologies and techniques are also in play. One of these is Apache's Hadoop, which offers open-source software tools for 'reliable, scalable, distributed computing'. As the project's website further explains:

> The Apache Hadoop software library is a framework that allows for the distributed processing of large data sets across clusters of computers using simple programming models. It is designed to scale up from single servers to thousands of machines, each offering local computation and storage. Rather than rely on hardware to deliver high-availability, the library itself is designed to detect and handle failures at the application layer, so delivering a highly-

available service on top of a cluster of computers, each of which may be prone to failures.

In essence, Hadoop makes hardware scaling and hardware failure a software rather than a hardware problem, which in turn makes these issues far easier and cheaper to manage. Hadoop was developed by the Apache Software Foundation, which created the open source software that powers about two-thirds of the servers that host the worldwide web.

At the time of writing, Hadoop is based on four modules. The first is the 'Hadoop Distributed File System' (HDFS), which facilitates the reliable, high-speed storage and processing of Big Data sets across clusters of server computers. There is then a set of management utilities called 'Hadoop Common', as well as a 'framework for job scheduling and cluster resource management' called 'Hadoop YARN' (the Hadoop 'Yet Another Resource Negotiator').

The final Hadoop module is a data processing framework called 'Hadoop MapReduce'. This is based on Google's initial search technology, and distributes or 'maps' large data sets across multiple servers. Each of these individual computers then performs processing on its part of the overall data set, and from this creates a summary. The summaries are finally aggregated in the so-termed 'Reduce' stage. This approach allows extremely large raw data sets to be rapidly pre-processed and distilled before more traditional data analysis tools are applied.

To provide a simple example of MapReduce in action, a security service may need to identify a suspect in a Big Data set comprised of thousands of hours of digital video. To achieve this, the data set would be divided up and distributed to hundreds or thousands of servers, each of which would apply face recognition algorithms to extract the 'landmarks' (human features) from every face in every frame. This would create a 'reduced' set of landmark data on each server, which would then be amalgamated into a final, single file that could be fairly easily checked against the facial landmarks of the suspect. Moreover, searching for any other known individual would subsequently also be straightforward, as the 'reduced' version of the Big Data set would already exist.

Hadoop is not the only Big Data technology, with similar alternatives including Apache Spark, Cluster Map Reduce, High Performance Computing Cluster (HPCC) and Hydra. However, Hadoop is currently used by most Big Data pioneers. For example, the business social network LinkedIn uses Hadoop to generate over 100 billion personalized recommendations every week.

Effective Hadoop or similar Big Data implementations are complex to implement and maintain, with most organizations unlikely to have the resources and expertise to create and operate their own solution. Once again this is where cloud computing providers may add value, as they can offer on-demand, plug-and-play services.

Increasingly, Big Data solutions should allow companies to close off their 'data exhaust'. Or in other words, they should allow businesses to stop excreting the data they have painstakingly gathered before they have even processed it. For many years large retailers like Walmart and Tesco pioneered the collection of customer data (from loyalty card schemes and other initiatives), but could process less than a few per cent of this great ocean of valuable information.

Reducing data exhaust presents a significant digital transformation opportunity that will facilitate 'management by knowing'. Until this point in history, 'management' has largely been an art practiced by those who could make the best guesses. But in the future, such 'management by hunch and intuition' is likely to fall by the wayside as those running organizations are empowered by digital systems that are able to capture, store and generate value from Big Data.

As a final point, it is worth highlighting that the companies to benefit most from tomorrow's Big Data implementations are likely to be those that seek data sets from beyond their own business. A firm that only applies AI to analyze its own production, stock and logistics records may learn how to become more efficient. But it will never understand exactly why the demand for its products or services fluctuates.

There are, however, already public Big Data sets available from the likes of Amazon and other cloud providers, and which include information on the economy, climate, social media sentiment, public health, the human genome, and a whole host of online activity. Smart firms will increasingly access these public Big Data sets and use AI to correlate them with their own, internal business information. This is indeed what the digital transformation trend of 'management by knowing' will really be about. According to analysts IDC, global revenues from Big Data analytics will exceed $200 billion by 2020, and it is not hard to understand why.

## BLOCKCHAIN

Alongside cloud computing and Big Data, a third digital development that has many computing pundits very excited is blockchain. This records transactions in a widely distributed and tamper-proof public ledger, and in doing so significantly increases trust in digital exchanges.

Because a blockchain ledger is shared and synchronized across a great many computers, it cannot be altered retrospectively. It also cannot be corrupted or hacked, as there is no single potential point of failure in a blockchain network, and no one, single file for a hacker to attack. All of this means that blockchain transactions – financial or otherwise – are always supported by a rock solid audit trail. This is why business likes blockchain and sees great potential in its widespread application. Or as IBM express matters, blockchain 'fosters a new generation of transactional applications that establish trust, accountability and transparency – from contracts to deeds to payments'.

Like many current developments in computing, blockchain has a strong parallel in nature. Every living thing has its biological blueprint encoded in DNA, and keeps this digital code safe by keeping a copy in every cell of its body. In an attempt to secure artificial digital codes and transactions, a blockchain network is designed to do exactly the same thing by widely distributing copies of its ledger.

Blockchain was invented in 2008 as the technology behind the cryptocurrency Bitcoin. Today, an increasing number of blockchain applications have nothing to do with Bitcoin or any other cryptocurrency. This said, an explanation of Bitcoin provides a nice example of blockchain in operation, and is hence worth including here.

Bitcoin is a virtual currency that only exists online, and which is not backed by any physical token of value (such as gold), or any government or bank. All Bitcoin transactions are recorded in the currency's single blockchain, which is very widely distributed across a great many computers. New Bitcoins are created by performing digital 'mining' operations. These manipulate Bitcoin's blockchain by compiling recent transactions (which keeps the system running), and reward miners by releasing a new coin when their computer solves a complex computation.

If you own a Bitcoin, this means that there is a record of a transaction in its blockchain that has allocated the coin to your Bitcoin wallet. If you want to buy something with the Bitcoin, this requires you to transfer it to another person's wallet, and a request for this transaction will be broadcast to the computers or 'nodes' that form the Bitcoin network. Your requested transaction will be validated by the network, and combined with others to create a new 'block' of data. This will then be permanently added to the 'chain' of blocks that make up the Bitcoin ledger, so indicating that your Bitcoin is now owned by another person. As you would expect, the whole system is protected with appropriate cryptography.

As the example of Bitcoin hopefully makes clear, blockchain is powerful not only because it facilitates secure and trusted transactions, but because nothing is ever deleted. A network's blockchain just grows and grows, which means that it is possible to trace the history of every transaction that ever occurred. Digital money can hence always be traced back to its source. And if somebody does try to corrupt or falsify a record, it will always be possible to find out when this happened.

To maintain integrity, the nodes in a blockchain network regularly communicate with each other to ensure that the distributed ledger is constantly reconciled. Or as the website BlockGeeks so nicely explains:

> . . . the blockchain network lives in a state of consensus, one that automatically checks in with itself every ten minutes. A kind of self-auditing ecosystem of digital value, the network reconciles every transaction that happens in ten-minute intervals.

Just as the Internet transformed communications by providing an infrastructure with no central control, so blockchain could transform digital transactions. As Bitcoin has already demonstrated, blockchain can facilitate financial exchanges that do not require trust to be vested in a bank or a nation's regulatory authorities. The technology may similarly be used to protect the integrity and security of anything else that has digital value, including stock and logistics records, contracts and other legal documents, and medical data. Or as Stewart Bond, a director at IDC, has reported:

> Just as blockchain and distributed ledger technologies are disintermediating financial transactions and disrupting financial services, they also have the potential to disintermediate and disrupt data management, integration and governance processes and technologies, thereby making data trusted, available, secure, and compliant for everyone. IDC believes that blockchain innovations will provide data with integrity: data that is trusted, secure, compliant, and available to all parties that have an interest.

When it comes to digital transformation, it could be argued that blockchain is far from revolutionary as it simply allows us to achieve old things in new, more secure ways. To some extent this is also true, as blockchain is no more and no less than a new digital security and validation technology. But critically, blockchain does have the potential to shift our locus of trust from respected human organizations – such as banks and governments – to shared digital systems. In turn, this means that blockchain could trigger one of the most fundamental digital transformations of the next decade.

## VIRTUAL & AUGMENTED REALITY

Back in the mid-1990s, many books on the future of computing focused on one topic. And that topic was virtual reality (VR). Taking their inspiration from William Gibson's novel *Neuromancer*, the 'holodeck' on *Star Trek*, and films like *The Lawnmower Man*, technology pundits painted grand visions of people 'travelling' to work by donning a VR headset, and taking vacations in amazing locations that consisted entirely of 3D computer graphics.

To some extent, those in the 1990s who predicted that we were about to start working and playing in virtual worlds were entirely correct. The only thing they did not foresee was how most 'digital places' would be accessed on 2D screens.

Today billions of us spend a significant proportion of our time *visiting* websites, *working* collaboratively with SaaS tools, and *socializing* in virtual locations. Though due to the extraordinary computer processing capacity of the human brain, we have developed the ability to do this without the assistance of totally immersive 3D technologies.

The above point noted, some do now claim that a 'second coming' of VR is on the horizon. I would, however, caution that many current VR advocates also recently told us that most people would be prepared to don special glasses in their living room in order to watch a 3D television. Certainly many computing companies want to sell us VR. But I am not aware that most people actually want to buy it.

Due to the development of increased computer processing power, better and cheaper motion sensors, and improved displays, we are certainly on the brink of being able to *deliver* VR experiences fairly similar to those predicted in the mid-1990s. This is also likely to transform computer gaming, as well as industrial design and some forms of education, medical care and training. Yet beyond these quite specific arenas, the extent to which VR will become a mainstream business and domestic technology remains in question. This is because modern VR interfaces still require their user to wear a headset that soon makes many people feel ill. I therefore suspect that it will not be until the era of Cyborg Fusion – when we are able to directly jack our brains into cyberspace – that immersive VR will become a widespread destination of choice.

When it comes to short- and medium-term digital transformation, we are likely to see an increasing focus on the development and application not of virtual reality, but of 'augmented reality' (AR). This enables a human being to see computer graphics superimposed on their vision of the real world. AR may also be delivered either by donning a headset, or by holding up a tablet, smartphone or other display that provides a digitally-augmented window on the real world.

Right now, Microsoft has proclaimed itself the leader in AR (or what it terms 'mixed reality') due to its development of a 'holographic' head-mounted display (HMD) called Hololens. This, so the company claims, will soon allow Windows users to treat the physical world as a 'digital canvas' that can be augmented with all manner of digital visual content. Also in the game are Google, which in July 2017 launched a new, enterprise version of its 'Google Glass' AR headset for use in the workplace. A month earlier, Apple also launched a set of software tools called 'ARKit'.

Even with these developments from Apple, Google, Microsoft and others, I believe that we are a considerable distance from either VR or AR becoming fluid and comfortable enough to take the world by storm. VR and AR also continue to be computing interfaces that demand human attention, and I happen to believe that cognitive interfaces *that attend to us* will dominate computing in the 2020s and 2030s. Beyond this timeframe, and as cyborg fusion allows users to abandon screens and headsets, VR and AR may well become exceedingly popular. In chapter 6 we will examine what this may mean, and the transformational potential of VR and AR in the 2040s and beyond.

## THE INTERNET OF THINGS

In recent years there has been a trend to add some level of digital technology to a broadening variety of physical items, and to hook them up to the global net. The result is the 'Internet of Things' or 'IoT', with an increasing number of online objects no longer being traditional computers. In fact, most IoT devices are online 'things' whose primary function is something other than being a computer, and which have not previously been used to receive, collect or transmit digital information.

Already the number of Internet-enabled devices is growing faster than the human population, and at the time of writing there are estimated to be slightly more online devices than there are people on the planet. By 2020, Gartner expect the number of Internet-enabled devices to reach 20 billion. Cisco are even more optimistic, and predict 50 billion online devices by 2020, with only 17 per cent of these being desktop PCs, laptops, tablets or smartphones. Also according to Cisco (who make a large proportion of the world's Internet routers), there are roughly 1.5 trillion items that could benefit from Internet connectivity.

The growth of IoT technology means that the objects in our lives will increasingly become sources of data (and indeed Big Data). Within IoT populated environments, both people and AIs will also be able to remotely control a great many things. Perhaps most obviously, and as pictured in figure 2.2, IoT developments are already allowing the creation of 'smart homes'.

In a smart home, a hardware device or online service called an 'IoT hub' coordinates the connection of many different devices. This can, for example, allow a central heating boiler and individual radiators to be adjusted in response to multiple temperature sensor readings and several streams of occupant location data. Lights, as well as appliances like washing machines, may also be remotely controlled using a smartphone or other computing device. An online fridge may even report its remaining contents to its user while they are out buying groceries. Other smart home IoT devices already include online switches and sockets, door locks, plant watering systems, curtain controllers, pet feeders and online electricity meters.

To my mind, labelling any collection of the aforementioned devices as 'smart' is stretching the definition of that word beyond any credible limit. Right now, most 'smart homes' are exceedingly dumb, and would be far better described as 'digitally connected' or 'digitally controlled'. This said, 'smart speakers' – such as Amazon's Echo and Google Home – are

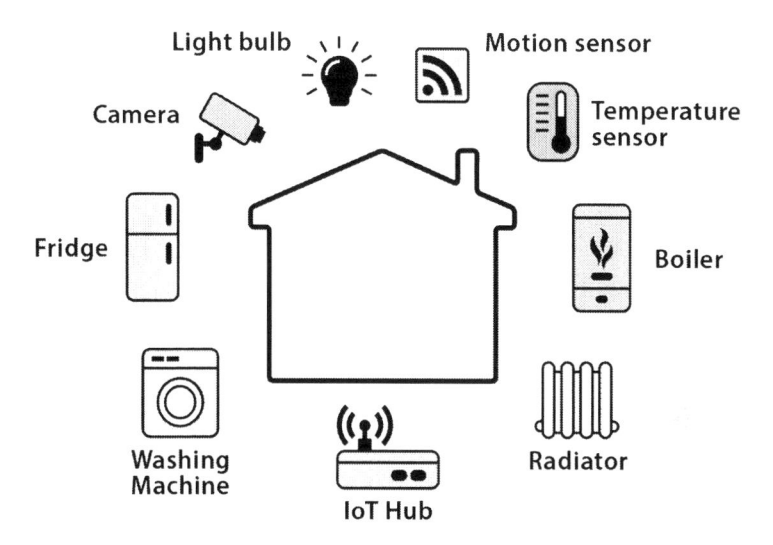

**Figure 2.2: IoT in the Home**

starting to be added into the smart home ecosystem, so finally introducing some level of AI into the mix. We will look at the possibilities this is starting to generate in the next chapter.

IoT technology also extends into wearable computing. Today 'wearables' include smartwatches (or in other words, watches with a computer and wireless connectivity), as well as health trackers that monitor their user's pulse, footsteps, sleep and other activities or bodily characteristics. In the near future, IoT health tracking is destined to become increasingly sophisticated, with personal sensors able to measure blood sugar levels and the status of a person's internal organs. Already heart surgery patients are being fitted with pacemakers that stream data over the Internet.

Consumer IoT technology still lacks a killer non-medical application. But out in industry, the situation is very different. Not least in logistics, the ability to turn almost any object into a connected sensor is being seized on to improve the 'visibility' of business operations. Indeed, in a recent report, DHL and Cisco highlighted how IoT implementations can 'light up' previously 'dark objects' to release valuable 'latent information'. As they went on to explain, a connected street light can provide information to city officials that allows them to optimize the flow of traffic. Or 'a connected forklift can alert a warehouse manager to an impending mechanical problem or safety risk, or [can] be used to create greater location intelligence of inventory'.

Increasingly, vehicles, parcels, components, shelves, motion sensors, doors, cameras and microphones are going to join humans as the eyes, ears and other sense organs of smarter and smarter organizations. As a consequence, transportation and storage will be optimized, energy and other resources saved, and production lines run and maintained at optimum efficiency. This may of course not be something that all human employees will welcome, as the increased monitoring and control of *things* will almost inevitably lead to the increased monitoring and control of *people*.

According to Cisco and DHL, by 2025 IoT technologies will have generated over $8 trillion of value added across the public and private sectors. This is clearly a very large claim, and I suspect a prediction that more accurately reflects the future value added of a great many digital technologies employed in combination. We really must not lose sight of the fact that most IoT developments are about extending the cloud to a wider and wider range of connected devices, and in the process generating an increasing quantity of Big Data that future AIs will process. It therefore should not surprise you that several large cloud computing and AI pioneers now offer an IoT platform. These include Amazon's AWS IoT and Microsoft's Azure IoT Suite.

Some – including Cisco – now refer to the Internet of Things as just one component of an even broader 'Internet of Everything' (IoE). This new term reminds us that it is not just physical things that are increasingly going to be interlinked online, but also people, other organic entities, AIs, robots and cloud applications. Indeed sometime this century the term 'digital technology' is going to become meaningless, as sooner or later every natural and artificial object, every intelligent being, and every virtual entity, is likely to fall under this banner.

## ARTIFICIAL INTELLIGENCE

Since the 1980s we have been pointing radio telescopes into deep space in the vague hope of finding another intelligent species. I find this somewhat amusing, as another intelligent species will soon be very easy to locate on our first planet. This second intelligent species will of course be artificial intelligence. I really have no doubt that, in the next two decades, AI will defy its critics and prove itself as the greatest innovation in history.

In futurist circles, the development of AI is strongly associated with a point in future history known as the 'Singularity'. This is a technological event horizon beyond which we cannot see, and that we will reach when exponential progress makes possible anything we can imagine.

As I explored in my 2015 book *The Next Big Thing*, we will arrive at the Singularity when the divide between 'technology' and 'magic' blurs. Or as I further explained, on a more practical level:

> ... the Singularity will be upon us when we are able to digitally program, replicate, repair and otherwise control all forms of living or inorganic matter. At the Singularity and beyond, we will also no longer face any resource constraints, as we will have learned how to turn waste products into fresh raw materials, or to access the very broad range of resources waiting for us beyond Planet Earth.

The technological progress implied in the above quotation is unlikely to be delivered by those who only possess the intellectual capacity of a human brain. Rather, our journey toward the Singularity will require the development of beyond human intelligence, and that is where AI will come into its own.

AIs are already uniquely equipped to evolve into smarter and smarter entities. This is because the application of AI facilitates the development of more sophisticated technologies (such as improved conventional microprocessors, quantum processors and biocomputers), with these in turn allowing even more sophisticated AIs to be created. This positive feedback system is known as the 'Singularity Loop', and is illustrated in figure 2.3. As the figure highlights, AI is unique as a digital transformation technology as its development will catalyze not just its own evolution, but also that of all other technologies and innovations.

Already the concepts and consequences of the Singularity Loop are raising concerns in some quarters. Not least, fears have been raised that any further development of AI will threaten the survival of the human race. Others – myself included – believe that without the future assistance of AI we are destined for terminal decline anyway, and hence that we need to advance smart technologies as rapidly as possible. We will return to these critical debates and related issues throughout the rest of this book. In particular, the next chapter explores a range of specific AI concepts, technologies, products and applications.

## ROBOTS

'Digital transformation' is just one of the technological buzz-terms currently doing the rounds in companies and business schools. Closely-related cousins are 'digital disruption', 'hyper-connectedness' and 'Industry 4.0'. The last of these has a focus on automation, and in particular the creation of 'cyber physical systems'.

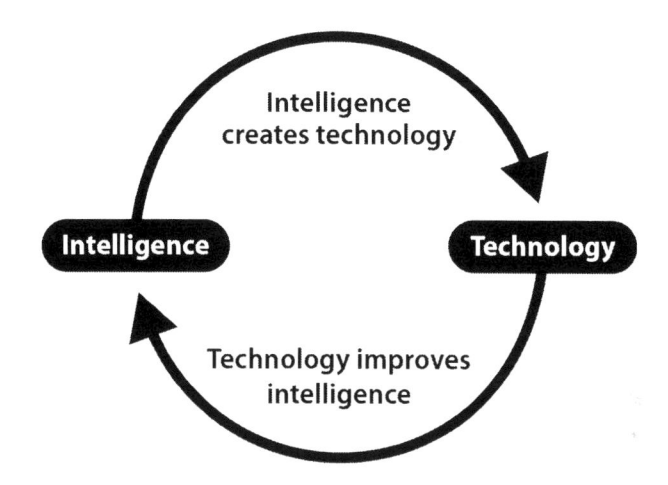

**Figure 2.3: The Singularity Loop.**

Cyber physical systems integrate computers, networking technologies and physical processes. They hence include production lines, robots and other mechanical mechanisms that are under smart digital control. According to the Industry 4.0 concept, we have previously experienced the revolutions of early mechanization, mass production, and the implementation of traditional computing and dumb automation. The introduction of cyber physical systems hence signals the arrival of our fourth industrial revolution.

As the Industry 4.0 model implies, for several decades computer-numerically-controlled (CNC) machine tools have been used in industry, with robots employed in large factories such as automobile manufacturing plants. But what is changing in the face of cloud computing, AI and IoT is the level of sophistication and smartness now attainable in a physical mechanism.

As we shall see in chapter 4, robots are on the rise. In the next two decades, independent cyber physical systems are also set to emerge from the factory floor to share previously human-only spaces, and to undertake previously human-only activities. This will be made possible by developments in attentive computing that will allow robots to develop an awareness of their environment, and to intelligently interact with the physical world. Around 2030, we should also expect an increasing proportion of robots to take humanoid form so that they can master the use of human tools and 'interpersonal' communication.

## AUTONOMOUS VEHICLES & DARK FACTORIES

Before humanoid robots populate our homes and public spaces, the most common cyber physical systems will be autonomous vehicles. The development of self-driving cars, trucks and tractors is indeed at the forefront of attentive computing. After all, before a vehicle is able to undertake journeys by itself without causing havoc, it will need to be highly attentive to what is going on around it. There is absolutely no doubt that autonomous vehicles will only be licensed for sale once they are able to respond exceedingly well to changing road and weather conditions, not to mention the 'random' actions of pedestrians and human drivers.

By the mid-to-late 2020s, both computing companies and traditional car manufacturers expect to be selling semi-autonomous and then entirely autonomous vehicles. When this happens, it will constitute a watershed not just for motoring, but for computing, robots and AI. The consumer sale of the first fully autonomous vehicle will indeed provide the first and best signal of our ability to make self-aware cyber physical systems that can safely and autonomously function within human society.

Meanwhile, away from the public gaze, during the 2020s industry will witness the increasing rollout of so-termed 'dark factories'. These manufacturing facilities do not need human operators, and can hence run 24/7 without any lighting on the factory floor. The idea may sound like science fiction. But already several businesses – and most notably some manufacturers in China – are pushing smart automation in this direction.

For example, the Changying Precision Technology Company – which produces cell phones – has already replaced most of the human workforce in its Dongguan plant with robot arms. The factory used to employ 650 workers, but now requires just 60, with this number expected to fall to about 20. None of the remaining staff are involved in hands-on production, but instead monitor the robots to ensure that everything is running as it should. In the wake of this extraordinary level of automation, productivity has increased by 250 per cent, while product defects have fallen by 80 per cent. Already the phone in your hand may have been assembled entirely by a robot.

Back in 1990, China manufactured about 3 per cent of the world's products. Today, this figure is 25 per cent, including 71 per cent of cell phones, and 63 per cent of shoes. But labour costs in China have been rising at 12 per cent a year since 2001, which is starting to make its factories less and less competitive.

Robots and dark factories have been identified as the digital technologies that will maintain and boost China's position as the largest manufacturer on the planet. To this end, the Chinese Government has set a goal for the country to overtake the manufacturing sophistication of Germany, Japan and the United States by 2049. We should therefore expect China to become the world leader in robotics long before this time. Further, we should confidently predict that the cyber physical systems it creates will drive digital transformation on a global scale.

## 3D PRINTING

As several of the previous sections highlight, many future digital innovations will transform the physical world rather than the online realm. Such developments include the application of Big Data, AI and IoT to improve logistics, as well as the mass roll-out of robots, autonomous vehicles and dark factories. In addition, several technologies will increasingly allow us to engage in 'local digital manufacturing' or 'LDM'. This refers to the automated transformation of digital data into a physical product in pretty much any location. Already several technologies may be classified as a form of LDM, although right now the one receiving the most attention is 3D printing.

3D printing turns digital designs into physical things by building them up in layers. The process begins with a model in a computer aided design (CAD) package, or a 3D scan. This is then vertically 'sliced' into a stack of cross-sections that are typically about 0.1mm thin. A 3D printer next outputs these slices one on top of the other. 3D printing is also known as 'additive manufacturing' (AM), as it is a production process that starts with nothing and adds only the material that is required.

3D printing can already fabricate objects in many different materials that include plastics, metals and ceramics. This is achieved using hardware based on a wide variety of processes, most of which fall within one of four broad categories.

Firstly, we have 3D printers that build objects by extruding a semi-liquid material from a computer-controlled nozzle. Such hardware most commonly outputs a heated thermoplastic, although material extrusion can also make things out of plastic-metal composites, clay, concrete, pure metals and various kinds of food. 3D printers based on material extrusion are currently priced from about $200 for entry-level desktop models, rising to in excess of $700,000 for the large-scale '3D Production Systems' used in some factories. Figure 2.4 shows a plastic elephant being created via material extrusion on an Ultimaker desktop 3D printer.

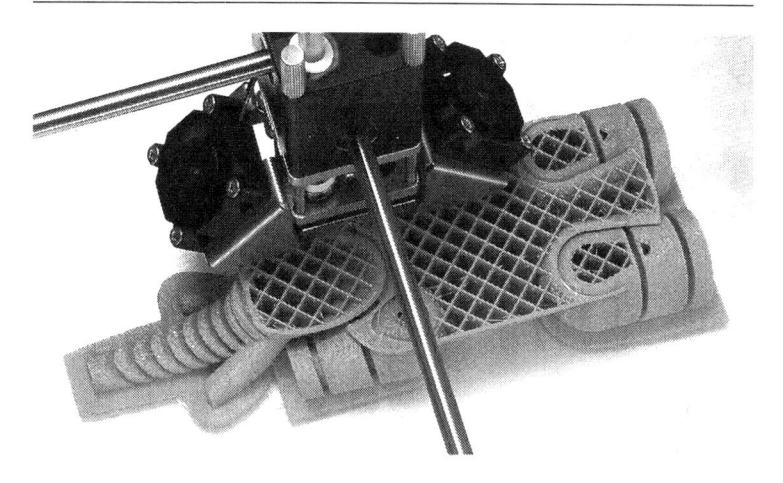

**Figure 2.4: 3D Printing on an Ultimaker 2.**

The second broad category of 3D printing technology creates objects via 'photopolymerization'. Here a light source is used to solidify a photocurable resin. Some 3D printers achieve this by using a laser to trace out each object layer on the surface or base of a vat of liquid photopolymer. The 'build platform' on which the object is being fabricated is then lowered or raised slightly, another layer is traced out and solidified, and so on.

Alternative photopolymerization 3D printers use a process called 'material jetting' to spray liquid resins from an inkjet-style print head, with each layer set solid with UV light before the next is added. The material jetting process is expensive, but has the advantage of being able to create multi-material, multi-colour objects by spraying and mixing different resins. Figure 2.5 shows a full-colour medical model produced via material jetting.

The third and broadest category of 3D printer builds objects via 'granular materials binding'. This means that it lays down successive layers of powder, and selectively sticks the granules together. Some powder-based hardware employs

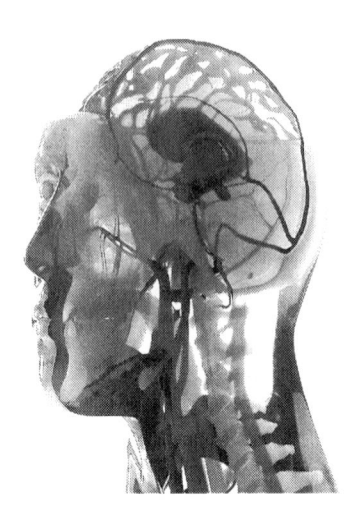

**Figure 2.5: A Medical Model 3D Printed Via Material Jetting**

a technique called 'binder jetting', which selectively sprays glue onto each powder layer. As illustrated in figure 2.6, this can allow the 3D printout of sand molds and cores for use in a traditional sand casting manufacturing process.

Other powder-based 3D printers use a laser, electron beam or other heat source to partially or completely fuse together the powder granules that form final object layers. This process goes by a variety of names depending on the hardware manufacturer, but is most commonly known as 'powder bed fusion' or 'laser sintering'. 3D printers based on this technology can fabricate objects using a wide range of materials that currently include nylon, stainless steel, aluminium, copper, titanium and cobalt chrome. Figure 2.7 shows a replacement human jaw bone laser sintered in titanium.

A final and less common 3D printing process is generically known as 'sheet lamination', and builds objects by sticking together cut sheets of paper, plastic or metal. Where cut paper is used as the build material, low-cost, full-colour models can

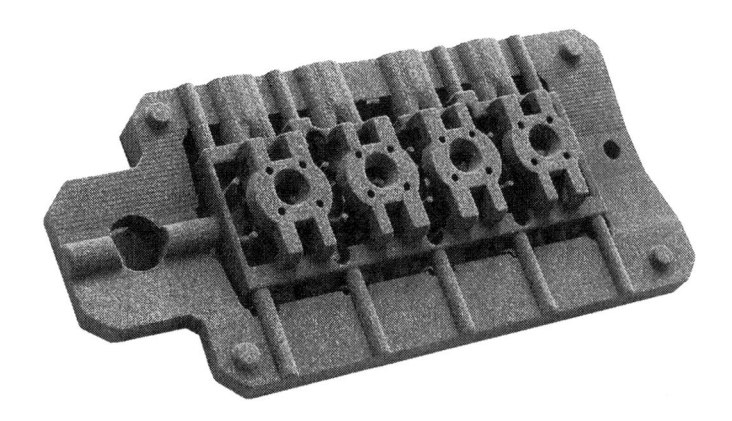

**Figure 2.6: 3D Printed Sand Core.**

be produced by spraying-on coloured inks during the 3D printing process. Metal-based sheet lamination also offers interesting possibilities, such as the fabrication of solid metal objects with embedded sensors. A pioneer of this technology is Fabrisonic, who have created 'ultrasonic additive manufacturing' (UAM). This welds together thin layers of metal tape using high frequency (20,000 hertz) vibrations.

For its first few decades 3D printing was dominated by those companies, such as Stratasys and 3D Systems, who invented its core technologies. These startup pioneers also largely sold hardware that was used for 'rapid prototyping' (RP). However, as we approach the 2020s, the 3D printing marketplace is changing dramatically. For a start, 3D printing is increasingly being used to make molds, jigs and other production tooling, as well as to fabricate final product parts. By 2020, it is indeed widely expected that most 3D prints will no longer be prototypes. And by 2025 or 2030, 3D printing may well be a mainstream manufacturing technology.

Reflecting the above, in the past few years several large, traditional manufacturers have either started to make their

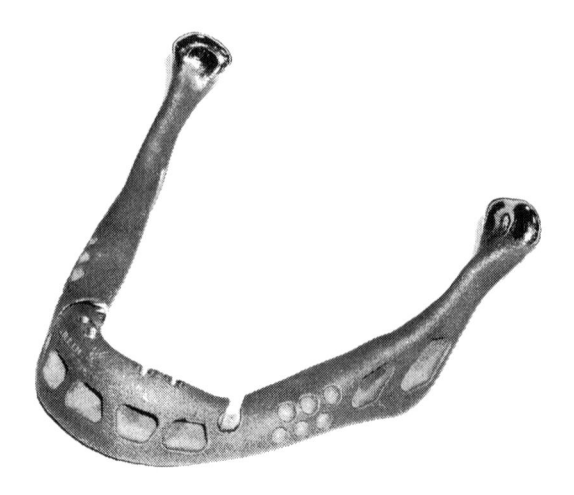

**Figure 2.7: Jaw Bone Laser Sintered in Titanium.**

own 3D printers, or have bought-out existing companies. Not least, in 2016 HP released its first industrial 3D printer, while GE spent around $1.4 billion purchasing the direct-metal 3D printer manufacturer Arcam, together with a 75 per cent stake in a similar company called Concept Laser. Following these acquisitions, GE formed a new division called GE Additive, which in June 2017 announced that it is developing the largest ever 3D printer for fabricating final parts in metal.

Another significant 3D printing trend is the rise of 'hybrid technology'. This refers to the creation of machines that combine 3D printing with robotic mechanisms or computer numerically controlled (CNC) tools. Companies that already have such hardware on the market include machine tool manufacturers Sodick and Mazak.

Capitalizing on the above trends and developments, in the past few years 3D printers have started to be used to produce final products or parts thereof. To cite just a few examples, Airbus, Boeing and GE are now all using 3D printers to make final aerospace parts, including aircraft engine fuel injectors. Local Motors are also working on a range of automobiles called LM3D that will be 75 per cent 3D printed by volume. Over in China, construction pioneer WinSun Decoration Design Engineering has even 3D printed several multi-story concrete buildings, and has plans for thousands more. Meanwhile, back in the United States, both Feetz and Prevolve have started to sell personalized shoes that are printed to match 3D scans of their customer's feet.

As the technology continues to improve, the opportunities to use 3D printing to directly manufacture all manner of things is going to be considerable. No longer will remote factories have to mass-manufacture standardized items that are then stored in vast warehouses in the hope that somebody will want to buy them. Rather, customized products (and spare parts to repair them) will be able to be printed-on-demand in a factory or bureau close to each customer's location. On some occasions, products may even be 3D printed in a local store or on a customer's own kitchen table. Tomorrow's cloud computing data centres are therefore likely to be stocked with physical items awaiting printout, in addition to Big Data containing other categories of information.

If the above were not revolutionary enough, several research teams are now learning how to 3D print organic tissue from a culture of living cells. This is known as 'bioprinting', and in the 2020s or 2030s will create replacement human tissues for transplant purposes. Proving the viability of the process, in November 2015 a Russian startup called Bioprinting Solutions revealed that it had bioprinted several thyroid glands and successfully transplanted them into live mice. The rodents were closely monitored following their surgery, and after 11 weeks had a completely restored thyroid function.

Another bioprinting pioneer is a Californian company called Organovo. Here a team under Gabor Forgacs has developed a bioprinter called the Novogen MMX. This builds organic tissue by placing tiny clusters of cells known as 'bio-ink spheroids' into protective layers of a water-based hydrogel known as 'bio-paper'. The bio-ink spheroids are comprised of an aggregate of many different types of cells, which have been cultured in the lab following a patient biopsy.

As illustrated in figure 2.8, once multiple layers of bio-ink spheroids have been printed, they self-assemble into solid tissue. Quite staggeringly, not only do the individual cells fuse together, but via natural, biological processes they somehow rearrange to end up in the correct anatomical location. So, for example, if a blood vessel is being fabricated, endothelial cells migrate to its inside, while smooth muscle cells move to the middle and fibroblasts shift to the outside of the 3D structure. If an entire kidney is being bioprinted, intricate capillaries even form naturally, rather than having to be printed as part of the design. While cells rearrange during the quite extraordinary, post-printout 'maturation phase', the bio-paper that initially held the non-fused cells in place either dissolves away or is otherwise removed.

In December 2010 Organovo used a Novogen MMX to create the first bioprinted human blood vessels. In November 2014 it then began to sell bioprinted human liver tissues for use in drug testing, and in September 2016 added bioprinted human liver tissue to its product range. A month later Organovo announced a formal program to develop bio-printed liver tissue for human transplantation, with its intention at that time being to apply for an FDA license for human trials 'in three to five years'.

As the aforementioned progress makes clear, in the coming decades digital technologies are set to transform not just the world of inorganic matter, but also the living substance of ourselves. This could lead to extraordinary innovations in healthcare, as well as the opportunity to redesign or augment

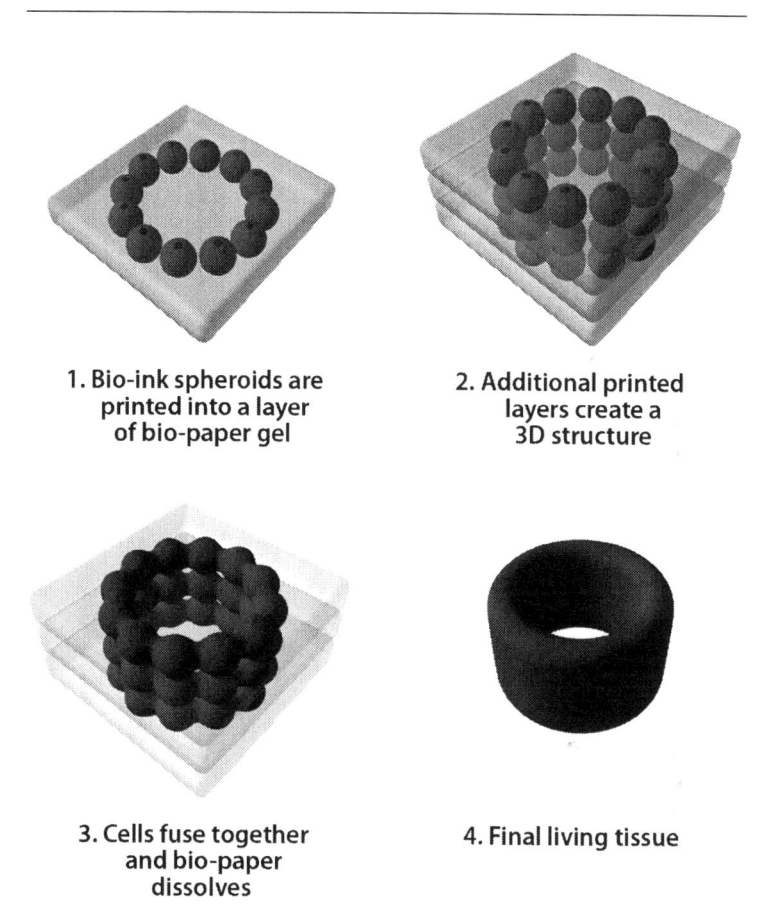

1. Bio-ink spheroids are printed into a layer of bio-paper gel

2. Additional printed layers create a 3D structure

3. Cells fuse together and bio-paper dissolves

4. Final living tissue

**Figure 2.8: Bioprinting with Bio-ink & Bio-paper.**

our bodies. Indeed, I know one bioprinting pioneer – Ibrahim Ozbolat at Penn State University – who believes that future patients may be fitted with several small, bio-printed pancreatic organs (rather than a single, replacement transplant) in order to provide 'redundancy cover'. Nature has been the master of human biology since our species first evolved. But this is not necessarily going to remain the case in the future.

## SYNTHETIC BIOLOGY

Talking of nature, take a walk in the countryside and you can see a great many cool digital things. These extraordinary items of hardware are generally known as 'plants' and 'animals', and have the remarkable ability to (re)manufacture themselves based on a digital code stored in their DNA.

For centuries human beings have capitalized on natural biological processes by cultivating crops, rearing animals, and fermenting products such as beer, cheese and yoghurt. But what if we could go further and digitally program new living things as an artificial production technology? Well, we have in fact already started to do this with the creation of synthetic biology or 'SynBio'. This takes an engineering approach to biology, with DNA broken down into a set of modular parts that can be rearranged in a computer and chemically pieced together.

Already synthetic biology is being used to develop novel microorganisms that can ferment sugar beet or other forms of starch into biofuels, bioplastics, bioacrylics and pharmaceuticals. Pioneers in the field include Amyris, who already use synthetic biology to produce a biodiesel called Biofene, a solvent called Myralene, and a drug to treat malaria. Randy Lewis of the University of Wyoming has even used synthetic biology to create goats that produce spider silk in their milk. This can be easily extracted by centrifuging the goat's lactations, and woven into a super-strong thread.

In May 2010, the J. Craig Venter Institute (JCVI) in the United States revealed that it had used synthetic biology to manufacture the first self-replicating, synthetic bacterial cell. Labelled 'JCVI-syn1.0', this was constructed from 1,078 DNA 'components' that the JCVI team designed and spliced together, and then transplanted into an existing *Mycoplasma capricolum* bacterium. They then electrically booted-up this cell to end up with a new form of life.

As JCVI explained, the creation of JCVI-syn1.0 proved that 'genomes can be designed in the computer, chemically made in the laboratory and transplanted into a recipient cell to produce a new self-replicating cell controlled only by the synthetic genome'. Or as J. Craig Venter, the Institute's founder and director went on to comment, JCVI-syn1.0 was 'the first self-replicating life form with a computer as its parent'.

In March 2016, JCVI produced the first 'minimal synthetic cell' – or in other words, the first synthetic cell that has had all of the 'redundant parts' of a natural living cell removed. The previous May, JCVI sister company SGI-DNA even launched the first 'DNA printer'. Known as the BioXp 3200, this is loaded with liquid reagents that turn a digital design into a new form of DNA in about 12-17 hours. Or as SGI-DNA further explain, the BioXp 3200 is:

> . . . a machine which will allow any biotechnology company or academic laboratory to create genes, genetic elements and molecular tools on their benchtop hands-free, starting with electronically transmitted sequence data.

As in other areas of computing, synthetic biology is now devising its own open standards. For example, the 'synthetic biology open language' (SBOL) provides a common data format for modular DNA parts. Open software applications for the design of biological parts have also been created. These include GenoCAD, which as the OMICtools website explains:

> . . . is built on the idea that DNA is a language to program biological systems. GenoCAD includes large libraries of annotated genetic parts, which serve as the words of the genetic language.

GenoCAD also includes design rules describing how parts should be combined to form functional genetic constructs.

Synthetic biology is a new nexus point where the *inorganic* digital world of computing, and the *organic* digital world of biology, are coming together. Just as 3D printers are increasingly set to turn digital designs into physical objects by building them up in layers, so synthetic biology is increasingly going to turn digital designs into physical things by harnessing the power of life itself.

In effect, what synthetic biology is doing is capitalizing on the natural process of 'self-assembly' that all living things use to put themselves together. No animal, plant or microorganism reaches for a set of machine tools to arrange its molecular components in the right places, and neither does synthetic biology.

## MOLECULAR SELF-ASSEMBLY

While synthetic biology offers amazing possibilities, later this century we may even develop hardware that will self-assemble inorganic, non-living physical things according to a digital template. This will involve the application of nanotechnology, which seeks to manipulate matter on the molecular scale. Today 'nanolithographic' processes are used to produce microprocessors and other silicon chips with components that are only a few hundred atoms across. Such nanotech manufacturing techniques are certainly amazing. But future inorganic 'molecular self-assembly' processes will be far more advanced.

Molecular self-assembly refers to a manufacturing process in which nanoscale parts fit themselves together without any external intervention. This becomes possible when each individual part of an object has a distinct set of bumps and hollows that allows it to correctly lock-on to other components when they are mixed together. So, in effect, the idea is to introduce Lego-brick-like, artificially-designed molecular parts into a vessel where they are shaken together until they form into the desired object. Or to put this another way, the concept is akin to putting all of the molecular components required to make a smartphone into a cocktail shaker, giving it a really good workout, and opening up the container to remove the latest, fully-assembled Samsung or Apple device. If this sounds absolutely crazy, just remember that molecular self-assembly is the process that life already uses to build every living thing on the planet, including complex computers like the human brain.

The first, experimental 'molecular 3D printer' based on the self-assembly process has already been created. Constructed at the University of Illinois by a team led by Martin D. Burke, this can fabricate highly complex, carbon-based small molecules 'at the click of a mouse'. The incredible hardware assembles the molecules in an additive fashion from simple chemical building blocks. The team have already managed to build 14 different classes of small molecules, with possible applications existing in the development of LEDs, solar cells and medications. We may be decades away from building everyday molecular self-assembly hardware. But the foundations for this future technology are now being laid.

In the decades ahead, and under the watchful control of ultra smart AIs, I predict that the three currently-identified forms of local digital manufacturing – 3D printing, synthetic biology and inorganic molecular self-assembly – will converge into a single technology. This will allow the creation of 'microfabricators' that will be able to turn almost any imaginable digital design into a physical thing. Over the past few decades, our economy and society have been transformed by machines – we call them 'microprocessors' – that routinely manipulate *information*. But later this century, we are in for a far more fundamental digital transformation as analogous machines called 'microfabricators' enter the fray. These will routinely manipulate physical matter on a grand scale, so fundamentally altering the way a great many things are produced.

## QUANTUM & ORGANIC COMPUTING

As we saw in the last chapter, from the late 1950s computer hardware came to be dominated by the transistor, and then the silicon chip. There are, however, limits to how far we will be able to advance this kind of technology. To produce future AIs, microfabricators, and other highly-transformative digital innovations, we will therefore need to start building computers in fundamentally new ways.

Right now, two avenues of research present themselves as the potential road ahead. The first is 'quantum computing', which capitalizes on the quantum mechanical properties of subatomic particles to deliver extraordinary new computational possibilities. The second is the creation of organic computers, or what has been termed 'artificial wetware'. These next-generation hardware developments are the specific subject of chapter 5, so I will say no more about them here.

## CYBERNETIC INTERFACES

Our final digital transformation driver is the invention (or synthetic evolution) of hardware and software that will directly interface a human being with a computer. As I signalled in the last chapter, my guess is that this kind of technology will come of age from around 2040. Not least this is because its development will be contingent on very significant advancements in AI, as well as fundamental and related progress in synthetic biology and organic computing.

The final chapter of *Digital Genesis* is called 'Cyborg Fusion', and details current and possible-future cybernetic interface developments. So once again I will leave my coverage of this topic until later in this book. This chapter has, I am pretty certain, already left us with more than enough to think about.

※ ※ ※

## THE FUTURE DIGITAL LANDSCAPE

Today, many people work, play and socialize using computer hardware, software and networks that would have been unbelievable just 20 years ago. As just one example, I earn a significant proportion of my living by uploading digital content to a platform (YouTube) that only came into existence in 2005, and which could not have existed much before that time. This fact alone ought to remind us that ongoing 'digital transformation' is very real, and that we ought to take its future potential and implications extremely seriously.

As we have explored across this chapter, in the years ahead digital transformation is destined to involve a great deal more than faster computing and the rise of new media. For this reason, I suspect that we will soon look back and realize how digital transformations to date have actually been quite minor. Many people today will, I am pretty certain, end up recounting tales of a past age in which 'computing' and 'digital' mainly involved an ancient information network called the 'Internet'.

Back at the start of this chapter, I defined 'digital transformation' as 'the use of computing and other digital technologies to create interconnection and smartness, and to deliver new manufacturing systems and working methods'. As I hope you now appreciate, the 'interconnection and smartness' part will come from developments in cloud computing, Big Data, blockchain, virtual reality, augmented reality, IoT, AI and cybernetic interfaces. In parallel, AI advancements, coupled with the ascendance of autonomous vehicles, robots, dark factories, 3D printing, synthetic biology, molecular self-assembly, organic computing and quantum computing, are set to 'deliver new manufacturing systems and working methods'. This second set of technologies will also weave their digital magic in a manner that will radically transform both the inorganic and the organic physical world, including the hardware of ourselves. Or in other words, this second set of technologies will take us on our journey to the Singularity.

This chapter has covered a lot of material. So much that, if you are new to this kind of stuff, you may want to place a cold compress on your head to provide a heat sink for your brain. The world of 'digital' is exploding with challenges and opportunities as never before. So just what are we to make of the myriad possibilities?

Well, I would suggest that the key takeaway from this chapter is that future digital transformation is going to be far more about manipulating the physical world than it is about processing and communicating information.

# 3
## THE DAWN OF AI

In 1950, computing pioneer Alan Turing published a paper called *Computing Machinery And Intelligence*. This hypothesized an 'imitation game' in which an interrogator would ask questions of two hidden subjects, one male and one female. Communication between the interrogator and the subjects was limited to typed messages exchanged via teleprinter. Relying solely on these text communications, the interrogator's apparent task was to determine which of the game's subjects was the man, and which was the woman.

The actual purpose of Turing's imitation game was to establish whether a machine could replace one of its human subjects without the interrogator knowing. A machine able to fool a person in this manner would subsequently be deemed capable of 'thinking'.

For many years, the ability to imitate a human being in a text-based communications exchange was taken as the benchmark of 'artificial intelligence' (AI). This is also extremely sad, as there is no reason to believe that the ability to imitate a human is a sound measure of 'intelligence'. Indeed, as even Alan Turing conceded, what later became known as the 'Turing Test' may be criticised because 'the odds are weighted too heavily against the machine'. Or as the great man himself wrote in his seminal 1950 paper:

> If the man were to try and pretend to be the machine he would clearly make a very poor showing. He would be given away at once by slowness and inaccuracy in arithmetic. May not machines carry out something which ought to be described as thinking but which is very different from what a man does?

'Intelligence' is a very hard concept to precisely pin down. Nevertheless, a definition of 'intelligence' is rather handy in any discussion of an 'artificial' variant. Herein I will therefore define intelligence as the ability to acquire information, to use that information in cognitive tasks including problem solving and learning, and to take actions or engage in communications as a result of such cognitive activities.

Most human beings are excellent at acquiring, applying, learning from, acting on and communicating information. As the second most intelligent species on the planet, dolphins are also pretty good at doing these things. This said, nobody expects a dolphin to be able to pass the Turing Test. Nor would they doubt a dolphin's intelligence because it is unable to mimic a human being in a text-based communications exchange.

We classify dolphins as 'intelligent' based on our observations of how they perceive, cognitively process, act on and reflect their own, non-human situation. I would similarly suggest that AIs need to be judged in precisely the same manner. I consequently propose that an AI should be defined as any artificial entity that is able to capture, cognitively process, learn from, act on or meaningfully report information. Or, if you like, we can just take the term 'AI' to refer to a smart machine.

This *Digital Genesis* chapter addresses the development of AI and its future applications and implications. In this context, I have opened with the above comments to stress how foolish it is to try and equate AI with HI (human intelligence). Will future AIs ever be able to 'think' and 'feel' just like a human? Probably not – although to be honest, almost certainly we will never know. And unless you are a philosopher, this does not and should not matter.

What does matter is that AI is set to become a viable alternative to HI in an increasing number of business and social situations. AI is also, I believe, the innovation that will drive and define our use of computing and other digital technologies across the next couple of decades. AI as a potential substitute for HI, and as the poster child of the Cognitive Computing Age, will therefore be our focus here.

## AI FOUNDATIONS

Since the days of Antiquity human beings have imagined the creation of artificially intelligent mechanisms. However, it was not until the invention of the first electronic computers that Alan Turing and others started to consider this an actual possibility. Writing software that could play games was considered a good place to start, and in 1950 an engineer and cryptographer called Claude Shannon published a research paper entitled *Programming a Computer to Play Chess*.

Shannon's work was based on the proposition that the strength of each chess player's position could be scored mathematically. This allowed a computer to select its next move by evaluating all possibilities, and then picking the one that would result in the best score. In 1951 this theory was put into practice when Dietrich Prinz wrote the first computer program that could play chess. A year later, Christopher Strachey also wrote a program that could play the simpler board game checkers (draughts). Both programs ran on the Ferranti Mark 1 computer at the University of Manchester, and are generally considered to be the first examples of AI.

The programs written by Prinz and Strachey evaluated every possible next move before selecting the one to play.

While Strachey's checkers program achieved a reasonable speed, Prinz's chess application was far slower than a human player due to the higher complexity of the game. Alan Turing and others subsequently realized that for AIs to become faster and more effective, they had to cease to apply all-encompassing, definitive rules, and to switch to 'heuristics'. The latter are problem-solving shortcuts, and are based on reasonable assumptions or observed patterns that allow an AI to discount many possibilities in order to save processing time.

Between 1952 and 1962, Arthur Samuel at IBM in the United States used heuristics to create an increasingly advanced checkers AI. This applied a number of heuristics according to a set of rankings, and could improve its performance by learning. To achieve this, the program constantly changed its heuristic rankings, and discarded those that resulted in a poorer performance.

Samuel speeded the learning process by pitting two copies of his AI against each other, so allowing them to play a great many games and improve via 'natural selection'. This approach laid the foundation for the development of 'genetic algorithms' (GAs). These are software programs that similarly 'evolve' by learning in order to become increasingly fit for purpose.

## NEURAL NETWORKS & DEEP LEARNING

Other early AI pioneers included Frank Rosenblatt, who in 1957 wrote a report called *The Perceptron: A Perceiving and Recognizing Automation*. This proposed the development of a machine able to 'recognize complex patterns', such as lights, sounds or other environmental stimuli, with the system having the ability to identify 'the "same" object in different orientations, sizes, colors, or transformations, and against a variety of backgrounds'.

What Rosenblatt was describing was the creation of an 'artificial neural network' (ANN). These are not explicitly programmed to accomplish tasks, but instead learn from observational data by being exposed to repeated examples that establish connective patterns. In 1960, Rosenblatt's Perceptron was constructed at the Cornell Aeronautical Laboratory, and was taught to recognize foot-high images of letters placed before an array of photocells.

ANNs function in a manner that is loosely modelled on the operation of the human brain. They are comprised of layers of 'artificial neurons' (or 'nodes'), each of which can carry a positive or negative numerical 'weight', and which are interconnected via 'artificial synapses'. Each artificial neuron adds up the input signals it receives, and if the result is high enough this triggers adjacent neurons. In aggregate, the signals from all of the neurons generates a final network output.

An ANN learns by comparing its output to correct data or expectations, and then modifies the weights of each artificial neuron in order to iterate toward the most successful result. When sufficient learning has occurred, the network can then be set to work. So, to provide a practical example, an ANN may be presented with several pictures of an object in order to learn to identify it correctly. It can then be used to search a far larger image database for sightings of the same object.

ANNs facilitate complex 'machine learning' (ML), and so remove the need for human beings to program AIs with specific rules and knowledge. Over the past 10 years, techniques that permit 'deep learning' have also been devised. These utilize ANNs with 'hidden layers' of artificial neurons and synapses sandwiched between their inputs and outputs. Figure 3.1 illustrates this concept for a very simple deep learning ANN. It should be noted that the largest ANNs already contain millions of neurons/nodes.

Complex ANNs and deep learning are instrumental in the development of AI in areas that include speech recognition, vision recognition and natural language processing (NLP). Many of today's most successful commercial AIs – including Alphabet's DeepMind and IBM's Watson – are subsequently based on this technology.

While AIs based on ANNs and deep learning can be extremely powerful, they are controversial in some quarters. This is because the internal operation of a large ANN can be impossible for a human being to understand. If an AI is created that learns via the evolutionary process of finding the most optimal heuristic rankings, then a human programmer can always inspect its final code to see which rules are most strongly being applied. But an ANN AI learns by recognising patterns of connectivity across its artificial neurons and artificial synapses. It can therefore be impossible for a person to 'open the black box' to find out *exactly* how a very complex deep learning AI actually delivers its results.

Recently I spoke at an AI conference where this issue resulted in some fairly heated debate. Specifically, an expert whose company supplied military and industrial AIs expressed reservations about using ANNs and deep learning. In particular, he noted that military clients always wanted to know every rule that their AIs would follow. Meanwhile others were more relaxed about 'closed black box AI', and argued that it will never be possible, or even necessary, for a human to comprehend how an AI processes very large quantities of unstructured data. This means that, as AIs become more complex, humans will increasingly have no choice but to trust their synthetic 'judgement'. So when a future autonomous vehicle drives into a pedestrian, its creators may never be able to reveal why it did so, or how a similar accident may be prevented in the future.

Although ANNs and deep learning are getting the majority of media attention, all of the aforementioned approaches to AI remain in active development. As a result, AI research continues to be a broad church, and is divided into

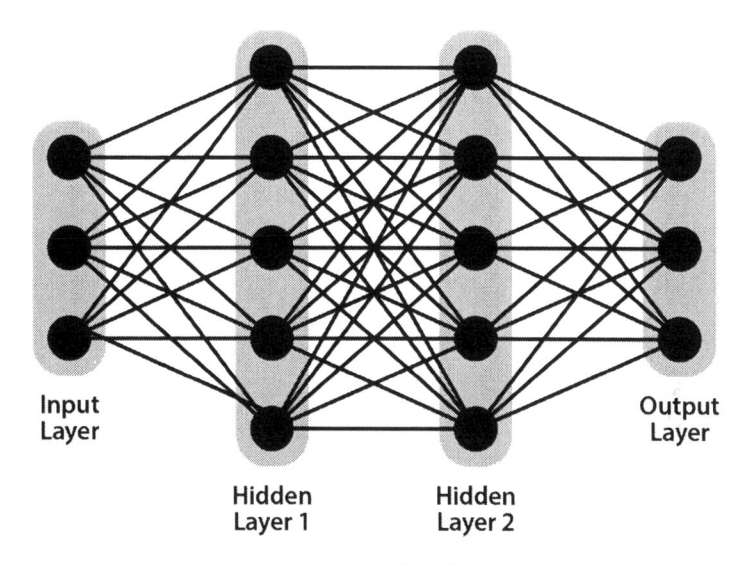

**Figure 3.1: A Deep Learning Artificial Neural Network**

what University of Washington AI guru Pedro Domingos calls 'tribes'. These comprise the 'symbolists' (who rely on rules and the mathematics of probability), 'evolutionists' (who focus on digital natural selection techniques), and 'connectionists' (who are nurturing the rise of ANNs and deep learning). Right now, as Domingos highlights, the 'connectionists are winning'. But, in the long term, AI advancements will probably continue to be delivered by all three of its core methodologies.

## NARROW & BROAD AI

Because 'artificial intelligence' continues to mean different things to different people, various attempts have been made to divide it into meaningful classifications. For example, you may have heard or read about AI being 'narrow', 'weak', 'applied', 'strong' or 'general'. So how do these different categories differ?

Well, unless you really want to split hairs, the good news is that there are only really two types of AI. The first is 'narrow AI', which refers to AIs created for very specific, constrained applications. The second is then 'broad AI', which aspires to create 'artificial general intelligences' (AGIs). The latter are very much a work in progress, but may one day have very wide-ranging cognitive capabilities similar to those of a human being.

The above noted, in some circles 'narrow AI' is referred to as 'weak AI' or 'applied AI', and may also be termed a form of 'expert system'. Meanwhile 'broad AI' is often called 'general AI'. In addition, narrow AI is occasionally referred to as 'vertical AI', which reflects the fact that it can accomplish a limited range of tasks. In the same context, broad AI may be labelled as 'horizontal'. If you are thinking that this is all a bit of a mess, then absolutely it is. But basically, we just need to remember that:

$$\text{narrow AI} = \text{weak AI} = \text{applied AI} = \text{vertical AI}$$
$$\&$$
$$\text{broad AI} = \text{general AI} = \text{horizontal AI} = \text{AGI}$$

Today, all forms of AI in commercial or personal application ought to be classified as narrow. Examples include aircraft autopilots, automated stock trading systems, vision recognition systems, voice recognition systems, language translators, website recommendation engines, AI systems for Big Data analytics, and the AIs that control most robots or (semi)autonomous vehicles. Also classed as narrow AI are the 'digital assistants' that we will examine in the next section.

Narrow AIs have accumulated some notable milestones. For example, back in 1962 Arthur Samuel's checkers program managed to win a game against a former state champion. Then, in 1997, world chess champion Garry Kasparov was beaten by an AI from IBM called Deep Blue, which caused quite a stir.

In March 2016, there was even more of a commotion when a DeepMind AI called AlphaGo beat the legendary Korean Go player Lee Sedol. This was a very significant watershed for deep learning ANNs, as Go is a far more complex game than chess, with considerably more potential move combinations. It is therefore impossible for an AI to master Go using a rules-based or heuristic approach. In January 2016 AlphaGo had already secretly defeated the top European Go champion Fan Hui. In May 2017, it then accrued further success when it beat the world Go champion, Ke Jie, three matches to zero.

In some respects the media attention and public amazement that surrounded the aforementioned events was rather curious. Today, nobody is remotely surprised when they travel in an airliner that takes off, flies to another continent, and lands with little or no human involvement. Nor are we shocked when pension funds trade stocks and shares automatically, or a motoring offence penalty is served by an AI that reads the license plate of a speeding vehicle. The fact that we regularly trust narrow AIs with people's lives and investments, and even allow them to sit in legal judgement, never seems to make the news. So maybe we just feel offended when an AI beats a human champion at an ancient game.

In the next 10 years, narrow AIs are destined to have an increasing impact on our lives, and not least because they will help us to save energy and other natural resources. For example, according to the *Financial Times*, in March 2017 DeepMind (which is part of the Google conglomerate Alphabet) was in 'early talks' with the United Kingdom's National Grid. Here the hope is to use a deep learning AI to save up to 10 per cent of the country's energy usage by predicting demand and optimizing electricity supply. Similar opportunities exist to use narrow AIs to optimize a great many business functions, and most notably logistics operations.

Narrow AIs are also poised to solve (or help solve) scientific and engineering challenges beyond human capabilities or comprehension. As I mentioned in the last chapter, the development of synthetic biology and inorganic molecular self-assembly will depend on AI to move them to the next level. Digital transformations involving Big Data, IoT, virtual and augmented reality, autonomous vehicles, robots, dark factories and cybernetic interfaces will also depend on narrow AI systems of one kind or another.

While the Cognitive Computing Age could quite happily rely on narrow AI alone, the development of broad AI remains the goal of some researchers and technology evangelists. For many, a 'true' artificial general intelligence or 'AGI' would have to be a synthetic version of a human mind that is able to think and maybe even feel like a person. As I argued at the start of this chapter, my own view is that there is no sensible reason to compare any form of AI with human intelligence. I would therefore consider a broad AI to be an artificial entity that is able to undertake a very wide range of cognitive activities, and which has the ability to develop expertise in a new field without human intervention. In this respect, at least some future AGIs may be tightly-knit collaborations of narrow AIs that are able to integrate further narrow AIs into their network as required.

Debates concerning the classification of AI, and the actual or potential creation of AGI, will probably rage for decades. However, such arguments are only likely to remain of significant interest to computer scientists, philosophers and other academics. Out in the marketplace, Amazon, Google, IBM, Microsoft and other computing pioneers are already far more focused on the practical roll-out of smart products and smart services. There are indeed likely to be very few customers who will care whether or not their digital assistant or autonomous vehicle has broad or narrow AI. Similarly, the main focus for a business that is thinking about substituting an AI for a human employee will be whether or not a 'digital worker' can get the job done at lower cost, rather than its precise technological classification.

## THE RISE OF DIGITAL ASSISTANTS

In public, the Cognitive Computing Age is being kick-started by the roll-out of increasingly sophisticated digital assistants. Right now, these software helpers most notably include Apple's Siri, Microsoft's Cortana, Google Assistant and Amazon's Alexa. Each of these has slightly different functionality, although all provide a voice interface for accessing web services and controlling IoT devices.

Siri was created by SRI International, who launched it as an iPhone app in February 2010. A few months later the digital assistant was purchased by Apple, and has since been integrated into its iOS, macOS, watchOS and tvOS operating systems.

Siri has the capacity to learn, and can already be used to do a fairly wide range of things without its user having to resort to a touchscreen or keyboard. Indeed, as Apple enthuse:

> Talking to Siri is an easier, faster way to get things done. It's always with you – on your iPhone, iPad, Mac, Apple Watch and Apple TV – ready to help throughout your day. Ask Siri to set an alarm or a destination. Book a ride or a meeting. Send a payment or a love note. Even change the lighting in your room. And the more you use Siri, the better it knows what you need at any moment. Just say it, and Siri does it.

In April 2014, Microsoft launched its own 'personal assistant' or 'digital agent' called Cortana. This is named after a 'synthetic intelligence' character in Microsoft's *Halo* video game, and runs on Windows PCs and Windows phones.

There are also Android and iOS Cortana apps, so making it accessible from a wide range of devices.

Just like Siri, Cortana can set and report appointments and reminders, and can send text messages or e-mails. It also provides voice access to the Bing search engine, and can open the applications installed on a PC. As Microsoft explain:

> Cortana is a personal digital assistant working across all your devices to help you in your daily life. She learns about you; helps you get things done by completing tasks; interacts with you using natural language in a consistent, contextual way; and always looks out for you. Cortana has a consistent visual identity, personality, and voice.

Microsoft and Apple were clearly the giants of the Personal Computing Age. It is therefore no surprise that Cortana and Siri now form an important part of their strategies for the future of their respective PC software platforms. In contrast, Google and Amazon are children of the Network Computing Age, and have conceived digital assistants that are less strongly associated with traditional computing.

In July 2012, Google launched a voice interface for its Android operating system called Google Now. In May 2016, Google Now was then joined by Google Assistant, which initially ran on a Google chat app called Google Allo, Google Pixel smartphones, and a 'smart speaker' called Google Home. However, by May 2017, Google Assistant was also available as an iOS app, and was starting to be included on smartphones running the Marshmallow or Nougat versions of Android.

Just like Siri and Cortana, Google Assistant can search the web, schedule alarms and events, and interact with its host hardware and its user's Google account. Interestingly, and in contrast to Apple and Microsoft, Google chose not to give its digital assistant a 'human' name or the illusion of a servant personality. As Jonathan Jarvis, a former creative director who worked on the project, explained to *Business Insider*:

> We always wanted to make it feel like you were the agent, and it was more like a superpower that you had and a tool that you used. If you create this personified assistant, that feels like a different relationship.

As mentioned above, Google Assistant can be accessed from a smart speaker called Google Home. This audio-only computer offers 'far field voice recognition', which in practice means that it has long distance microphones able to pick up a user's voice across a large room. Google would like its customers to populate their residences with several Google Home devices. This would then allow them to say 'OK Google' and access Google services wherever they are in the building.

The fundamental idea behind Google Home is that a user will no longer have to get out a smartphone, or go to a computer, in order to conduct a web search, send a message, purchase a product, or listen to music. Google Home and Google Assistant can also stream video to a TV equipped with a Google Chromecast device, as well as controlling IoT devices including smart light bulbs, power sockets, door locks and heating systems.

Since November 2014, Amazon has offered similar functionality with its Alexa digital assistant. This can be accessed from Amazon's own hardware, which began with a smart speaker called Echo. Like Google Home, this has wide-field microphones to allow it to listen out for commands across a large room, and resembles a high-tech spray can. Additional Echo devices now include a far smaller, $50 unit called the Echo Dot, a device with a seven inch touchscreen called the Echo Show, and a nifty piece of hardware called the Echo

Look that includes a camera. The latter can allow Alexa to comment on a user's appearance or selection of clothing, or to visually keep track of the dog.

As well as being accessible from Amazon's own dedicated hardware, Alexa can be summoned from an iOS or Android app, and even from some Ford automobiles and LG refrigerators. Like Google and Microsoft, Amazon has also opened up its digital assistant to computing enthusiasts so that they can incorporate Alexa into their IoT devices and maker projects.

As you would expect, Alexa can access information services, interact with a calendar, play music, and control smart devices in the home (or car). At the time of writing, Alexa was the fastest growing digital assistant, with over 15,000 voice controlled applications (or 'skills') created by its user community.

Like other digital assistants, Alexa is currently not that sophisticated, but is rapidly improving. To highlight continual progress, in July 2017 Dave Limp – the Amazon vice president responsible for Alexa – did an interview with the BBC. As he explained, a recently rolled-out feature allows Alexa to answer follow-up questions. This means that Alexa now understands some simple pronouns. So if you ask 'what's the weather in London?', and then subsequently question 'what's the population there?', Alexa will know that you are referring to London. In July 2017, Amazon also partnered with UBS Wealth Management to enable its digital assistant to answer financial queries for some of its European users.

Other companies staking a claim in the growing digital assistant marketplace include Samsung, which in March 2017 announced a smartphone AI called Bixby. Back in August 2015, Facebook also started trials of a digital assistant named 'M' that lives within its Messenger App, and which can provide reminders and suggestions.

In July 2017, Chinese e-commerce giant Alibaba additionally entered the fray when it launched a smart speaker – the Tmall Genie – that amongst other things allows customers to use a voice interface to purchase items from its Tmall store. A month earlier, Chinese electronics manufacturer Xiaomi also launched its 'Mi AI Speaker'. This offers Alexa/Echo-style functionality for a lot less money, including voice control of a user's air conditioning, lights, TV and robot vacuum cleaners. Also in June 2017, Apple upped the ante by announcing its own smart speaker called the HomePod, although at the time of writing this has yet to hit the market.

## ATTENTIVE & OMNIPRESENT COMPUTING

As the last few pages have hopefully demonstrated, large computing companies are investing heavily in digital assistants and related hardware. In part, this is because these AI innovations could turn out to be tomorrow's most common digital interface. They hence present old computing giants like Microsoft with a significant opportunity to develop new revenue streams.

New sources of income are also needed, as users no longer expect to pay for operating systems like Windows or macOS, or even basic productivity applications. Granted, many companies still blindly dish out wads of cash for Microsoft Office. But given the quality of free, open source alternatives, even Microsoft cannot expect its customers to go on paying indefinitely to use a word processor and a spreadsheet.

While Siri, Cortana, Alexa, Google Assistant and their digital friends are currently free, if they get useful enough their corporate masters could start to charge for their services. However, I suspect that this will never happen. Rather, I imagine that the goal of our computing overlords is to garner a strong following for their own digital assistant, and then to make money by charging companies who wish to advertise and sell their wares via its AI interface.

According to market analysts Verto Analytics, 'AI-driven personal assistants' are 'already shaping digital consumer habits'. As the company's CEO, Hannu Verkasalo, explains, AI apps such as Amazon Alexa, are 'providing a next-generation user experience for digital content' as well as 'a more contextually-driven, seamless way for consumers to perform tasks'.

If voice controlled AIs do trump the world-wide web to become the e-commerce and digital content interface of choice, so online search and online marketing will radically change. Today, companies fight and pay handsomely to appear in the top ten listings in a Google search (or even a Bing search, if they are that desperate). But when a user conducts a voice search using a digital assistant, they are extremely unlikely to be provided with or remember more than one or two results.

Today, most people who conduct a web search self-scan the output and apply their own intelligence. This happens because a screen is used as an intermediate interface between the user and the digital world. But, in the future, almost all of the cognitive process involved in a search-and-purchase activity is destined to be handled by an AI. People will simply get used to saying 'get me some new socks' or 'book me an enjoyable holiday', with the expectation being that things will be taken care of by a trusted and well informed digital servant that will not land them in too much debt.

If the above sounds crazy or alarming, it is worth reflecting on how much time many people currently spend staring at smartphone apps or browsing the web. These time-zapping pursuits are entirely new human activities, and hardly seem to be increasing the happiness or wellbeing of most individuals. Indeed, attending to screens – and having our lives governed by smartphones and other computing devices – is in many instances destroying quality social time, cultivating ADHD, heightening anxiety levels, and eroding some people's mental health. When digital assistants and other AIs become competent enough *to attend to us*, I therefore suspect that many people will gladly surrender digital control. Since the days of Alan Turing, people have been attending to the needs of computers. So it really is high time for the technology to attain a level of maturity that will allow it to start attending to us.

Today's digital assistants may be very rudimentary. But they are the advance troops of the attentive computing revolution. Indeed, the initial roll-outs of smart speakers like Google Home and Amazon's Echo range are already starting to create domestic 'omnipresent computing' environments in which an AI is constantly listening out for human commands. As previously noted, the Echo Look is even equipped with a camera so that it can visually monitor its user's activities, family and property.

Add in a personal robot, a swarm of IoT devices, and an online autonomous vehicle, and 10 years from now some people will start to enjoy all of the digital access and control they desire without ever having to go near or pick up a 'computer'. Google currently advertise Google Home as a voice activated 'remote control to the real world, whenever you need it'. So the desired direction of travel from the supplier end is abundantly clear.

Outside of the home, opportunities to apply attentive and omnipresent computing are extremely wide ranging. For example, experiments are now taking place in which cameras and AIs are being used to recognize the faces of commuters at railway stations. In the future, such vision recognition systems could allow ticket barriers to be removed, with passengers charged solely on the basis of a visual identification. Just one company developing this kind of technology is a Chinese startup called Face++, which is already valued at roughly $1 billion.

Some future in-store systems are likely to employ vision recognition AIs to establish who enters the premises, what items they pick up and take with them, and hence how much to deduct from their bank account. Such AI implementations would clearly need to be highly accurate. But this could be achieved by developing systems that would verify a shopper's identity on multiple occasions as they moved around a store, so reducing the risk of an error being made. Data on a person's identity could also be correlated against other Big Data sources, such as an individual's last known location. So, for example, it would be impossible to 'face pay' in a shop in London if, 10 minutes earlier, another AI had just verified your presence in New York. In September 2017, Chinese e-commerce giant Alibaba actually launched a 'smile and pay' service, with the first commercial roll-out in a KFC KPRO fast food restaurant in Hangzhou.

Already public spaces are populated with a great many CCTV cameras, including around 30 million in the United States, and over 5 million in the United Kingdom. Add in the electronic eyes (and ears) of future robots, autonomous vehicles and IoT devices, and it may well be possible for future AIs to constantly attend to the vast majority of the population. Almost everybody's location could therefore be constantly known, with their actions and desires predicted. In such a world, nobody would need to carry money. Crime could also be very low as there would be no place to hide, with criminals and terrorists very easily apprehended.

What I have just described is the most extreme future vision of omnipresent, attentive computing, and one that may make some people very uncomfortable. Yet it is a logical extension of where the roll-out of digital assistants and related hardware is already taking us. Until recently, the only omnipresent entities were the Gods of human religions. But in the future, both at home and out in the wider world, omnipresent AIs may be watching over us 24/7.

## CLOUD AI SERVICES

All digital assistants provide AI from the cloud, with the devices that deliver them – including smartphones, PCs or smart speakers – being very dumb computers. Beyond the realm of the digital assistant, this technological model is also starting to be far more widely applied, with several large technology companies now offering a broad range of 'cloud AI services'. As a Microsoft Technology Evangelist recently informed me, such services are rapidly 'democratizing AI', as they are making it possible for those with little technical skill to embed smartness into their products and services.

In short, Cloud AI services deliver cognitive capabilities over the Internet. More specifically, they allow software applications or connected objects to upload structured or unstructured data, and to receive a cognitive response. Figure 3.2 illustrates the concept, with a web page sending some text in English to a cloud AI service that translates it into French, and a smart speaker sending an audio stream to a cloud AI service that converts it into a command.

Cloud AI services may be categorized into four quadrants on a two-by-two matrix. On one axis we have the type of 'client' involved – which may be a software application, or a physical object or 'thing'. On the other axis we have the type of data uploaded – which may be structured or unstructured. Figure 3.3 illustrates such a cloud AI services matrix.

Rotating around the grid, in the top left we have software applications sending structured data (such as information from a customer database) to the cloud. As suggested in the figure, this may be an e-commerce website that sends data on visitor activity to a cloud AI that then reports back personalized recommendations. Amazon has been doing this kind of thing for years, displaying content in the form of 'other visitors who bought this item were also interested in this'. But now, thanks to cloud AI, it is becoming easy for any

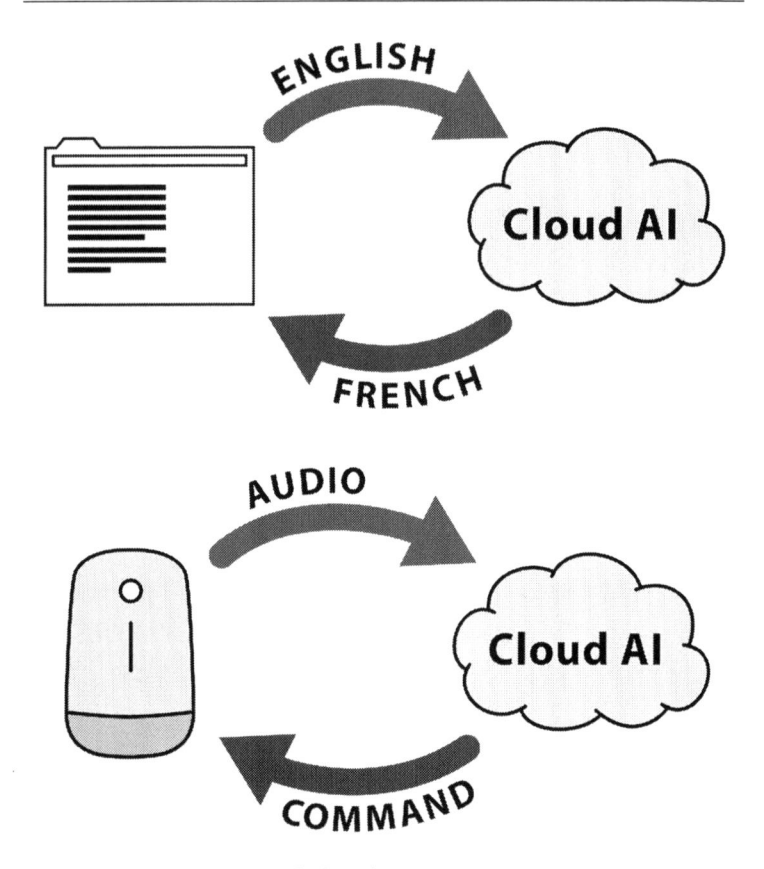

**Figure 3.2: Examples of Cloud AI Services.**

website to offer the same kind of highly sophisticated recommendations functionality.

In the top right of the grid we have software applications sending unstructured data (such as video or audio feeds) to a cloud AI. So, for example, a web page may capture a visitor's image via a camera, and stream this data to the cloud in order to learn more about them. Such data could include the visitor's age, dress sense and state of happiness, with this data then used to help deliver the best personalized service. In the

## TYPE OF DATA UPLOAD

|  | STRUCTURED | UNSTRUCTURED |
|---|---|---|
| **APP** | EXAMPLE Recommendations engine for website | EXAMPLE Face recognition service |
| **THING** | EXAMPLE IoT-driven logistics engine | EXAMPLE Smart speaker voice service |

TYPE OF CLIENT

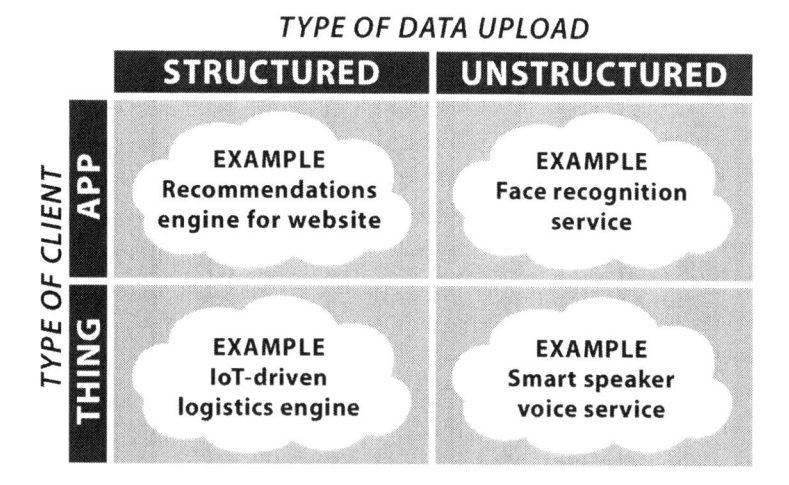

**Figure 3.3: The Cloud AI Services Matrix.**

relatively near future, websites even may use such cloud AI vision recognition services to establish visitor identity.

In the bottom right quadrant of the cloud AI services matrix, online objects upload unstructured data to the cloud. So, for example, this could be a smart speaker, automobile, robot or other item of hardware that uploads an audio stream that is converted into identifiable commands.

Finally, in the bottom left of the grid, we have the scenario of hardware that supplies structured data to a cloud AI. Here, for example, a cloud AI logistics service may be sent data from IoT sensors embedded in a factory's production equipment. It would then send back intelligence that would allow the factory to optimize its use of energy and scheduling of resources.

The aforementioned examples of cloud AI are generic and represent just a few of the possibilities that lie ahead. To help us to gain a deeper understanding, we will therefore now look in turn at the cloud AI services that are already on offer from four of the largest providers. You will also not be surprised to learn that these companies are IBM, Microsoft, Google and Amazon.

## IBM Watson

IBM's 'cloud-based cognitive services' are based around a very powerful AI called Watson. This deep learning system was first showcased in February 2011, when it took on two human champions in the US TV game show *Jeopardy*. The challenge was difficult for an AI to master, as *Jeopardy* contestants are supplied with linguistically complex answers for which they have to provide the questions. Nevertheless, over three matches, Watson emerged as the victor, so securing another victory for AI in its apparent battle with the human race.

In January 2014 IBM announced the creation of the Watson Group as a 'new business unit dedicated to the development and commercialization of cloud-delivered cognitive innovations'. As the company went on to explain, its investment of more than $1bn signified 'a strategic shift by IBM to accelerate into the marketplace a new class of software, services and apps that think, improve by learning, and discover answers and insights to complex questions from massive amounts of Big Data'.

Fast forward to today, and Watson is being advertised as 'the AI platform for business'. Like other AI cloud services, it is accessed via a set of standard application programming interface (API) tools that allow companies to 'integrate the world's most powerful AI into their applications'.

As a deep learning AI, Watson adopts what IBM describe as the 'human learning process of observing, interpreting and analyzing data' in order to expose patterns and insights and make informed decisions. This allows Watson to 'achieve mastery' over a given subject so that it can perform as well as the best human employees whose knowledge was used to train the system in the first place.

At the time of writing there are 15 Watson products and services available under the six categories of 'conversation', 'discovery', 'vision', 'speech', 'language' and 'empathy'. Here, the 'vision', 'speech' and 'language' SaaS apps do what you would expect, and allow companies to apply cloud-based deep learning to classify and search visual content, perform text-to-speech and speech-to-text operations, interpret natural language, and perform language translation.

Watson's 'conversation' tools additionally allow businesses to 'quickly build and employ chatbots and virtual agents' with 'no machine learning experience required'. In the United States, Staples has used these and some other Watson APIs to create an 'an intelligent ordering ecosystem that business customers can use to order supplies easily using voice, text or e-mail'. As Ryan Bartley of Staples noted, the development 'was a wake-up call for us' and one that proved 'that cognitive solutions are real and the tooling around them powerful'.

As another example, the Royal Bank of Scotland (RBS) in the United Kingdom has used Watson Conversation and related tools to build a chatbot called Luvo. Following a successful two-month trial, in October 2016 this was rolled-out, as RBS describe, to 'support employees, and perhaps bring some tender loving care (TLC) with it'. Luvo is able to understand customer questions, filter them through 'huge amounts of information in a split second', and then respond with an answer.

On the occasions where Luvo is unable to provide an answer, it passes the support query on to a human member of staff. According to RBS, Luvo has 'a unique psychological profile [that] means it has a warmth to its personality'. RBS also describe their chatbot as 'approachable' and 'creative', and note that it 'uses a combination of intuition and reasoning when answering questions'.

IBM are clearly very keen for businesses like Staples and RBS to use Watson to build AI customer interfaces, and has outlined some of the potential advantages on its blog. According to IBM, these include the fact that chatbots 'can deliver a level of responsiveness that isn't humanly possible', 'only have to be trained once', and offer a consistent and 'totally personalized service'. The use of chatbots may also engender a self-service mentality among customers. In this context, IBM note that the majority of millennials seek to avoid situations that 'require a human interaction', preferring instead to use self-service digital messaging systems that are pretty easy to automate using AI.

Several major research firms agree with IBM's analysis that 'by 2020, 85 per cent of all customer interactions will be handled without a human agent'. For example, in January 2017 Forrester published a report on customer service trends in which it predicted that 'companies will continue to explore the power of intelligent agents to add conversational interfaces to static self-service content'. In May 2017, Juniper Research even estimated that 'chatbots will help businesses save more than $8 billion per year by 2022'.

Moving on to other services, Watson's 'discovery' AI tools allow users to 'unlock valuable insights from unstructured data'. Such Big Data analysis AI capabilities have a wide range of potential applications. Most notably at present, these include the use of the Watson AI in healthcare, as we will explore later in this chapter.

The final set of Watson tools – at least for now! – allow users to analyse the meaning of text, predict the personality of its human author, and even to understand their 'emotions, social tendencies and perceived writing style'. With the development of these services, IBM is clearly attempting to provide Watson with skills that humans would term 'hunch' and 'intuition'. There is no doubt that practical AI research is continuing to dig deeper and deeper into the subtle and complex intricacies of human communication.

## Microsoft AI Platform & Cognitive Services

Like most of Microsoft's product line, the company's suite of cloud AI tools are offered under a plethora of changing brands and banners that even Microsoft employees admit can be somewhat confusing. But in simple terms, at the time of writing the company offers an 'AI Platform' that allows users to 'innovate and accelerate with powerful tools and services that bring AI to every developer'. These tools include a 'Bot Platform' for creating chatbots, as well as the 'Microsoft Cognitive Toolkit' for building and training 'deep learning models at massive scale'.

Another element of the AI Platform is Microsoft Cognitive Services, also referred to as Azure Cognitive Services. As of September 2017, this offers a suite of thirty very-impressive, API-based cloud AI tools under the service categories 'vision', 'speech', 'language', 'knowledge' and 'search'.

Here the vision tools are particularly powerful, and are already able to recognize objects, people and places in a photograph or a real-time video stream. Microsoft's Emotion API can additionally even classify the emotion of one or more individuals based on their facial expressions. This may, for example, allow a store to monitor its CCTV camera output, and to automatically determine those displays of goods that make its customers the most happy, sad, surprised, angry or contemptuous.

Microsoft's speech and language cognitive services offer the expected variety of text and spoken language recognition and translation tools. These include some sophisticated sentiment analysis apps that can, for example, rapidly analyse customer feedback. The 'knowledge' tools then include a rather useful website recommendations API, a 'custom decision service' for personalizing web content, and the Academic Knowledge API. The latter interprets text-based natural language in an academic context. It can, for example, be used to compare the meaning of two literature sources, so allowing the creation of a smart plagiarism detection system.

## Google Cloud AI & TPU Chips

Like its competitors, Google offers a wide range of plug-and-play, API-accessible AI services, here via the Google Cloud Platform. These include the Cloud Video Intelligence API, which 'allows developers to extract actionable insights from video files without requiring any machine learning or computer vision knowledge'. There is also the Cloud Natural Language API for analyzing and learning from text, the Cloud Vision API for analyzing photographs, the Cloud Speech API, and the Cloud Translation API. Also of particular note is the Google Cloud Machine Learning Engine, which enables users to 'easily build machine learning models that work on any type of data, of any size'.

As I am certain you have now gathered, the current giants of computing are all competing in the same space to offer a similar suite of plug-and-play cloud AI tools. Quite who offers the best services is difficult to ascertain, and not least because the market and its technologies are advancing extremely quickly. Right now, IBM claims that Watson is the most advanced online AI. Meanwhile Google suggests that it offers the best machine learning (ML) tools for 'injecting AI into your business'. Or as they further explain:

> Google Cloud's AI provides modern machine learning services, with pre-trained models and a service to generate your own tailored models. Our neural net-based ML service has better training performance and increased accuracy compared to other large scale deep learning systems. Our services are fast, scalable and easy to use. Major Google applications use Cloud machine learning, including Photos (image search), the Google app (voice search),

Translate, and Inbox (Smart Reply). Our platform is now available as a cloud service to bring unmatched scale and speed to your business applications.

To support its cloud software developments, Google is working on new, AI-optimized computer hardware. This includes the development of AI chips known as 'tensor processing units' or 'TPUs'. A TPU is a microprocessor created from the ground up for executing neural network computations, and in particular for running the machine learning software 'TensorFlow'. Also created by Google, TensorFlow is an 'open-source software library for machine intelligence', and is becoming increasingly popular in the AI community.

In May 2017 Google revealed that it will launch a new cloud computing service that will provide exclusive access to its latest TPU 2.0 or 'Cloud TPU' hardware. While Google's first TPU was optimized to run machine learning models as quickly and efficiently as possible, its neural networks still had to be initially trained on conventional computer hardware. However, the big breakthrough with the TPU 2.0 chip is that it is able to both train and run machine learning models. Google has also designed its new TPUs to be networked into clusters of what it calls 'TPU pods'. Each of these contains 64 TPU 2.0 chips which function as a 'machine learning supercomputer'.

Like many AI pioneers, Google has previously used graphics card chips (known as graphics processing units or 'GPUs') for running some of its most intensive machine learning applications. But its Cloud TPUs and TPU pods are now far more effective. As it explained in May 2017, using its TPU pods:

> . . . we've already seen dramatic improvements in training times. One of our new large-scale translation models used to take a full day to train on 32 of

the best commercially-available GPUs – now it trains to the same accuracy in an afternoon using just one eighth of a TPU pod.

As the above developments indicate, Google has very serious intentions to dominate the evolving AI ecosystem at both the hardware and the software level. But the company's ambitions do not stop there. For example, Google is also attempting to get individual makers onboard via a DIY initiative called 'Google AIY'. This provides hardware and software support for anybody who wants to experiment with Google cloud AI. Or as the AIY website explains:

> We want to put AI into the maker toolkit, to help you solve real problems that matter to you and your communities. These kits will get you started by adding natural human interaction to your maker projects.

## *Amazon AI Services*

As one of the largest cloud computing providers, it is no surprise that Amazon now offers a range of cloud AI services. These provide businesses (and potentially individuals) with an increasingly powerful set of smart web tools. Or to quote the Amazon AI website:

> Amazon AI services bring natural language understanding (NLU), automatic speech recognition (ASR), visual search and image recognition, text-to-speech (TTS), and machine learning (ML) technologies within the reach of every developer. Based on the same proven, highly scalable products and services built by the thousands of machine learning experts across Amazon, Amazon AI services

provide high-quality, high-accuracy AI capabilities that are scalable and cost-effective.

In addition, the AWS Deep Learning AMI provides a way for AI developers and researchers to quickly and easily begin using any of the major deep learning frameworks to train sophisticated, custom AI models; experiment with new algorithms; and learn new deep learning skills and techniques on AWS' massive compute infrastructure.

The above summarizes what is on offer pretty effectively, and given that I have already outlined the competing cloud AI suites from IBM, Microsoft and Google, I do not have a lot more to add here. Suffice it to say that, like Microsoft and Google, Amazon is working very hard to get individuals as well as corporates experimenting with its cloud AI provision, and is achieving particular success in this area by promoting free access to its Alexa digital assistant. This said, the other players in online cognitive computing are not far behind, with the cloud AI marketspace continuing to evolve very rapidly indeed.

Finally here, it is worth noting that IBM, Microsoft, Google and Amazon are far from the only players in cloud AI. Also notable is Facebook which runs its own lab called Facebook AI Research (FAIR). Facebook also owns a company called Wit.ai that provides cloud AI services which allow developers to make applications and devices 'that you can talk or text to'.

In addition, the large SaaS and PaaS cloud computing provider Saleforce has developed a cloud AI service called Einstein that 'helps everyone blaze new trails with artificial intelligence'. Right now, Einstein is dedicated to helping with sales and marketing processes, such as coaching sales reps and assisting human service agents.

## AUTONOMOUS VEHICLES

Some, including *Wired*, have labelled today's smart speakers the 'Trojan horses' of the Cognitive Computing Age. Given that many of these devices are being cost-competitively offered as 'gifts' to gain consumer and business interest, this is also a reasonable description. However, if smart speakers and related online cognitive services are AI Trojan horses, then so too will be the first fully autonomous vehicles.

A car, truck or tractor that is capable of operating entirely independently has to be equipped with an extremely effective attentive AI. In fact, when an empty car is able to turn up at your house, pick up a passenger, and deliver them to a location a few hundred miles away with no en route instruction or human intervention whatsoever, then we will be certain that attentive computing has arrived. The AIs driving such vehicles will, after all, need to be able to know their location, perceive their environment, and react rapidly and safely in response to the actions of human drivers, pedestrians and natural phenomenon. Further, when the human race trusts autonomous 30 tonne trucks and other self-driving vehicles to cruise public highways, it will be a very strong signal that our civilization has accepted attentive computing systems as coexisting intelligent entities.

AI-on-wheels is expected to arrive gradually throughout the 2020s, with governments around the world already granting it the legal right to drive. Many computing companies are now also developing autonomous vehicles. For example, in 2009 Google initiated its Self Driving Car Project. In 2016 this became a separate company called Waymo, which falls under the control of the broader Google conglomerate Alphabet. Also from the world of computing, both Apple and Baidu are reported to be working on self-driving technology, while in March 2017 Intel invested $15.3 billion to purchase the Israel-based driverless car technology firm Mobileye.

Most traditional automobile manufacturers are also working on self-driving vehicles, including Audi, Daimler, GM, Honda, Hyundai, Tesla, Toyota, Volkswagen and a Renault/Nissan Alliance. Ford is also developing self-driving cars, and according to the April 2017 *Navigant Research Leaderboard Report* on automated driving, is currently at the forefront of autonomous vehicle development.

All of the aforementioned companies have built prototype driverless cars, and face a complex, dual challenge. Firstly, they need to develop a suite of sensor technologies that can allow a vehicle to gather sufficient data on the world around it. They then also need to create and train an AI that is capable of processing this sensor information in a manner that allows it to safely drive. Sensor technologies currently in use include GPS navigation, multiple cameras and LiDAR (light detection and ranging). The latter detects objects by projecting a laser beam and measuring the time taken for it to reflect back, and can allow a car to accurately sense an object up to about 100 feet (30 m) away.

Due to the challenges involved in creating and training suitable 'AI drivers', autonomous vehicles are expected to arrive in phases. Already some cars feature automated systems like adaptive cruise control and self-parking. Around 2020, such cars will be joined by 'semi-autonomous' vehicles that will be capable of independently cruising or edging along in traffic. Next, around 2025, most experts predict that 'high autonomy' vehicles will start to become available. These will be able to operate autonomously for large portions of a journey, but will require the constant presence of a human able to rapidly take control. Finally, towards 2030, fully autonomous vehicles will begin to appear. These may not feature any human controls, and could enhance the mobility of millions.

In addition to private cars and taxis, driverless commercial vehicles are in serious development. For example, in May

2015, Daimler unveiled its Freightliner Inspiration as the first autonomous truck licensed to drive on public highways in the United States. In October 2016, a Volvo truck equipped with Uber self-driving technology also took its place in history when it drove 120 miles across Colorado to deliver 50,000 cans of Budweiser. This was the first commercial cargo to be shipped by a self-driving vehicle on a public highway, and understandably made many truckers rather nervous.

Away from public roadways, in 2012 Rio Tinto Zinc revealed that 150 autonomous trucks had been set to work at its Nammuldi iron ore mine in Australia. Meanwhile, in August 2016, Case IH revealed a prototype autonomous tractor that will allow farmers to 'rethink productivity'. I have also spoken with a large company in the construction sector that anticipates the roll-out of autonomous road maintenance vehicles. These will be able to place and remove traffic cones, as well as being equipped to automatically remove and replace a road surface.

By the late 2020s, the digital 'drivers' of autonomous vehicles will be far from the only AIs to have taken control of common machinery. Not least, as noted in the last chapter, connected domestic devices will increasingly allow the creation of 'smart homes' in which a friendly AI will control the heating, lights, entertainment system, vacuum cleaner, lawn mower and door locks.

In the medium-term, it is highly likely that many people will be served by a single AI that will not just run their computer and their home, but which will also monitor their health, drive their car, and assist them with their work. There really is no logical reason for an AI to remain physically imprisoned in a single body such as that of a vehicle. Indeed, given that most future AIs will be cloud based, they are unlikely to be embodied at all. Highlighting this fact, in January 2017 Intel introduced a new software and hardware platform called GO to deliver a 5G wireless 'automotive solution spanning car, connectivity and cloud'.

As the above example once again signals, in the 2020s the dominant cloud AI services are destined to become our interfaces to everything. There will therefore be great rewards for those companies that develop the AIs that most people end up using to control their computer and their home, to make online purchases, and to drive them around. For at least a decade or more, we should therefore expect to go on living in a world of AI Trojan horses.

## FRIEND OR FOE?

Over the past few years, several notable individuals have expressed their fears concerning the impact of AI. For example, in December 2014, Professor Stephen Hawking told the BBC that 'the development of full artificial intelligence could spell the end of the human race'. In his view, this is because human beings are 'limited by slow, biological evolution' and will 'be superseded'.

In October 2014, SpaceX and Tesla Motors CEO Elon Musk similarly pronounced that creating AI is akin to 'summoning the demon'. In July 2017, Musk again made this point when he informed a group of American governors in Rhode Island that AI constitutes the 'biggest risk we face as a civilization'. As he went on to suggest:

> Until people see robots going down the street killing people, they don't know how to react because it seems so ethereal. AI is a rare case where I think we need to be proactive in regulation instead of reactive. Because I think by the time we are reactive in AI regulation, it's too late.

In his 2014 book *Superintelligence: Paths, Dangers, Strategies*, Nick Bostrum of Oxford University also argues that the development of AI presents a danger to us all. As he explains, it is only mental superiority that has allowed human beings to gain a dominant position over all other species. In turn, this has resulted in physically stronger animals – like gorillas – having their survival placed in human hands. But when a super intelligent AI emerges, so human beings may end up with no more influence over their destiny than gorillas, with the future of our civilization dependant on the actions of machine intelligence.

The above fears and warnings are on the face of it rather powerful. Granted, they assume the creation or evolution of sentient AGIs in strict isolation from the human species, and this may never happen. Though even if we do assume that such isolated super intelligence will emerge, ought we really to fear its coming? The human race has long furthered its progress by creating more and more powerful tools, and never before have these mechanisms by themselves threatened our survival. Indeed, almost always we have reaped great rewards from the innovation of more powerful technologies. So why should we fear AI?

Over the following few pages I will outline some of the more probable advantages and disadvantages of AI. Given the fears of those who believe that AI could lead to our physical destruction, I have also chosen to begin by considering the likely impact of smart technology on human health.

## KEEPING PEOPLE WELL

The medical sector is one of the biggest industries on the planet, and is likely to grow as the population ages. The medical sector also captures an extraordinary quantity of data, and could be far more efficient if it employed AI to learn from its massive binary stash. Highlighting the opportunity, in 2011 the McKinsey Global Institute predicted that the US healthcare sector alone could save about 8 per cent of its budget (or about $300 billion every year) 'by using Big Data creatively and effectively to drive efficiency and quality'.

Such AI-enhanced creativity would use deep learning to precisely predict and plan for human illness, rather than building hospitals and training doctors in the fairly vague expectation of actual medical demand. There is also a very large quantity of data exhaust that could assist in such prediction and planning.

For example, when a camera is inserted into a patient, most hospitals today only store any resultant video recording for a few days, weeks or months. Even still image scans are only kept for a number of years. The logic is that, after the requisite period, the value of such data *to the individual patient* has passed. Yet what if all such digital information could be amalgamated into a huge Big Data set and analysed by a swarm of AIs to predict the future health of the nation?

Already the power of AI in health diagnosis has been proven. For example, a San Francisco pioneer called Enlitic is using deep learning to develop what they term 'data driven medicine'. As the company explains:

> Every time a doctor sees a patient, they are solving a complex data problem. The goal of each case is to arrive at an optimal treatment decision based on many forms of clinical information, such as the patient's history, symptoms, lab tests, and medical images. The quality and quantity of this data is rapidly improving – it's estimated to grow over 50-fold this decade, to 25,000 petabytes worldwide by 2020. [Our mission is] to improve patient outcomes by [applying] deep learning to distill actionable insights from billions of clinical cases.

Enlitic Founder and CEO Jeremy Howard believes that the application of machine learning presents the 'biggest opportunity for positive impact' that he has seen in more than 20 years in the medical field. Early results also suggest that he may be correct. For example, in one batch of x-rays scans used in an Enlitic test, about 7 per cent of patients given a clean bill of health by a human radiologist were later found to have cancer. But when the company's AI performed a diagnosis on the same batch of scans, it did not make one error. A transition to AI diagnostics should therefore result in cancers being detected earlier, so improving patient outcomes and saving healthcare costs. In the future, you will want your medical scans to be checked by an AI rather than a person.

Similarly working to improve diagnosis and 'get patients from test to treatment faster' are DeepMind Health. Here, for example, a machine learning app called Streams has been created, and is already being trialled at the Royal Free Hospital in London. Streams is an 'instant alert app' that addresses the 'failure to rescue' problem that arises when the right medical professional does not get to the right patient in time. This occurs when conditions like sepsis or acute kidney injury are missed because warning signs are not picked up. While the Streams trial is still in its early phase, already some patients have had conditions identified and treated faster thanks to the app. Some nurses have also estimated that the deep learning system is saving them up to two hours a day.

The AI might of IBM Watson is also being applied in the medical sphere. Here 'Watson Drug Discovery' is providing a cognitive platform that is accelerating the work of life sciences researchers, while 'Watson for Oncology' is assisting with cancer diagnosis and care. The latter system has been trained by expert human clinicians, and can now help consultants by analysing patient data and rapidly providing evidence-based treatment options.

At the University of Adelaide in Australia, a research team is even working on an AI that can predict a patient's lifespan by examining organ scans. Results suggest that the AI is just as good as a human doctor, and has great potential to improve. By the late 2020s, the use of wearable and implanted IoT devices additionally has the potential to turn medicine into a predictive rather than a diagnostic science. No longer will we have to wait until we have pain or other symptoms before we visit a doctor. Rather, we will be sent an alert and an appointment when the digital assistant that constantly monitors our body anticipates a problem.

Looking further into the future, AIs are likely to catalyze the development of gene therapies that will 'correct' diseases such as cancer by reprogramming a patient's DNA. The quantities of data and analysis that are involved in treating health problems genetically are always likely to remain beyond the capabilities of the current human brain. But AI and deep learning will rapidly get very good at this, and in time may learn to understand and maintain the hardware of the human body at the genetic and even molecular level. Genetic analysis is indeed a field to which Enlitic are already applying their AI expertise.

The opportunities to use AI to improve human health are very great indeed. Or as IBM express matters, AI systems like Watson can 'arm health heroes with the technology and expertise they need to power thriving organizations, support vibrant communities and solve health challenges for people everywhere'.

Without a doubt IBM and other AI pioneers have latched onto the healthcare sector as an ideal industry in which to demonstrate the capabilities of their new, smart technology. Partially as a consequence, there are already concerns that amalgamating individual patient records to create diagnostic AI Big Data sets will compromise medical confidentiality. Even so, it is difficult to argue that anybody in need of medical care should fear rather than welcome AI.

## AUTOMATION OR AUGMENTATION?

While AI is poised to extend our quantity and quality of life, it also looks set to steal many jobs. According to a 2016 World Bank Development Report, the percentage of jobs 'at risk from automation' ranges from 35 per cent in the UK, to 47 per cent in the US, 69 per cent in India and 77 per cent in China. In March 2017 PwC forecast different figures, suggesting that up to 38 per cent of US jobs, 30 per cent of UK jobs, and 21 per of Japanese jobs, are 'susceptible to automation' by 2030.

I could go on to cite many similar studies, none of which include exactly the same numbers. Nevertheless, all such reports do agree that a significant percentage of jobs in all nations are likely to be automated by the end of next decade. Of course, not all of this automation will be of the mental variety, with robots set to take on many physical human labours as we shall see in the next chapter. But there is no doubt that a large number of 'mental jobs' that currently require human intelligence (HI) will shortly be able to done by an AI – and in many instances an AI that learnt from a person.

Exactly how this will happen, what it will mean, and whether it is a 'good' or a 'bad development', is a matter of increasing debate. This said, most of those involved fall into one of two camps. The first of these groups is spearheaded by business academics and business journalists, who generally claim that while human jobs will be lost to AI, this will lead to the creation of other forms of more interesting employment, with everything working out just fine. The other camp is then generally headed by technologists, who are usually far more pessimistic.

Two key proponents of the 'promise of AI' are Thomas Davenport and Julia Kirby, who have conducted several studies and published many articles in the *Harvard Business Review* and the *MIT Sloan Management Review*. Their baseline proposition is that a great many mental processes that are currently undertaken by human workers will soon be able to be automated. Indeed, as they have argued, virtually all jobs at all levels in fields like regulatory compliance, record keeping and tax accounting are 'crying out for automation'.

You may be wondering why Kirby & Davenport are classified as 'positive' proponents for the promise of AI. The reason is that they believe future humans and AIs will end up working together in teams, with the technology set to 'augment' rather than replace most human occupations. As they argue, in the future there will still be 'unlimited ways for humans to contribute tremendous value'. They also believe that many people will work in collaboration with smart machines 'to do things that neither could do well on their own', and that this will 'deepen' human work, rather than diminishing it.

Another pair of esteemed academics – Mary Lacity and Leslie Willcocks – agree with Kirby & Davenport, and cite detailed case studies. These demonstrate how people working in teams with AIs are often far more productive. For example, at London-based XChanging, 500 insurance notices that used to take a human team 'several days' to process are now completed by some AIs and a 'few humans' in 30 minutes. Meanwhile at the Associated Press, AIs now write corporate earnings reports, which has 'freed up time for the equivalent of three full-time journalists'.

What Kirby, Davenport, Lacity, Willcocks and a great many other business academics somehow fail to spot is that, in every practical example of 'augmentation' they provide, less human labour ends up being required. Their message that everybody will not just be alright, but will enjoy 'deepened' work, is therefore hardly of much comfort to those who will no longer have a job.

I have already stated several times in this book that many people in business are in 'AI denial'. The aforementioned common argument that 'everything will be OK because AI will augment rather than automate' is also partly to blame for perpetuating this head-in-the-sand attitude. Absolutely, many people will have their jobs augmented and will end up working in human-AI teams. But such teams will usually have fewer human members than before the AIs arrived.

So now we get to those technologists and others who are currently predicting a human workforce armageddon. For example, Marshall Brain – the founder of *How Stuff Works* – argues that smart technology is poised to 'evaporate' human labour in many service sectors. As you have probably guessed, I would sadly place myself in this far more pessimistic camp, as it does seem inevitable that a tsunami of mental automation is going to sweep across the world in the 2020s.

As highlighted by the earlier content in this chapter, if you are a driver, personal assistant, customer service agent, sales rep, accountant or medical consultant – let alone anybody who can undertake all of their job using a computer – then AI will soon constitute a threat to your future employment. So just what should you do? Well, I am asked this question a lot, and my advice is to develop your non-digital skills, and to try to gravitate toward at least some work that cannot be undertaken digitally.

The above is particularly important for young people in developed nations, who in five years time risk becoming the least employable generation in history if they do not start spending less time online. For 25 years I taught and directed degree programmes in a leading university. When I left academia in 2015, it was also already obvious that an over-reliance on digital skills was starting to prevent some graduates from obtaining a job.

I am absolutely not suggesting that digital literacy is unimportant. To the contrary, the ability to work in a team with AIs and robots is going to be a critical future skill. We will also need human systems analysts, programmers and hardware engineers for some time to come. But if your first reaction when you enter a room full of strangers is to check your smartphone rather than attempt a human conversation, I would really start to worry. Over the next decade, everybody in the workplace is going to be in competition for a job with other human *and non-human* resources, and we all need to decide what we are going to do about this.

## AGI INTENT & THE FUTURE HIVE MIND

I have now argued that AI is set to be good for our physical health, but bad for human employment. Yet even if AIs take 20 or 25 per cent of human jobs by 2030, this need not imply that we should fear them rising up to subjugate the human species. As I argued at the start of this chapter, artificial intelligence is not remotely like human intelligence, and probably never will be.

For an army of sophisticated, future artificial general intelligences to 'take over the world', they would need to have developed such an *intent*, and to me at least this seems rather unlikely. Will some future AIs restrict some human actions? Yes, I am quite certain that they will. For example, by 2050, a great many people are likely to be banned from driving because they will be far more likely to cause an accident than an AI driver, and would pilot a vehicle to a far lower level of fuel efficiency. Nevertheless, I am pretty sure that it will be human lawmakers who will restrict what human beings can do in the future (if with some well-informed advice from their Big-Data-crunching digital assistants).

Another of the flaws in the argument of those who proclaim that super intelligent AIs will wipe out the human race is their assumption of a binary divide between future human beings and machines. As I suggested in chapter 1, future reality is likely to be more complex than this, with the Cognitive Computing Age followed by the era of Cyborg Fusion. By this point in time, at least some computers will be organic, with an increasing number of people possessing an internal connection to the global digital network. I therefore suspect that, while some future super intelligences will be pure AIs, the majority will be human-computer hybrids. This means that what 'normal' human beings should fear – if anything – is the emergence of more intelligent and more advanced 'post-humans' or 'transhumans', who will be part of a global hive mind.

Will future enhanced humans pose a threat to their traditional, unmodified cousins? Well yes, absolutely they will – just as the arrival of *Homo Sapiens* spelt very bad news for Neanderthals. But this is an issue of evolution and natural selection, and not a problem directly associated with the future development of AI.

In developed nations today, average life expectancy is around 70, compared to little more than 35 a century ago (when infant mortality was very high). The fact that most of us live 'unnaturally' long lives is also due to us leveraging the power of technology to improve our food, medical care, and sanitation infrastructure. I am also pretty certain that nobody a century ago sensibly feared the future mass roll-out of modern drainage systems and antibiotics. In a similar vein, nobody today ought to fear for our race's future survival due to the continued development of AI.

*\* \* \**

## THE COGNITIVE COMPUTING AGE

While reading this chapter you may have experienced a wide range of emotions. After all, we have pondered the differences between artificial and human intelligence; have investigated the nature of AI technology; have looked at some of those digital assistants and other cloud AI services already on the market; and have anticipated the likely impact of AI on our health, employment and the human species. Just one of the maddening things about AI is that it is already clear that it is going to cause dramatic things to happen, but not so clear that we can determine exactly what those dramatic things will actually be.

What is certain is that IBM, Microsoft, Amazon, Google and other giant computing corporations have decided that AI is the Next Big Thing. Personally, I am also delighted that they have made this decision. In part, this is because I am curious to experience the kinds of AI services that they will deliver. But mainly it is because I am certain that the human race faces tough times ahead.

If we are to maintain our current population level while tackling challenges like climate change, resource depletion, global hunger and antibiotic resistance, we need all of the help we can get. I therefore believe and hope that AI is set to play an important and positive role in optimizing humanity's future. Granted, we will have to deal with the impact of AI on human employment. But you never know, the rise of AI may result in the replacement of capitalism with something even better. Well OK, that is probably a thin hope.

While all of the major computing corporates are currently competing to get a slice of the future AI action, you may be surprised and pleased to learn that they are also cooperating. Specifically, back in September 2016, the so-termed 'Partnership on AI' was formed with the aim of 'benefitting people and society'. The founding partners were Amazon, Apple, DeepMind, Facebook, Google, IBM and Microsoft, and a year later these companies have been joined by Intel, Sony, Salesforce, and various consultancy organizations and learned societies.

The mission of the Partnership on AI is 'to study and formulate best practices on AI technologies, to advance the public's understanding of AI, and to serve as an open platform for discussion and engagement about AI and its influences on people and society'.

To the above ends, the Partnership has established a number of tenets. These include seeking 'to ensure that AI technologies benefit and empower as many people as possible', 'open research and dialogue on the ethical, social, economic, and legal implications of AI', and striving 'to create a culture of cooperation, trust, and openness among AI scientists and engineers'. Never before in digital history have we witnessed the creation of such a powerful group so early in a technology's mainstream development, and I am therefore hopeful that those actually delivering AI are on the right track and intent on remaining so. You can read more about the Partnership on AI at partnershiponai.org.

As a final piece of information, you may also be interested to discover that, in February 2016, IBM created the IBM Watson AI XPRIZE. This $5 million competition challenges teams globally 'to develop and demonstrate how humans can collaborate with powerful AI technologies to tackle the world's grand challenges'. The intention is to accelerate the adoption of AI technologies and 'spark creative, innovative, and audacious demonstrations of the technology that are truly scalable and solve societal grand challenges'.

The IBM Watson AI XPRIZE runs until 2020, and it will be fascinating to see what those who have entered come up with. AI really is going to be an extraordinary tool, and our main task ahead is learn how to employ it most effectively.

# 4
# ROBOT HORIZONS

Since the Industrial Revolution we have built machines to replace human labour. We have also constructed mechanisms to manufacture things that human flesh and bone are unable to produce. In the future, such tools are going to get increasingly smart and highly automated, with 'robots' destined to become a very common technology.

In the workplace, most robots currently labour in factories, with the remainder mainly operating in warehouses, healthcare and the military. In all of these areas, the use of robots will increase in the 2020s and 2030s, with a greater proportion of manufacturing, logistics and military operations falling under computer control. However, the biggest change will be the introduction of robots to customer-facing and other commercial service roles that have previously only been occupied by humans. For example, we are likely to see robots taking front-of-house jobs in care homes, shops, restaurants, hospitals and security.

In the domestic sphere, robots are poised to evolve into embodied digital assistants. In the last chapter, I suggested that individuals are likely to end up with just one 'virtual servant', and this may well turn out to be a robot. Such a mobile descendant of the Amazon Echo or the Google Home will be able to provide information, make online purchases, clean your house, cook your meals, care for your relatives, tend your garden, and drive your vehicle. Indeed, it may even be your vehicle if you a frequent traveller, or just enjoy sitting in, polishing or talking to a car.

Other personal AIs may be embodied in far smaller mobile contraptions, including those with rotors that will allow them to fly. Yet more AI servants will take humanoid form so that they can work most effectively in human habitats. Many future digital assistants are also likely to transition between different bodies as their user's demands dictate. Or alternatively, as cloud-based entities they may multitask to occupy multiple bodies at the same time.

## MONSTERS THAT BECAME REAL

The word 'robot' was coined by Czech writer Karel Capek for his 1921 play *R.U.R.* This stood for 'Rossumovi Univerzální Roboti', or 'Rossum's Universal Robots', and told the tale of a global robot-human war. Capek based the term 'robot' on the Czech word for 'forced labour', with his writing being more of a statement on communism, capitalism, and the role of the worker, than a technological tale. Nevertheless, As Adrienne LaFrance discusses in a 2016 article in *The Atlantic*, his play 'helped set the tone for the modern conception of robots [as] adversaries [and] potential killers'.

Since Capek's seminal play, many works of fiction have portrayed robots as the bad guys. Indeed, as LaFrance argues, we have had a century 'of pop culture momentum making robots evil, making them villains'. Robots are of course not the only monsters to have terrified us from the page and screen. However, unlike werewolves, vampires, and the Creature from the Black Lagoon, they remain the only fictional monster to have actually become real.

Right now we cannot visit a 'mechanical labour pool' and hire out a servant robot like the *Star Wars* droid C-3PO. Even so, since Karl Capek introduced his new word, many automated mechanisms have been referred to as 'robots'. This has resulted in a 'robot' becoming a tricky creature to define, and increasingly so. For a start, in addition to labelling physical automatons as robots, a fair few people now include chatbots and other online applications in the 'robot' camp. As I have already indicated, we also face the quandary that driverless cars could and perhaps *should* be classified as robots.

The above points noted, I am keen to avoid becoming too bogged-down in a linguistic mire. I am therefore choosing to define a robot as a computer-controlled mechanism that can perform sophisticated physical tasks without human intervention. Increasingly, this means that 'robots' will be mechanical mechanisms that embody an AI, or which are remotely operated by a cloud AI service.

The above definitions exclude chatbots and related online applications, and I think rightly so. In my view, a 'robot' really does need to possess a physical body. Or as Cornell University roboticist Hadas Kress-Gazit stated in 2016, a robot is 'something that can create some physical motion in its environment. It has the ability to change something in the world'. Just in case you are wondering, all of this leaves chatbots and their disembodied, online chums to be collectively classified as 'bots'.

## OUR GROWING MECHANICAL WORKFORCE

The first industrial robot was called Unimate, and was installed on a General Motors production line in 1959. The automaton had the job of taking die castings from machines and performing welding operations. It also proved a success, and by 1961 a successor called the Unimate 1900 became the first industrial robot to be mass produced.

Like all early industrial robots, Unimates were hydraulically powered and pretty dumb. But, since the 1980s, a transition has taken place to electrically powered machines with greater intelligence and improved capabilities. Most commonly today, industrial robots are multi-axis articulated arms that cost between $50,000 and $80,000. The price can, however, easily rise to over $100,000 once application-specific peripherals have been added. According to the International Federation of Robotics (IFR), over 250,000 industrial robots were sold in 2015, with the figure for 2016 being around 290,000. Based on its latest projections, the IFR estimates that about 414,000 industrial robots will be sold in 2019.

The majority of industrial robots are used for applications that include welding, cutting, injection molding, materials handling, parts-assembly, painting, meat processing and packing. By far the largest market for such robots is China, which now makes 27 per cent of all purchases. Worldwide, most industrial robots are installed in automotive, electrical and electronics manufacturing plants, with other large-use industries including raw materials processing and food production.

While almost all manufacturing robots are fixed in a static location, away from the production line the use of 'autonomous mobile robots' (AMRs) is growing rapidly. For example, in some warehouses AMRs are now being used to pick, move around, pack, palletize and load items. By January 2017, Amazon alone had 45,000 AMRs working in its fulfillment centres – an increase of 50 per cent from a year earlier.

Many of Amazon's warehouse robots are from a company called Kiva Systems that Amazon purchased in 2012 for $775 million (and which now forms part of Amazon Robotics). The Kiva 'Mobile-robotic Fulfillment System' relies on hundreds of robots to automate picking and packing processes. Each robot is about 16 inch (40 cm) tall, and is capable of transporting 317 kilograms of packages at 5 miles an hour.

Another successful manufacturer of AMRs is Symbiotic, who offer a modular robot hardware and software platform to 'simplify material handling from manufacturer to store shelf'. As they claim, their 'bots' can be installed in existing warehouses, where they can 'randomly access any case, at any time, in any sequence, at speeds up to 25 miles per hour'.

Similarly offering 'automated material transport' solutions are Fetch Robotics, who manufacture AMR systems that include VirtualConveyor. This uses a combination of robots, charging docks and fleet management software to enable the automated transportation of items from any point in a warehouse to any other.

Figure 4.1 illustrates three Fetch Robotics robots, two of which are 'Freight' models, with the other known as a 'Fetch'. The former have a lower centre of gravity and are designed for speed, while the latter is equipped with an articulated picking arm that can lift items that weigh up to 6 kilograms. The two classes of robot can work together, with the Fetch autonomously picking items which the freight then transports around. Alternatively, Freight robots can automatically follow a human around a warehouse, and then transport their pickings to the required location.

As DHL noted in the 2016 edition of its *Trend Radar* report, the adoption of robotic solutions in logistics 'is likely to intensify over the next three years'. This will include the further roll-out not just of small AMRs, but also large robots able to load and unload trucks and containers, and potentially even robots that will assist humans with final deliveries. Or as DHL went on to predict:

> Logistics is on the brink of a new wave of automation. Driven by rapid technological advancements, next-generation robots and automated solutions are entering the logistics workforce, supporting zero-defect processes and boosting productivity. Robots in particular will adopt collaborative roles in the supply chain, assisting workers with warehouse, transportation, and even last-mile delivery activities.

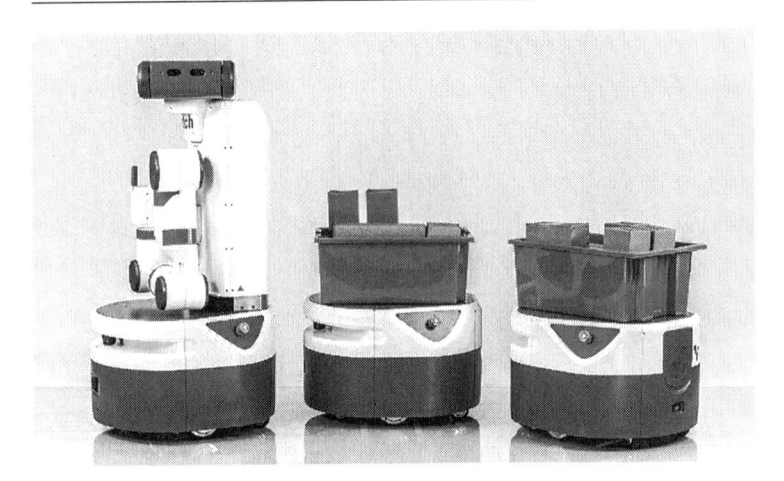

**Figure 4.1: One Fetch & Two Freight Robots Manufactured by Fetch Robotics.** Image courtesy of Fetch Robotics.

In common with manufacturing and logistics, the medical sector is turning to robots to automate or assist physical processes that require high levels of repeat precision. Here the involved hardware includes robots that are used in surgery, as well as robots that help to conduct experiments in research labs. As on the factory floor, the development of vision recognition AIs is having a growing impact in medicine, as it is allowing the creation of automated systems that can 'see' objects and manipulate them with mechanical arms or surgical tools.

One day medical robots may even operate entirely independently *inside* the human body, and on a very small scale. Like their larger robot cousins before them, such 'nanobots' are just starting to move from science fiction to science fact. In the future, they may even navigate our bloodstreams to effect internal repairs.

Right now, most work in this area is focused on the creation of microscale and nanoscale drug carriers that can more precisely deliver medicines than traditional tablets or injections. For example, in 2014 at the Department of Nanoengineering at the University of California, a team of researchers used tiny cylinders propelled by zinc-based micromotors to deliver a drug to the stomach of a mouse. This said, at the Institute for Robotics and Intelligent Systems at ETH Zürich in Switzerland, researchers are working on microrobots and nanorobots that within 10 years may perform delicate surgery within the eye or other organs.

## OUT IN THE FIELD

Whether static or mobile, today practically all manufacturing, logistics or medical robots work in structured environments. In other words, they operate in large spaces or isolated work cells that have been built or adapted for robot occupation. However, the development of AIs with attentive computing capabilities is now starting to facilitate the roll-out of robots in far less structured spaces. In time, these environments will include entirely unstructured spaces, such as domestic residences. This said, before robots go mass-market in the home, they are likely to invade semi-structured working environments. Or, as Travis Deyle, CEO of robot maker Cobalt, explained in a March 2017 article:

> There's a massive, untapped market for robots to be used in commercial spaces such as hotels, hospitals, offices, and retail stores. Commercial spaces could serve as a great stepping stone on the path toward general-purpose home robots by driving scale, volume, and capabilities.

Some of the first robots to labour in semi-structured environments are security droids. For example, a Californian company called Knightscope now advertises how 'there's no need to spend hours on those boring and monotonous patrols', as its security robots can 'guide themselves through even the most complex environments'. As Knightscope explains on its website:

> Knightscope Autonomous Data Machines (ADMs) are autonomous robots that provide a commanding but friendly physical security presence. The K3 and K5 gather important real-time, on-site data through their numerous sensors, which is then processed with advanced anomaly detection software to determine if there is a concern or threat in the area. If so, an event is created with an appropriate alert level and a notification is sent to the proper authorities through the Knightscope Security Operations Center (KSOC), a browser based user interface.

Some of Knightscope's robots are illustrated in figure 4.2, and are already autonomously patrolling client locations that include office buildings, data centres, malls and arenas. The robots are used in parallel with human security personnel, who are freed to focus on less mundane tasks than endless surveillance.

Several companies are now also putting robots to work in hospitals. These include Aethon, which has developed an autonomous mobile delivery robot called TUG to transport medications, meals and materials. As the company explain, they are 'passionate about automating the internal logistics in hospitals to help make healthcare more efficient and effective'. Aethon is also proving successful, with its TUG robots in operation in over 140 hospitals worldwide, and making over 50,000 deliveries every week.

Meanwhile, out in the countryside, other firms are working to automate agricultural production. As we saw in the last chapter, already major agricultural machinery manufacturers, including Case IH, have prototyped autonomous tractors. According to Goldman Sachs, by transitioning from very

**Figure 4.2: Knightscope ADM Security Robots.**
Image courtesy of Knightscope, Inc.

large manned vehicles to fleets of smaller automated tractors, farmers could plough more land more efficiently, reduce labour costs, and 'lift their revenues by more than 10 percent'. Goldman Sachs also estimates that the broader use of autonomous agricultural vehicles, farm robots and drones – and the precision planting, fertilizing and irrigation they would facilitate – 'could result in farm yields potentially rising by more than 70 percent by the year 2050'.

Examples of the kinds of thing Goldman Sachs have in mind are AgriBot and BoniRob. Here, AgriBot is a robot 'that autonomously does all the work in orchards and plantations'. Unlike a human labourer, the robot can toil night and day, and has a mechanical arm at both ends so that it can perform two tasks at once.

Meanwhile BoniRobi is a 'multi-purpose robotic platform for applications in agriculture' that has been created by a

Bosch start-up company called Deepfield Robotics. The robot has four independently steerable drive wheels, and straddles rows of plants as it navigates its way down a field. It can even adjust its track-width to account for the type of crop planted.

As well as toiling on future farms, robots will increasingly participate in the field of battle. Military robots already come in a wide range of form-factors that include unmanned aerial vehicles (UAVs) such as robot planes, helicopters and drones, as well as unmanned ground vehicles (UGVs) with wheels, tracks or legs. It will not surprise you to learn that the United States has more military robots than any other nation, with the total number being in excess of 20,000.

Over the past few years the US Defence Advanced Research Projects Agency (DARPA) has sponsored many robot initiatives and competitions. As with so many other computing developments across history, military expenditure has therefore become a key driver of robot development and application. It will indeed not be long before autonomous military hardware has the mental capability to decide who to kill, coupled with the physical hardware required to execute its own self-determined actions.

So alarming is this proposition that the United Nations has established an expert group to look at the implications of 'lethal autonomous weapon systems'. In August 2017, over 100 robot and AI companies from 26 countries also wrote an open letter to the United Nations expressing grave concerns. Within, they urged the United Nations to find a means to prevent an arms race in autonomous weapons, 'to protect civilians from their misuse, and to avoid the destabilizing effects of these technologies'. Their letter then ended as follows:

> Lethal autonomous weapons threaten to become the third revolution in warfare. Once developed,

they will permit armed conflict to be fought at a scale greater than ever, and at timescales faster than humans can comprehend. These can be weapons of terror, weapons that despots and terrorists use against innocent populations, and weapons hacked to behave in undesirable ways. We do not have long to act. Once this Pandora's box is opened, it will be hard to close. We therefore implore the High Contracting Parties to find a way to protect us all from these dangers.

The above letter did not call for autonomous killer robots to be completely banned, and sooner or later such 'death machines' are going to exist. Indeed, as I am sure you are aware, the US military has on many occasions already used remotely-controlled drones for 'surgical strikes' in foreign war zones.

Talking of drones, some of these flying quadcopters are intended to become autonomous delivery vehicles. To this end, Amazon has established its 'Prime Air Service', and in December 2016 successfully completed its first trial when it delivered a TV streaming device and a bag of popcorn to a garden in Cambridge in the United Kingdom. Such an 'autonomous aerial delivery service' (AADS) could one day allow small items to be with a customer within an hour of their digital assistant placing an order. This said, there are many logistical and legal practicalities to overcome before the skies are full of flying delivery robots.

## TAKING HUMANOID FORM

You may have noticed that so far in this chapter I have said comparatively little about personal and domestic robots. These already exist in the form of toys, vacuum cleaners, robot lawn mowers, and personal drones that can follow you around and take aerial selfies. We are also just starting to see the arrival of digital companion robots, such as Buddy from Blue Frog Robotics in France. As pictured in a small herd in figure 4.3, this cute, roughly two-foot (560 cm) wheeled contraption can assist with tasks that include video messaging, schoolwork and home security, and may also act as a memory aid for the old. A similar robot called Zenbo is sold by Asus.

Robot companions like Buddy and Zenbo may become fairly popular, and especially amongst those who want a cat or dog but without the hassle and the mess. Even so, I cannot imagine that any of the types of domestic robot so far mentioned are going to have a fundamental impact in the home.

While many companies would like to sell domestic servant robots, the challenges they face remain very significant. For a start, the home is a totally unstructured environment. Even more significantly, almost all physical activities undertaken in the home are complex and often ad-hoc. I therefore expect that really useful domestic robots will not become common until they have taken humanoid form.

For thousands of years we have been crafting artificial environments for human occupation. In factories, warehouses and some other workplaces, it is not too difficult to adjust our ways and to redesign and alter things for robot cohabitation. But the home, I would suggest, is different, and likely to remain so. However endearing R2D2 may appear in *Star Wars*, his form-factor of a trashcan-on-wheels is never going to master cooking, ironing, making a bed, changing a nappy, cleaning the toilet, generally clearing up, or helping an elderly person to get out of bed and get dressed. Robot domestic servants and carers really do need to be equipped with a roughly-human arms-and-legs combination in order to manipulate human artefacts, human tools and the bodies of their human users.

The future creation of androids that can manipulate their user's body is likely to raise a great many possibilities and questions. Substantial research is currently focused on de-

**Figure 4.3: The Buddy Personal Robot from Blue Frog Robotics.** Image credit: Blue Frog Robotics.

veloping domestic care assistance robots, and this could clearly prove very useful as our population ages. In addition, robots able to interact with people on a tactile basis may be able to take on a wide range of service roles outside of the home. For example, such robots may one day become hairdressers, masseurs, physical therapists, nurses, medics or undertakers.

Future humanoid robots could potentially even function as escorts, prostitutes, sex workers, or whatever the most appropriate term may be. Indeed, given that a Canadian company called Abyss Creations already makes 'RealDoll' sex mannequins that can move and talk, I suspect that this is exceedingly likely to happen. Many technologies and media – including super-8 film, VHS tapes and DVDs – were given a significant boost by the sex industry, and humanoid robotics may well be similarly advanced.

Beyond constructing robots to complete tasks that require a humanoid body, there are three other reasons for building AI-controlled mechanical mechanisms that resemble ourselves. The first is to provide a better robot-to-human interface, so narrowing the communications divide between people and machines. Or as I explained in *The Next Big Thing*:

> No factory worker seriously pauses to share a moment with a robot co-worker that welds car parts. Yet, as several experiments have already demonstrated, when a humanoid robot turns its head toward you, let alone holds out a hand, a shared context for communication is established. A great deal of human communication is non-verbal, and hence only readily replicated via a humanoid form.

In 1970, Japanese robotics professor Masahiro Mori wrote an article in which he asserted that humanoid robots are more endearing than any other design. Mori did, however, go on to suggest that there was a limit to how humanlike a robot ought to become, and termed this the 'uncanny valley'. This proposes that while most people's empathy increases as a robot's design becomes more human, it abruptly veers into revulsion when a robot's physicality approaches, but fails to attain, a totally human appearance.

Many studies have proven Mori's uncanny valley proposition, with most people finding robots that look like animated corpses to be disturbing and creepy. Hence, while we should predict the widespread rollout of humanoid robots in the 2030s, we should still expect them to look like robots, rather than synthetic copies of ourselves.

Beyond maximizing a robot's capacity to work and communicate in a human environment, a third reason to create android beings will be to train and otherwise improve AI. Not least, embodiment in a humanoid form ought to allow an AI to empathize a little better with humanity, and to more greatly understand our habits, aesthetics and culture. The creation of sophisticated robots that feel and see the world roughly as we do may therefore be considered essential if AI is to advance in a manner that most people consider safe and acceptable.

The final reason to create humanoid robots is medical symbiosis. This refers to the complimentary exchange of technologies and ideas between the medical and robotics sectors, which is increasingly going to occur as medical science, mechanical engineering and synthetic biology converge. The creation of humanoid robots is set to accelerate this crossover, and particularly as we enter the age of Cyborg Fusion in which human beings will augment their bodies with digital technology. So, for example, in the 2040s a pair of robot legs may be transplanted to allow a disabled person to walk.

The above idea may sound extremely far-fetched. It is therefore worth noting that, in November 2015, Honda began leasing a 'Walking Assist Device' to hospitals and other medical establishments. This revolutionary robotic technology attaches to a human patient as a rehabilitation aid, and arose out of research into artificial bipedal motion that was undertaken to help create the ASIMO robot that we will look at in the next section. The first instance of medical symbiosis resulting from humanoid robot development has therefore already taken place.

As we shall explore in the next chapter, decades hence we may even start to bioprint or artificially grow robot components and other computer hardware from organic materials. If and when this happens, opportunities for crossovers between the worlds of medicine and humanoid robotics may become very significant indeed. Our current human 'wetware' has evolved via natural selection over millions of years. It would hence be logical for the AIs tasked with creating organic robots to capitalize on this natural machine learning archive, and this will be easiest to achieve if they end up crafting a new variety of organic humanoid.

In turn, the limbs, eyes, skin, bone and other components mass-fabricated for organic androids may be able to be used as functionally-direct replacements for some human organs. In the second half of this century, such extraordinary possibilities may be an everyday part of the Brave New World of Cyborg Fusion. We will therefore be delving further into such matters in the final chapter of this book.

## ANDROIDS ARRIVE

The challenge of creating viable humanoid robots has been occupying great minds in some pioneering companies for many decades. My best estimate is that such hardware will become an everyday domestic and business appliance around 2030, with a typical humanoid robot costing about as much as a car. I subsequently expect the market for robot assisted living (RAL) to become very large indeed. In addition, around 2030 I predict that humanoid robots will be regularly employed to automate many low-level manufacturing and service jobs that require a humanoid form.

Currently, the development of robots that are either fully humanoid, or which possess at least some humanoid features, falls into three distinct categories. Firstly, there are static, two-armed factory robots that can labour at a human workstation. Next we have mobile robots that are largely humanoid but non-bipedal. And finally, there are an increasing number of fully-humanoid automata. Personally I find the development of all such robots absolutely fascinating, and not least because it provides us with a glimpse into our robotic future.

### *Two-Armed Pedestal Robots*

Robots that can labour in place of a human at a factory workstation have so far been built by pioneers that include Kawasaki Robotics, Hitachi and Epson. All of their creations are SCARA devices, or in other words 'selective compliance articulated robot arms'. So, for example, the 'duAro' from Kawasaki features two articulated arms that are mounted on a box that is about the same size as a two-drawer filing cabinet.

DuAro can be wheeled into a position where a human would sit, where its arms extend out in front of its pedestal to reach over a bench or similar flat work surface. As Kawasaki explain, the 'robot's area of motion is the same as that of a person, with motions similar to those of human arms and independent movements for each arm'. As they continue:

> ... this configuration can easily perform operations similar to those of a person using both arms within a one-person space. Equipped with a collision detection function and a safety function that slows down its motion when near a person, the robot can be reliably operated in tandem with the operations of workers adjacent to the machine.

The duAro has learning functionality that allows it to be quickly set to work to complete a range of different tasks. Typical applications include component assembly, machine tending, material handling, material removal and sealing or dispensing.

Looking somewhat more humanoid (because they have a recognizable head and torso) are the 'Autonomous Dual-Arm Robot' from Epson, and the NEXTAGE 'Humanoid Dual Arm Industrial Robot' from Hitachi. The first prototype of the Epson robot was unveiled at the International Robot Exhibition (IREX) in Tokyo in November 2013, and can be seen in figure 4.4.

Epson explain that their Autonomous Dual-Arm Robot is intended to 'expand the range of tasks that can be automated on the production floor'. To this end, the robot is

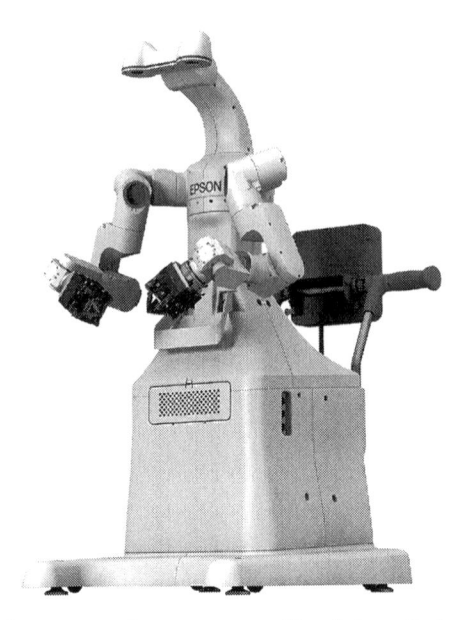

**Figure 4.4: The Epson Autonomous Dual-Arm Robot.**
Image credit: Seiko Epson Corp.

'equipped with vision and force sensing functions that allow it to autonomously execute tasks by recognizing objects, making decisions, and adjusting the amount of force applied'. When demonstrated at IREX, the robot apparently caused quite a stir.

Hitachi's NEXTAGE has similarly been developed to work in a factory or other location alongside humans. Like its Kawasaki and Epson brothers, it does not have human hands. But with 15 axes of movement (six in each arm, plus two for its neck and one for its waist), it is highly dexterous and can perform delicate assembly and materials handling operations.

NEXTAGE is equipped with four cameras (two in its head, and one at the end of each arm) that allow it to measure distances and identify tools, workpieces and markers in its environment. As Hitachi explain in a really cool YouTube video called *Humanoid Dual Arm Industrial Robot NEXTAGE*, out of 'consideration for people working next to it', the robot has been designed so that its arms (or mechanical elbows) do not protrude. Also according to Hitachi, NEXTAGE 'liberates humans from menial, repetitive tasks' and 'takes robots from being equipment to being partners'.

## *Non-Bipedal Humanoid Robots*

Moving to the next level, we have mobile robots that are largely humanoid but non-bipedal. Creating such hardware is clearly a pragmatic decision, as bipedal motion is complex to engineer and control. It therefore makes sense to build a humanoid robot with wheeled locomotion if it is not required to move over rough terrain, climb stairs, or do demanding physically-manipulative tasks.

To date, the most famous robot of this variety is Pepper. As illustrated in figure 4.5, this four foot (120 cm), 28 kilogram robot glides around on a skirt-like pedestal, above which it has a humanoid torso, a head, two arms and articulated hands. Pepper was created by French pioneer Aldebaran Robotics, and was launched by SoftBank Mobile in Japan after it acquired a majority stake in Aldebaran. SoftBank subsequently established a division called SoftBank Robotics in July 2014.

Pepper is described by SoftBank as 'a genuine day-to-day companion' and the first humanoid robot capable of recognising human emotions. In practice, this means that Pepper is able to analyze a person's voice, facial expression, body movement and language, and will alter its behaviour as a result. As the SoftBank website further explains:

> Pepper is capable of identifying the principal emotions: joy, sadness, anger or surprise. He is also capable of interpreting a smile, a frown, your tone

of voice, as well as the lexical field you use and non-verbal language such as the angle of your head, for example. The combination of all this information enables the robot to determine whether his human interlocutor is in a good or a bad mood

As the above implies, Pepper has been given human form to enhance its communication with people, rather than to allow it to dexterously manipulate the physical world. The robot first went on limited sale to the general public in June 2015, with the initial 1,000 units snapped up in under a minute. This rapid sell-out repeated when further Pepper batches were released, with the robot priced at $1,600 plus a $360/month telecoms data plan and insurance contract.

As of May 2016, over 10,000 Pepper robots were 'out in the world', with many of these in business roles. The latter include about 2,000 Pepper robots deployed in SoftBank's own stores to 'create interest, generate traffic to the stores, greet customers, present company offers and provide entertainment'. Also in Japan, since December 2014 Nestlé has begun to 'integrate Pepper' into its stores, with a roll-out of about 1,000 robots planned.

Internationally, Pepper is being sold or hired out for business use. For example, Robots of London now offers Pepper to businesses for a range of applications that include 'receptionist'. Here, the robot can 'welcome every visitor as soon as eye contact is made', before sending an e-mail or text to inform an organizer of the visitor's arrival. While the visitor is waiting the robot will showcase its dancing skills, before entering into a 'free and autonomous' chat on one of over 90,000 different topics.

A competitor to Pepper is a fascinating robot from Hitachi called EMIEW3, which stands for 'Excellent Mobility and Interactive Existence as Workmate'. EMIEW3 is about three feet or 90 cm tall (so that its eye level is the same as somebody

**Figure 4.5: SoftBank Robotics Pepper Robot.**
Image courtesy of Philippe Dureuil/TOMA - SoftBank Robotics.

sitting in a chair). It is also 15 kilograms in weight, and is designed as a 'human symbiotic robot that actively communicates with people'. The robot has a cloud-based 'remote brain', and has been developed to provide 'services such as greeting customers or giving guidance in public spaces like stations and airports'.

EMIEW3 has a fully humanoid body, although it cleverly avoids the complexities of bipedal locomotion by having wheels at the front and back of its feet, so removing the need for it to move forward by taking steps. The robot hence travels around as if it is on rollerskates. This said, it is able to move its legs to allow it to corner, lean forward, sit down, stand up, and overcome floor height differences of about six inches (15 cm). EMIEW3 can even right itself after a potential fall.

Again to save on complexity, EMIEW3 has been equipped with paddle-like gripper claws rather than fingered hands. Like Pepper it has hence been designed for expressive human communication rather the physical manipulation of objects or people. In common with Hitachi's NEXTAGE, EMIEW3 has also become a YouTube star. To see it in action, just search the video platform for 'EMIEW3'.

EMIEW3's cloud-based approach allows it to use nearby networked cameras as 'eyes'. It can also share information with other EMIEW3 units, and has complex speech capabilities, including language translation. In September 2016, Hitachi began proof-of-concept tests of EMIEW3 as a meet-and-greet robot at Haneda Airport.

### *Fully-Humanoid Robots*

Fully-humanoid robots – or robots with a humanoid frame that is capable of independent bipedal motion – are very much a work in progress. Nevertheless, they are steadily increasing in number and becoming ever-more complex. Chief amongst such creations is ASIMO from Honda, which is illustrated in figure 4.6. The robot's name stands for 'Advanced Step in Innovative MObility'.

In 1986, Honda began its quest to create a 'two-legged humanoid robot' that could 'genuinely help people' when it

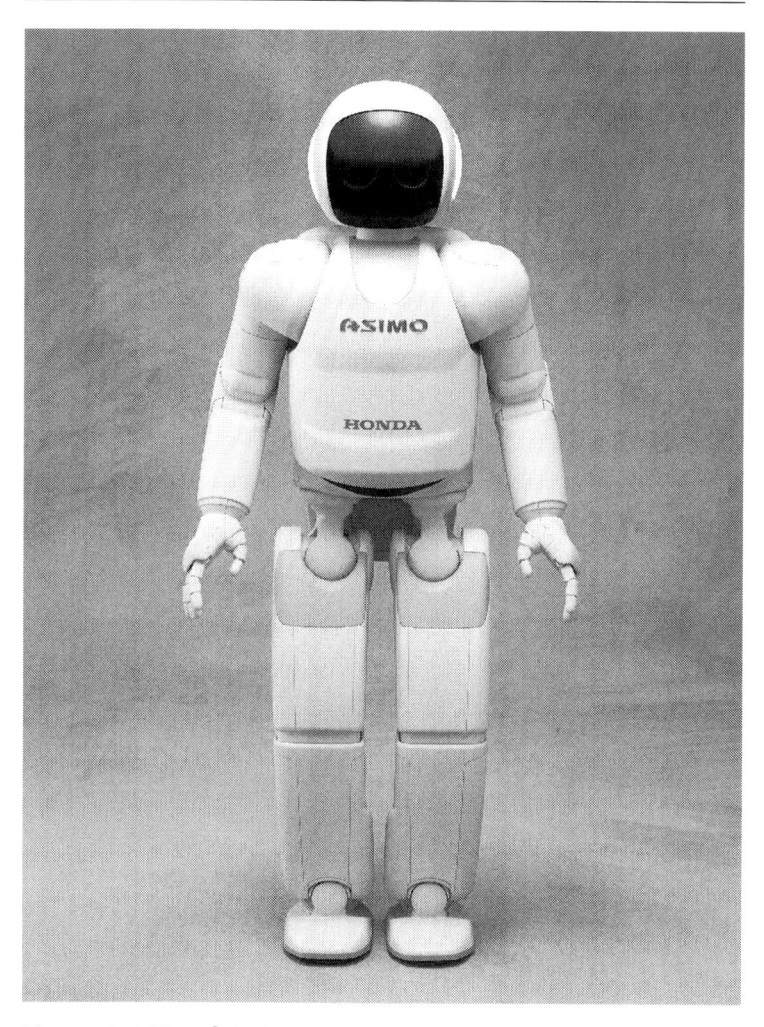

**Figure 4.6: Honda's ASIMO.** Image courtesy of Honda.

created a biped box-on-legs robot called the E0. This was capable of walking, if only in a straight line, and took 5 seconds to calculate and take each step. Between 1987 and 1993, six further iterations followed (the E1 through to the E6), which helped Honda to master stable bipedal walking.

Beginning in 1993, three fully humanoid robots were then built (the P1 to the P3), the first of which was about 6 feet (1.88 m) tall and weighed 130 kilograms.

Finally in 2000, ASIMO was released. At 4.25 feet (1.3 m) high, and weighing 48 kilograms, the shiny white robot is less imposing than its forebears, and intentionally so. Initially the hardware was a programmable 'automatic machine', but in 2011 it became an autonomous machine with 'the decision-making capability to determine its behaviour in concert with its surroundings'. Specific AI developments that allowed this to happen included the development of a 'high-level postural balancing capability' (which means that ASIMO can stick out a leg to stop itself from falling over); an 'external recognition capability' (that allows ASIMO to gauge and predict the movement of people around it); and the ability to 'generate autonomous behaviour' without operator intervention.

ASIMO can now walk, run, climb stairs, communicate via sign language, and alter its behavior to accommodate the intentions of others. For example, ASIMO will step aside to allow a human being to pass, or will change its own trajectory to walk around them. ASIMO also has integrated face and voice recognition, so allowing it to know who is giving it spoken commands. Honda state that their 'dream' is still to deliver a robot that can provide 'peace of mind and physical care for family members', as well as 'assistance with housework'.

Another innovator of amazing humanoid robots is Boston Dynamics. This was recently part of Alphabet (Google), but in June 2017 was purchased by SoftBank. The company's Atlas hardware is billed as 'the world's most dynamic humanoid', and is able to walk bipedally over rough terrain, or to climb using all four limbs. The robot is 5 feet (1.5 m) tall, weighs 75 kilograms, and is intended for heavy industrial and military applications, such as providing relief support after natural disasters.

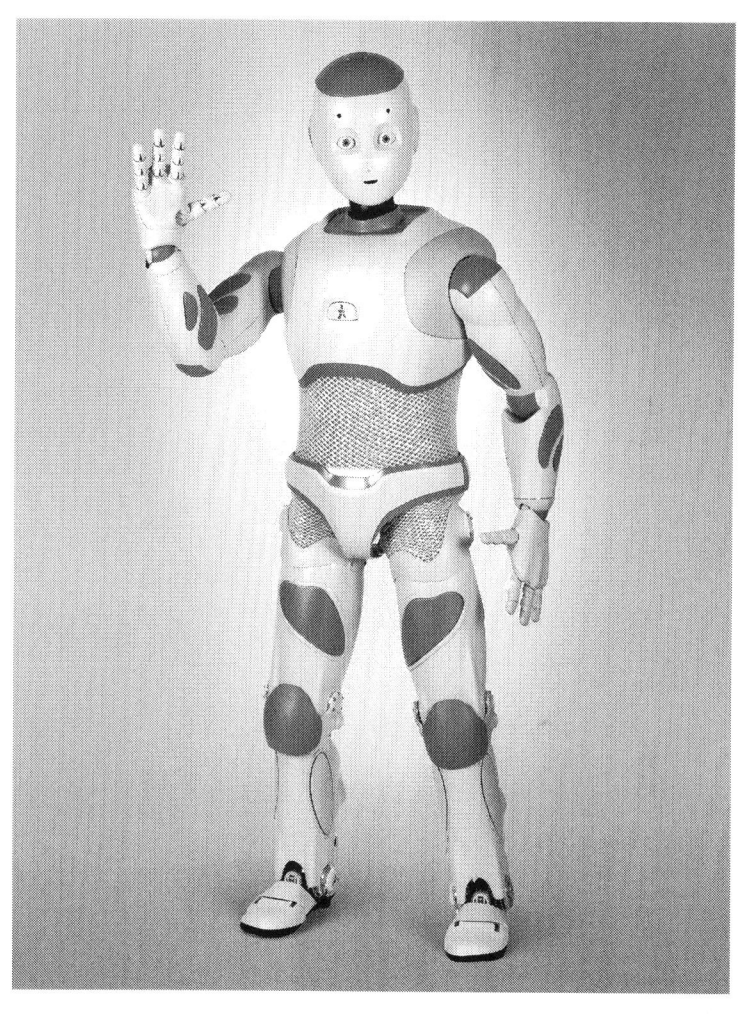

**Figure 4.7: SoftBank Robotics Romeo Robot.**
Image courtesy of SoftBank Robotics.

Another fully-humanoid robot from the SoftBank stable is Romeo. As shown in figure 4.7, this five foot (1.5 m) machine is totally humanoid, save for the fact that it only has three fingers on each hand. Development was initiated in

2009 at Aldebaran Robotics in France, with funding from French national and regional governments. Romeo was designed to 'explore and further research into assisting elderly people and those who are losing their autonomy'. In 2013, a second-phase of research and funding kicked-in with the objective of evaluating, over time, the use of a humanoid robot in providing domestic assistance.

Also developing a humanoid robot are NASA, with a model called Valkyrie or 'R5'. As pictured in figure 4.8, this has soft coverings (so that it does not feel cold to human touch), stands 6.2 feet (1.9 metres) tall, and weighs 136 kilograms. The hardware was initially designed by NASA's Johnson Space Center (JSC) to complete disaster-relief manoeuvres, and for potential use in future deep space exploration. It has, for example, been suggested that before any future human mission to Mars, a contingent of R5 robots would first be despatched to prepare a base. An earlier version of the R5 robot, called the R2, has already visited the International Space Station (ISS).

Given the development of R2 and R5 by NASA, you will not be surprised to learn that a Russian humanoid robot has been built for potential use in space. Known as FEDOR – or the 'Final Experimental Demonstration Object Research' – this imposing machine was designed by Android Technics and the Russian military's Advanced Research Fund. Already FEDOR is able to drive a vehicle and to use tools like an electric drill. As Andrey Grigoriev of the Advanced Research Fund explained in April 2017:

> FEDOR was designed as an android able to replace humans in high-risk areas, such as rescue operations. For this purpose, it was necessary to teach him to work independently in an urban environment, navigate the terrain, drive a car, to handle special tools, first aid and other actions.

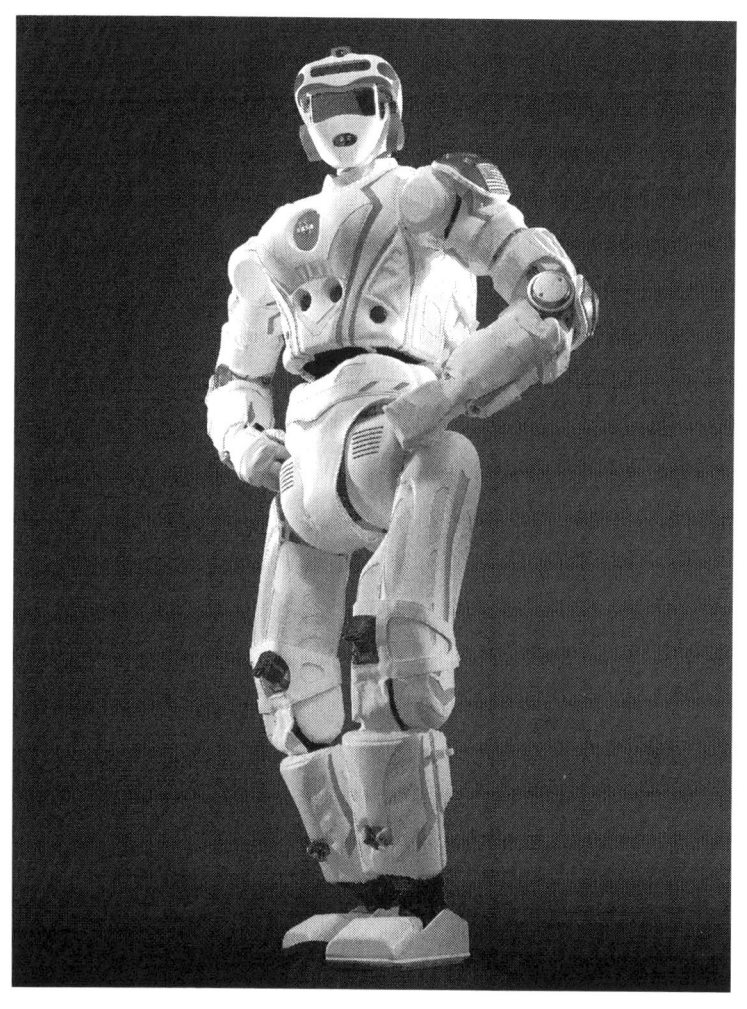

**Figure 4.8: NASA's Valkyrie (R5) Robot.** Image courtesy of NASA.

In various online videos, FEDOR can be seen walking, crawling, using a syringe, and accurately shooting live ammunition from firearms held in each hand. Like R5, the robot is very much a work in progress, and is usually seen operating with a tether. Even so, FEDOR appears to be an extremely robust machine with very significant potential. So much is this the case that, after the online footage of two-handed shooting was posted, Russia's Deputy Prime Minister, Dmitry Rogozin, took to Twitter to provide reassurance that 'we are not creating a Terminator, but artificial intelligence that will be of great practical significance in various fields'.

Other humanoid robots include the child-sized iCub. This was created as an 'open source cognitive humanoid robotic platform' as part of a European Union project called RobotCub, and is in use in 20+ research labs worldwide. Some iCubs have even been fitted with capacitive skin on their fingertips and palms to provide them with a sense of touch and so permit the development of 'safe grasping strategies'. Other open humanoid robot initiatives include the Poppy Project (an 'open source platform for the creation, use and sharing of interactive 3D printed robots'), and the Inmoov 'open source 3D printed life-size robot'.

## COMPETING WITH ROBOTS

As the last few pages have demonstrated, humanoid robots of various complexities are now operating in the lab, and to a limited extent in the field. Within 10 to 20 years, they are hence likely to be joining the growing legion of robot arms and autonomous mobile robots that will be populating many future industrial, commercial, military and domestic environments. Like it or not, there are going to be far more robots in the world in the 2020s and 2030s, and their 'physical digital transformation' will have very significant implications.

In the home robots ought to empower the old, protect the very young, and save time and energy for at least some people in the middle. On the battlefield and in other dangerous situations, robots will hopefully also reduce risks and save lives. There is additionally little doubt that robots will allow many companies to reduce their costs. Certain forms of service quality and brand consistency are also likely to be improved, with fast food chains and other businesses finally able to guarantee that every customer will be greeted and served in precisely the same manner. Yet as a consequence of these commercial and other benefits, human jobs are going to be lost.

A growing number of commentators are predicting that the 'substitution' of robots for manual human workers will create mass unemployment. Other pundits claim that this will not occur, as new forms of employment will be created to compensate for the jobs that robots take away. As such optimists argue, since the Industrial Revolution we have been replacing human beings with machines, and yet the total number of people in employment around the world is greater than ever before. History may therefore be interpreted to teach us that everything will work out just fine. There is, however, no guarantee that the next round of mass physical automation will create sufficient new jobs for all of the human workers it displaces.

While nobody knows exactly what is going to happen, many reputable organizations have made informed predictions. For example, in December 2016 President Obama's outgoing administration published a report on AI, automation and the economy. This revealed that, between 1993 and 2007, robots had added 0.4 per cent to the gross domestic product (GDP) of 17 countries studied. This is clearly a positive message, although some of this growth had been achieved by 'employing fewer workers at some facilities'.

In June 2017 Forrester predicted that, by 2027, many people will work side-by-side with robots. It also estimated that, in the United States alone, 25 million jobs will be lost due to the increased use of robots, with 15 million jobs to be created, and hence a net impact of 10 million people unemployed.

While robots are likely to lead to job losses in developed nations, they will also allow manufacturing to return to their shores. This may well be good for rich countries, but disastrous for the developing world. In November 2016, the United Nations Conference on Trade and Development (UNCTAD) signalled how the rise of robot-automated manufacturing in developed nations may trigger a wave of 'premature deindustrialization' in many developing nations. As it went on to note:

> The increased use of robots in developed countries risks eroding the traditional labour cost advantage of developing countries. If robots are considered a form of capital that is a close substitute for low-skilled workers, then their growing use reduces the share of human labour in total production costs. Adverse effects for developing countries may be significant.

UNCTAD went on to cite 2016 World Bank statistics which suggest that two thirds of all jobs in developing nations are at risk due to future 'significant automation' in the developed world. In chapter 2, we similarly noted how China is intent on remaining competitive by replacing hundreds of millions of manual workers with robots. For large numbers of people around the world, the rise of the robot is therefore highly likely to result in dark times as well as dark factories, and this is something that governments need to start planning for and fast. Or as British MP Tom Watson wrote in *The Guardian* in March 2016, 'technology is bringing profound, unstoppable change to society [and it is] vital that government faces this'.

## ROBOT LAWS & RIGHTS

Something else that governments and society need to start thinking about are the regulatory changes that will be needed as robots emerge from the factory floor. In his classic novels and short stories, science fiction master Isaac Asimov famously explained how our future mechanical creations will need to be carefully controlled, and went on to champion three 'Laws of Robotics'. In summary, these state that a robot may not injure a human; that a robot must obey human orders unless this would break the first law; and that a robot must protect its own existence unless this conflicts with the first two laws.

Isaac Asimov's fictional ideas have had a powerful influence on the inventors of real robots. Not least, Joseph Engelberger – the 'father of robotics' who co-created the Unimate – is reported to have been motivated by Asimov's Laws. It also stands to reason that smart, synthetic mechanisms will need to be subject to laws of some kind before they are let loose in public spaces and the home. This said, encoding absolute, hard-and-fast rules into deep learning systems is not easy.

Even if we do manage to program robots with operational red lines like those proposed by Asimov, there can be no guarantee that criminals and others will not hack their way around them. After all, today most commercial software applications, music and videos are copy protected, and this does not prevent digital content from being cloned. 'Kill switches' built into future robots may also be subject to illegal hacking, and so will not be able to protect us with 100 per cent certainty.

In the fairly near future, we will also have to decide just what legal status robots ought to enjoy. For a start, if a robot does accidentally or purposefully kill a person, should it be held responsible? Or should its owner be accountable? Or its manufacturer or retailer? Asimovian robot laws may be all well and good. But I suspect that, for many decades to come, we will insist on holding humans to account for robot actions. So if you buy or rent a robot in the future, your biggest worry may be the liabilities it could expose you to, and the cost of appropriate insurance.

The other way around, as robots and AIs become smarter and more 'self aware', there may be pressures to give them their own rights. If somebody turns off another person we call it 'murder'. So if a person removes the power from a robot and deletes years of deep learning, ought this to be treated as 'digital murder' and legally punished in a similar manner? Granted, if a robot is controlled by a cloud AI, it will be difficult to erase and ought to be backed up. But even so, sooner or later I suspect there will be calls for the intelligent, synthetic species that we are starting to create to be given not just responsibilities, but also the right of citizenship.

If all of this sounds bizarre, I would point out that for many years the South Korean government has been talking about establishing rights and responsibilities for robots and AIs. It's latest ministerial meeting on the subject took place in February 2017, with Minister of Science Choi Yang-hee announcing that many South Korean ministries and government agencies would, within a year, be defining new legal standards, statuses, responsibilities and ethical codes related to AI, self-driving cars and similar technologies.

Perhaps even more significantly, in June 2016 a draft motion drawn up by the European Parliament's Committee on legal affairs called for a debate on granting rights of 'personhood' to robots. Specifically, the draft motion asked the European Commission to consider 'that at least the most sophisticated autonomous robots could be established as having the status of electronic persons with specific rights and obligations'.

The 'robot personhood' motion in question is very unlikely to gain parliamentary backing, let alone to enter into any form of law even if it does. For a start, a related 2016 European Parliament policy report entitled *European Civil Law Rules in Robotics* concluded that 'assigning person status to a non-living, non-conscious entity' would 'be an error' as 'humankind would likely be demoted to the rank of a machine'. The 2016 report even concluded its argument with the words 'robots should serve humanity and should have no other role'. Nevertheless, I suspect that the 'rights for robots and AIs' movement will grow as smart digital technology continues to advance.

\* \* \*

## FUTURE ROBOT EVOLUTION

Over the next few decades robots will complete their slow metamorphosis from fiction to reality. Several key technology developments will drive this evolution, with these most notably including the rise of cloud AI, the availability of low-cost sensors, and the advancement of 3D printers and other local digital manufacturing technologies.

For robots to become autonomous, they clearly need either an onboard AI, or access to one or more cloud AI services. Over the past year or so the latter have started to advance very rapidly, so allowing robots with fairly minimal computer processing hardware to be equipped with complex AI capabilities. Naturally, such cloud-based robots require good Internet connectivity. But 5G is on the near horizon, which ought to give a shot in the arm to cloud robotics. Indeed, to cite a June 2017 GTI report from SoftBank, China Mobile, Huawei and others, once 5G and related low-latency network technologies arrive, 'there will be an explosion in use of cloud robotics across businesses of all types, and in the home'. Indeed, as the report further stresses:

> The market for robots is about to change dramatically. Traditional factory robot arms will be joined by a huge variety of highly capable robots fulfilling many more types of function. These new robots will make use of cloud-based resources to become more intelligent. These resources will include artificial intelligence, machine learning and deep learning, to provide image and face recognition, and natural language processing.

Regardless of the level of AI they have available, robots need good sensors if they are to operate effectively in semi-structured and unstructured environments. Over the past 10 years, the cost of orientation and motion sensors has fallen dramatically due to their inclusion in most tablets and smartphones. This has been a godsend for robotics, and in particular for the development of bipedal walking mechanisms. All sophisticated bipedal robots walk not just by executing programmed commands, but by practising the art of 'controlled falling over' that is used by humans. To achieve this, bipedal robots hence depend on motion and orientation sensors to constantly monitor the position of their body parts and centre of gravity.

While smartphones have made orientation and motion sensors low-cost stock components, future robots are also going to depend on other kinds of sensors. These will include very high definition cameras, potentially LiDAR to accurately map their environment, and haptic sensors to provide a sense of touch. Today LiDAR is used in many self-driving vehicles, but remains very expensive. Haptic sensors – such as force-sensing resistors – are also far from a mature technology, and hence as these improve, so will the robots for which they become available.

As well as relying on effective AI and sensors, robots require all of their physical components to be fabricated, and until recently this was very expensive. It is therefore fortunate that another digital transformation technology has come to the rescue, and that technology is 3D printing. In recent years this has started to allow one-off and low-run robot mechanisms to be fabricated for hundreds or thousands of dollars, rather than tens or hundreds of thousands. Robots and robotics research projects that would have been financially unviable even five years ago have hence become realistic, and this is helping to drive more rapid robot evolution.

No species – artificial or otherwise – can exist for a long period without a means of self-repair and procreation, and this has to be true for robots. At the present time, 3D printers that can fabricate items out of metals and plastics appear to be the obvious mechanism for robot self-repair and procreation, and it is not impossible to imagine some future robots either having a 3D printer built in, or more likely attached to them as part of their wider cloud network. In time, synthetic biology, bioprinting and molecular self-assembly may provide additional digital mechanisms for robot construction, repair and replication. As we have seen so many times across this book, the technologies of digital transformation are all synergistically intertwined.

As robots, let alone self-replicating robots, become a common sight in our workplaces, public spaces and homes, so the human race will need to adjust to living with another intelligent species. Granted, in parallel we will also be adjusting to living with disembodied AI. However, I suspect that it will be physically manifested synthetic intelligence that will take the most getting used to.

Even today, dumb robot toys – let alone more sophisticated automata like ASIMO, FEDOR, Pepper, EMIEW3, Buddy and Zenbo – can appear to be 'alive'. Absolutely we know that they are totally dead. But for millions of years our brains have been deeply programmed to recognise complex, moving mechanisms as living things. At least at the subconscious level, we are therefore now facing a psychologically fraught period of history as our world comes to be populated by robots, and in particular by robots with humanoid bodies. In the near future, some of our co-workers, domestic co-inhabitants and even friends are going to be artificial mechanisms. Some very interesting times and experiences therefore lie ahead.

# 5

# QUANTUM & ORGANIC FRONTIERS

In April 1965, Gordon E. Moore wrote an article for the 35th anniversary issue of *Electronics* magazine. Within, he observed that the number of transistors on an integrated circuit had been doubling roughly once a year. Moore predicted that this trend would continue, with digital hardware expected to increase in power and reduce in cost at an exponential rate.

In 1968 Moore co-founded a semiconductor manufacturer called NM Electronics with his colleague Robert Noyce. Their company was quickly renamed 'Intel', and went on to become the world's largest microprocessor manufacturer. Moore's prediction that the number of transistors on an integrated circuit would increase exponentially also grew in stature, and became known as 'Moore's Law'. In 1975, Moore gave a speech in which he revisited his earlier work, and noted that the exponential growth of computer power would continue, if at a slower rate.

Specifically, in 1975 Moore predicted that by 1980 the number of transistors included on the most sophisticated microprocessors would double approximately every two years. Since 1980, this prediction has also proved to be accurate, with computer technology doubling in power roughly every 18 to 24 months.

At the end of his 1975 address, Moore indicated that his predictions meant that we would have 'integrated structures containing several million components . . . within ten years'. In actuality, in 1985 Intel introduced the 80386 microprocessor containing 275,000 transistors. Ten years after that, in 1995 it was releasing the Pentium Pro with 5.5 million. By 2004, an Intel Itanium 2 microprocessor had 292 million transistors, while by 2015 their Xeon chips featured over 5.5 billion. Today Intel is able to fabricate a staggering 100 million transistors per square millimetre of integrated circuit, and markets a Xeon Broadwell-E5 processor with 7.2 billion transistors.

The above figures and progress are almost too large to comprehend. Yet these staggering improvements in microprocessor technology are what have delivered us the PC, the modern data centre, the tablet, the smartphone and the Internet. Quite simply, every major computing development that has occurred since 1980 has depended on the continual, exponential development of the microprocessor. It is, however, naive to believe that transistor-based, silicon chip technology can and will continue to provide us with exponential leaps in computing performance.

Already we are starting to approach practical constraints imposed by the laws of physics. At the time of writing, the latest Intel microprocessors use a 14 nanometre production process. One nanometre is just one billionth of a metre, with the 14 nanometre process producing components only 14 nanometres apart, with interconnects (wiring) as tiny as 52 nanometres across, and a minimum component feature size of 42 nanometres. While this is extraordinary, Intel has not stopped yet. By 2023 the company hopes to be using a 5 nanometre manufacturing process. What this implies is that, by the early-to-mid 2020s, Intel is planning on the sale of mainstream consumer products with some internal components measuring less than 100 atoms across and spaced at roughly 25 atom intervals.

What Intel and others have continually managed to achieve in their integrated circuit fabrication plants is nothing short of miraculous. Yet it does not take a genius to work out that such continual improvements in miniaturization cannot go on forever. At some point in the 2020s or 2030s, Moore's Law really has to start failing. Just as significantly, there are already certain kinds of future computing activities – such as molecular and biological modelling – that traditional, transistor-based computers will never be able to tackle. In this chapter we will therefore examine the potential way ahead for the most sophisticated computer hardware, and in particular the development of alternative and radically different future computing technologies.

## NEXT GENERATION HARDWARE

In chapter 1 we charted the rise of large IT systems, followed by personal and interpersonal computers. In the future, all such hardware will continue to advance, with tomorrow's smartphones, tablets and laptops destined to be a lot more powerful than those we have today.

The humble desktop PC is also set to evolve but also to shrink. I indeed suspect that few of us will harbour a large tower on or under our desk in ten years time, with most PCs destined to become rather small boxes, or else an integral part of a monitor. Tiny 'single board computers' (SBCs) like the $35 Raspberry Pi are already more capable than many desktop PCs from 10 years ago.

Today, the only real reason for desktop PCs to remain as large as they were is to accommodate spinning hard drives, DVD and other optical drive mechanisms, and large power supplies and cooling systems. But as solid-state drives (SSDs) take over from hard drives, most optical disks go the way of the dodo, and all forms of hardware are integrated and use less power, so the classic desktop PC will inevitably become smaller.

Regardless of their future size and form factor, it is important to appreciate that the power of most end-user computing devices is going to get less and less significant. This is because, as more and more computing migrates to the cloud, most end-user devices will become little more than an interface to a remote data centre system. It is hence the racks of servers operated in their millions by the likes of Amazon, IBM, Google, Microsoft and Apple that constitute the next-generation computer hardware frontier. The new technologies necessary to push beyond the limits of Moore's Law are therefore very unlikely to be directly operated by end-users. And it is to two such revolutionary technologies that we will now turn our attention.

## QUANTUM COMPUTING

The first hardware innovation that could deliver staggering new levels of computational power is quantum computing. This capitalizes on the 'quantum mechanical' behaviour of matter and energy, and is already starting to deliver an entirely new kind of computational platform. A detailed explanation of *exactly* how quantum computing works would require us to delve into the highly technical field of quantum mechanics, and is hence beyond the remit of this book. So below I will simply outline the key principles involved.

Conventional or 'classical' computers are based on miniature transistors that can be turned 'on' or 'off' to represent a numerical value of either '1' or '0'. This allows classical computers to store and process data using 'binary digits' or 'bits'. But it also places some limits on their capabilities.

In contrast, quantum computers work with 'quantum bits' or 'qubits', which are represented by the quantum mechanical properties of subatomic particles. These quantum mechanical properties allow qubits to exist in more than one state – or 'superposition' – at exactly the same point in time, so allowing a qubit to assume a value of '1', '0', or both of these numbers simultaneously. In turn, this allows a quantum computer to process a far higher number of data possibilities than a classical computer that is limited to working with just 'on' or 'off' data values. Not least, qubit superpositions can enable quantum computers to process a very wide range of probable solutions simultaneously, rather than having to compute each possible solution in turn.

The fact that qubits are more 'smears of possibilities' than definitive, black-and-white certainties is exceptionally weird. Flip a coin and it cannot come up both heads and tails simultaneously, and yet the quantum state of a qubit can in some senses do just that. It is therefore hardly surprising that renowned nuclear physicist Niels Bohr once stated that 'anyone who is not shocked by quantum theory has not understood it'.

In addition to assuming superpositions, qubits can become 'entangled'. Such 'entanglement' is another quantum mechanical property, and means that the state of one qubit can depend on the state of another. This is useful and powerful, as it means that observing one qubit can reveal the state of its unobserved pair.

By capitalizing on the way in which qubits can assume superpositions and achieve entanglement, quantum computers should in the future be able to tackle computational challenges that cannot be handled by classical, transistor-based hardware. Such challenges include logistical problems that involve large-scale optimizations or exponential complexity, as well as the development of more sophisticated deep learning AIs. Right now, experimental quantum computers are no more powerful than the best classical computers except in very specific situations. But sometime in the 2020s, quantum computers could potentially outperform any classical computer at many tasks.

## QUANTUM COMPUTING PIONEERS

Several companies – including IBM, Google, Microsoft, and a Canadian start-up called D-Wave – have for years been experimenting with quantum computing. For years many pundits have also questioned their achievements, and have even queried whether quantum computing will ever become a practical proposition. However, in the last 18 months, very clear progress has been made, with fairly near-term business intentions reported.

For example, in May 2016 IBM made an experimental quantum computer publicly available over the Internet. In March 2017, it then announced a new initiative called 'IBM Q' that will build commercial quantum computers and deliver their services from the cloud. Given the perceived state-of-play in quantum computing only five years ago, this is really big news. It also suggests that we should start our review of quantum computing pioneers by turning to the old 'Big Blue'.

### *IBM Q*

IBM has been developing quantum computers for over 35 years, and has built several experimental quantum processors. These include the 5 qubit system that was made available for public experimentation in May 2016, and which has already been used to conduct more than 300,000 experiments. In May 2017, IBM also announced new 16 and 17 qubit prototype quantum processors. As the company explained, its latest 16 qubit hardware is freely accessible to developers through its IBM Q Experience website. However, the 17 qubit model is 'IBM's first prototype commercial processor', and will leverage:

> . . . significant materials, device, and architecture improvements to make it the most powerful quantum processor created to date by IBM. It has been engineered to be at least twice as powerful as what is

available today to the public on the IBM Cloud and it will be the basis for the first IBM Q early-access commercial systems.

According to IBM senior vice president Arvind Krishna, the aforementioned engineering improvements 'will allow IBM to scale future processors to include 50 or more qubits and so enable 'new applications and new frontiers for discovery'. In this context it should be noted that a 50 qubit quantum computer is anticipated to demonstrate 'quantum supremacy'. Or in other words, quantum hardware with this many qubits is expected to be able to outperform a classical computer at any task.

Unsurprisingly, quantum computers are extremely difficult to build, with no industry-wide consensus for how they should be constructed. IBM's solution is to build 'approximate universal quantum computers' (or, in other words, quantum computers able to run any type of program) based on 'universal quantum gates'. IBM also argues that this is the only approach that will result in useful quantum computers.

IBM's quantum processors need to be supercooled down to approaching -273 °C. The actual operational temperature is only 0.015 degrees Kelvin, or a tiny smidge above the temperature of 'absolute zero' at which all atoms stop moving.

Within the quantum processor, qubits are created and maintained within superconducting devices called 'Josephson junctions'. Microwave resonators are then used to observe and address their quantum states. The technology really is mind-numbingly sophisticated. Figure 5.1 shows part of the interior of an IBM quantum computer with its refrigeration casing removed.

### *D-Wave Systems*

While IBM is making steady progress in creating 'approximate universal quantum computers', one of it's main rivals

**Figure 5.1: IBM Quantum Computer Interior.**
Image credit: IBM Research.

takes an entirely different approach. This pioneer is a Canadian Company called D-Wave Systems, which builds 'adiabatic quantum computers' based on 'quantum annealing'. IBM notes that this simpler approach results in the 'least powerful and most restrictive form of quantum computer' which can 'only perform one specific function'. Many other commentators have also been rather dismissive of the activities of D-Wave, whose claims have subsequently proved controversial in some quarters. This has especially been the case since 2011, when D-Wave became the first company to actually sell a quantum computer.

Without getting too deeply into the quantum mechanics, one of the key differences between the 'universal gate' systems made by IBM, and the 'quantum annealing' hardware produced by D-Wave, is that the latter has a lower level of 'quantum coherence'. This means that the qubits in a D-Wave system degenerate more quickly than those in an IBM quantum computer. However, D-Wave's approach has allowed it to produce working hardware with far more qubits, which in certain contexts may make up for the reduced quantum coherence limitation.

A second and even more fundamental difference between the two approaches is that while quantum annealing utilizes the quantum states of its qubits to perform computations, it does not try to control them. In contrast, universal gate quantum computers do try to control the quantum states of their qubits. This makes the gate model of quantum computing much harder to implement, but broadens its range of applications by allowing it to run a much wider range of quantum algorithms. It is for this reason that IBM describe quantum annealing as 'restrictive'.

D-Wave first demonstrated a 16 qubit quantum computer in 2007. Its first commercial (if still experimental) system was then a 128 qubit machine called the D-Wave One that it sold for $10 million to a Lockheed Martin research facility. In May 2013, D-Wave announced that a 512 qubit D-Wave Two had been supplied to NASA, Google and the Universities Space Research Association (USRA) to establish the Quantum Artificial Intelligence Lab (QuAIL) at the Ames Research Center in California. At present QuAIL is focused on demonstrating the future potential of quantum computing to solve currently unfathomable aeronautic optimization problems.

In 2015 D-Wave broke the 1,000 qubit barrier with its D-Wave 2X, one of which was also supplied to QuAIL. However, the company's latest machine is the D-Wave 2000Q. This went on the market in January 2017, and is based on a 2,000 qubit quantum processing unit (QPU). This contains a lattice of 2,000 superconducting devices, which like IBM's quantum hardware are supercooled to just 0.015 degrees Kelvin.

The D-Wave 2000Q is an extraordinary feat of engineering, with its QPU environment shielded to reduce its internal magnetic field to 50,000 times less than that of the Earth. The QPU also functions in a vacuum, with its operating pressure being 10 billion times lower than typical atmospheric pressure.

As already noted, D-Wave's hardware is based on quantum annealing, which does limit its application to certain kinds of computing activities. Nevertheless, these tasks include optimization and sampling problems that are very hard for classical computers to handle at a very large scale.

Optimization problems are common in logistics and AI, and involve finding the best solution to a problem with a great many possible permutations. Such problems can be framed as so-termed 'energy minimization problems', which a quantum annealing system can solve because all physical systems (and hence its qubits) tend toward minimum energy states.

As D-Wave explain, users of their computers turn their computational problem into a search for the 'lowest energy point in a vast landscape'. In turn 'the processor considers all possibilities simultaneously to determine the lowest energy and the values that produce it'. Multiple solutions are then 'returned to the user, scaled to show optimal answers'.

In addition to optimizations, D-Wave's quantum annealing hardware can solve 'sampling problems'. These can be especially useful when developing AI systems, and sample many low energy states to come up with those 'probabilistic representations of the world' on which deep learning relies.

According to D-Wave Systems, in benchmark optimization and sampling tests, its 2000Q QPUs 'outperformed competitive classical algorithms by 1,000 to 10,000 times in pure computation time'. D-Wave also note that the D-Wave 2000Q is 100 times more efficient that a classical computing system in terms of performance per watt. As the company further reports, the D-Wave 2000Q uses only 24.8 kilowatts, compared to about 2,500 kilowatts for a comparable classic supercomputer. The power usage of D-Wave's systems has also 'remained constant in successive generations, and is expected to continue to do so while the computational power increases dramatically'.

In January 2017 the first customer for a D-Wave 2000Q was cyber security firm Temporal Defence Systems (TDS). In March 2017, NASA and Google's QuAIL facility also elected to upgrade its hardware to a D-Wave 2000Q. In May 2017, Recruit Communications Co in Japan then announced a collaboration with D-Wave 'to apply quantum computing to marketing, advertising, and communications optimization'.

The above announcement followed a collaboration with Volkswagen, which became the first company to apply quantum computing to a traffic flow optimization problem. In July 2017, D-Wave Systems additionally made an agreement with the US Government's Oak Ridge National Laboratory (ORNL). This will provide ORNL scientists with cloud access to a D-Wave 2000Q, with the intention being to develop hybrid (classical and quantum) computing architectures 'as a way to achieve better solutions for scientific applications'.

As you can see, D-Wave Systems has for several years been operating as the world's only commercial quantum computing company. In August 2016, a peer-reviewed scientific paper published in *Physical Review X* also reported that certain algorithms ran up to one hundred million times faster on a D-Wave 2X than on a single-core classical processor. The authors of the research behind this claim further concluded that 'we are optimistic that the significant runtime gains we have recovered will carry over to commercially relevant problems that occur in tasks relevant to machine intelligence'.

Rather sadly, some have questioned the validity of the *Physical Review X* paper results because the astonishing speed advantage of the D-Wave hardware only applies when running certain, very specific computational algorithms. This is also a somewhat bizarre criticism, as D-Wave has never claimed otherwise, and has always marketed its technology as a complement to classical computer systems. The debate concerning whether or not D-Wave's approach to quantum computing is, as IBM claim, 'a dead end' will I am certain continue. But I am equally certain that D-Wave Systems remains a quantum computing pioneer to watch.

### *Google Quantum AI Lab*

Beyond the walls of IBM and D-Wave Systems, several other pioneers are beavering away to turn quantum computing into the Next Big Thing. Some such work is almost certainly classified, with both the American and Chinese military believed to be working on quantum computing projects. Meanwhile, out in the reasonably public eye, most of the usual computing suspects are doing work of note, and deserve a mention here.

For a start, Google is a quantum computing pioneer. Given the company's core focus on search technologies and AI, this is also hardly a surprise. As we have just seen, in conjunction with NASA, Google was one of the first purchasers of D-Wave quantum hardware.

As well as experimenting with D-Wave technology, Google is in parallel working on its own quantum computers. The company's current technological solution is a sort of hybrid between the quantum annealing approach taken by D-Wave, and the 'gate model' design strategy of IBM. At the time of writing (in August 2017), Google was testing a 20 qubit quantum processor, and by the end of the year hoped to be testing a 49 qubit machine.

In March 2017, researchers from Google's Quantum AI Laboratory published an article in *Nature* that suggested short-term returns from investments in quantum computing ought to be possible 'within the next five years'. They also proposed that:

> . . . within a few years, well-controlled quantum systems may be able to perform certain tasks much faster than conventional computers based on CMOS (complementary metal oxide–semiconductor) technology.

Google's 2017 *Nature* article was clearly a corporate statement of intent. Indeed, as it noted in a section that discussed business opportunities:

> If early quantum-computing devices can offer even a modest increase in computing speed or power, early adopters will reap the rewards. Rival companies would face high entry barriers to match the same quality of services and products, because few experts can write quantum algorithms, and businesses need time to tailor new algorithms.

### *Microsoft Station Q*

Given the above analysis, it is hardly surprising that Microsoft wants in on the forthcoming quantum computing action. To this end, in 2006 it established a quantum computing research capability by creating 'Station Q Santa Barbara' at the University of California. The approach taken by Microsoft is to develop 'topological quantum computing', in which the motions of pairs of sub-atomic particles are controlled to manipulate entangled qubits.

Rather than creating qubits using electrons and superconductors, topological quantum computing utilizes subatomic particles called 'Majorana fermions' or 'anyons'. This makes things easier to control, and potentially to scale to commercial proportions. As Microsoft's Peter Lee told *TechRadar* in December 2016, superconducting qubits [such as those used by IBM and D-Wave] 'still hold a lot of potential', but could be 'leapfrogged' by topological qubits. As he further explained:

> Superconducting qubits are to quantum computing what vacuum tubes are to digital computers – but topological qubits are to quantum computing what transistors are to digital computing. When we were building computers out of vacuum tubes they were very useful – you could compute a better missile trajectory – but it was never going to be a scalable technology.

Over the years, Microsoft has made significant investments across a range of international research groups. These include the Niels Bohr Institute in Copenhagen, and the University of Sydney. Meanwhile another Station Q team, called the Quantum Architectures and Computation (QuArC) group, is based on Microsoft's Redmond campus. As you can see, Microsoft's strategy with quantum computing is to spread its money around to ensure that it does not have all of its eggs in one basket.

In June 2017, Microsoft additionally announced a long-term collaboration with Netherlands-based quantum computing pioneers QuTech. This is part of the Delft University of Technology, where Microsoft has opened the Station Q Delft lab. As Ronald Hanson, Director of QuTech, stated in a press release:

> . . . in science, we have made enormous leaps in quantum technology in recent years and are now on the verge of actually being able to use the technology. To achieve this, it is essential that we bring together cutting-edge science from universities and advanced engineering from high-tech companies like Microsoft.

### *Quantum Computing at Intel*

As you may expect, as the world's largest microchip manufacturer, Intel has also taken an interest in quantum computing. Indeed, in an interview with *PC World* in February 2017, CEO Brian Krzanich described his company as 'investing heavily' in the area. In part Intel is adopting Microsoft's strategy of backing external research institutes and centres. Indeed, in common with Microsoft, Intel has invested tens of millions of dollars into research projects at the Delft University of Technology and QuTech in the Netherlands.

Intel is, however, also ploughing its own furrow, and hoping to apply its expertise at making microchips to the development of quantum computers. In December 2016, Intel even revealed plans to create 'silicon qubits' inside transistors on standard integrated circuit wafers. Though just to hedge its bets, Intel is apparently also conducting its own in-house research into creating qubits using the more 'conventional' superconductor approach.

### *The CAS - Alibaba Quantum Computing Laboratory*

Another large, commercial organization intent on becoming a leader in quantum computing is the Chinese Internet giant

Alibaba. In July 2015 the company signed a memorandum of understanding with the Chinese Academy of Sciences (CAS) to form the 'CAS – Alibaba Quantum Computing Laboratory'. This has been charged with conducting 'pioneering research in quantum theory with a view to discovering ground-breaking security techniques for e-commerce and data centers' as well as 'enhancing computing performance'. Or as Professor Jianwei Pan from CAS explained at the time:

> The CAS – Alibaba Quantum Computing Laboratory will undertake frontier research on systems that appear the most promising in realizing the practical applications of quantum computing . . . so as to break the bottlenecks of Moore's Law and classical computing.

In March 2017, *The Next Platform* reported that the CAS – Alibaba Quantum Computing Lab is working to coherently manipulate 30 qubits by 2020, and to run quantum simulations more quickly than a classical supercomputer by 2025. The intention is to then work toward 50 to 100 qubit hardware by 2030.

Given that military and industrial quantum computers could tip the balance of world power, China's commitment to developing quantum computing should not be underestimated. Already the country has a better track record than any other nation in making long-term technology investments. It is hence perfectly possible that the world's first commercial quantum computers will be made in China, and not the United States.

## QUANTUM COMPUTING IMPLICATIONS

In 2012 I published a book called *25 Things You Need to Know About the Future*. One of its chapters dealt with quantum computing, although at the time the only organization making any real, practical headway was D-Wave Systems. After decades of research, back in 2012 even IBM appeared to be in the last chance saloon. In fact, in late 2010, IBM had 'rededicated resources and personnel to its quantum computing project in the hope that a five-year push [would] produce tangible and profound improvements'.

Only half a decade later the quantum computing landscape has changed dramatically, with IBM, D-Wave, Google, Microsoft and others all strongly participating in the game. After decades of doubt, across the board there appears to be a growing consensus that commercial quantum computers will be delivering services from the cloud by the late 2020s. So just what, exactly, ought users to expect?

Well, for a start, all of the major players agree that quantum optimization will vastly improve the capabilities of future deep learning AIs. Hartmut Neven, a director of engineering at Google, has even stated that 'quantum machine learning may provide the most creative problem solving process under the known laws of physics'.

There is also a widespread consensus that quantum simulation is set to accelerate progress in medicine and materials science. Today, the atomic-scale simulation of most molecules and their interactions is not possible with any existing or theoretical classical computer. This is perhaps surprising, but is due to the exponential number of mathematical possibilities involved. Quantum computers will, however, be able to model and analyze complex atomic and molecular systems, and this could revolutionize fields like synthetic biology. Or as Google expressed matters in its 2017 *Nature* article:

> Modelling chemical reactions and materials is one of the most anticipated applications of quantum computing. Instead of spending years, and hundreds of millions of dollars, making and characterizing a

handful of materials, researchers could study millions of candidates in silico. Whether the aim is stronger polymers for aeroplanes, more-effective catalytic converters for cars, more-efficient materials for solar cells, better pharmaceuticals or more breathable fabrics, faster discovery pipelines will bring enormous value.

Opportunities to run very complex simulations are also expected to be highly beneficial in the aerospace sector. As noted earlier, Lockheed Martin was the very first company to purchase a D-Wave quantum computer. In 2015, Airbus Defence and Space also established a quantum computing unit at its Newport plant in the United Kingdom. Here the hope is to improve the modelling of airflow over a wing – a process that can currently take years, but which a quantum computer may be able to achieve in weeks.

Quantum computing services delivered from the cloud are additionally expected to prove beneficial in logistics, and indeed in all fields where digital optimization algorithms have become the key to delivering the best customer service. To again cite Google, quantum computing is likely to be used to improve 'online recommendations and bidding strategies for advertisements', as well as allowing companies to 'optimize their scheduling, planning and product distribution'.

What the above implies is that most individuals will in the late 2020s come into contact with quantum computing without even knowing it. Just as today we casually click on a web link and move a hard drive head in a remote data centre, so in the future some distant qubits will deliver insights to our digital assistant or browser window. Meanwhile, a little quantum entanglement may speed the delivery of the autonomous robot or driverless vehicle that is delivering our package.

Another thing that future quantum computers are expected to be very good at is cracking digital encryption. This is because quantum computers should be able to factor large numbers into prime numbers far more quickly than classical computers. Given that all current digital encryption technologies rely on prime number calculations, this is highly significant. It is indeed for this reason that the Chinese and the United States military do not want to be the second to be in possession of a quantum computer that could very rapidly hack every classical computer on the planet. Or as Patrick Tucker wrote in the July 2010 edition of *The Futurist*, 'if cyberwarfare is the Cold War of the new millennium, quantum computation may be the hydrogen bomb'.

While the military may place code breaking high on their agenda, as Google notes 'most private enterprises are uninterested in breaking encryption systems'. They hence see molecular modelling, the development of better deep learning AIs, more advanced search engines, improved cyber security, and improved financial management systems, as the most likely drivers of the quantum revolution.

## ORGANIC COMPUTING

Quantum computing may one day turn out to be as significant as the creation of the microprocessor. However, we should not get too hung up on quantum technology as the only post-Moore's-Law new computing solution. As I mentioned back in chapter 2, it is not only inorganic mechanisms that are able to store and process digital information. Life is also rather adept at this, and has been manipulating digital codes stored chemically in deoxyribonucleic acid (DNA) for billions of years. Given that we have only been using transistors and silicon chips to store and process information for a few scant decades, this also has to be significant. Most of the computation that has ever taken place on Planet Earth has utilized DNA. We should therefore expect at least some future computers to be made from living cells.

The art and science of 'organic computing', 'biological computing', 'biocomputing' or 'DNA computing' is not as advanced as the quantum field, with even the name of the discipline yet to really settle. It should also be noted that many computer scientists currently use terms like 'organic computing' and 'biological computing' metaphorically. So, for example, if you look up the term 'organic computing' on Wikipedia, it informs you that 'organic computing is computing that behaves and interacts with humans in an organic manner'. The term is hence used to describe the operational characteristics of a system, and not to imply that it is constructed from organic materials.

Granted, Wikipedia should never be relied upon as a source of scientific information. But given that a lot of current, classical computer scientists would agree with its definition, we do have a problem. I therefore want to make it absolutely clear that the remainder of this chapter is about the future creation of biological computer hardware. Whatever Wikipedia may currently say, 'organic computing' is the art and science of fabricating machines that perform computation using organic materials.

The idea of cultivating rather than manufacturing future computers may sound ludicrous. It is therefore worth pointing out that we already know that biological computers can work very well indeed. You are, after all, using a biological computer right now to read this book.

Further, we know that those items of 'wetware' that we call 'human brains' are currently the most proficient mechanisms for 'machine learning', not to mention the best platform for running the thought programs of an intelligent entity. The idea of creating 'wetware 2.0' – or in other words 'artificial' organic computers – should therefore not come as a surprise.

## WETWARE 2.0

There are three potential ways in which living matter may be artificially employed to perform computation. The first is to construct individual circuit components from living materials, and to somehow assemble them into a 'biocomputer'. A second option is to use DNA to make a 'non-deterministic universal Turing machine' that would function somewhat like a quantum computer. Finally, we could design an entire living, computational entity from scratch, artificially fabricate its entire genome, and bioprint or grow a 'pre-constructed' biocomputer, potentially in a host animal.

All of the above are radical propositions. The construction of a useful, cost-effective organic computer based on any of these methods also lies way beyond the capabilities of existing science or technology. We should, however, not dismiss a computing innovation just because it will rely on technologies and production processes that we have yet to invent. As we saw in chapter 1, in the late 1800s Charles Babbage and Lady Ada Augusta came up with several computing propositions that were many decades ahead of available science and engineering, but which proved to be entirely reasonable.

The potential benefits of creating organic computers are immense, and not least because they may be the best mechanisms for hosting the most sophisticated future AIs. Deep learning artificial neural networks are, after all, modelled on the networks of neurons that operate very successfully in human and all other animal brains.

As you may recall from chapter 2, the new science of synthetic biology takes an engineering approach to living matter. It does this by breaking DNA into a set of modular parts that can be rearranged in a computer and chemically pieced together like Lego bricks. As we saw, there is now even a desktop printer – the BioXp 3200 from SGI-DNA – that can take a biological CAD file and turn it into novel genes or genetic components. This means that we already have at least some of the tools necessary to build organic computing parts.

All living cells are also already computational devices that survive and thrive by reacting to their environment. Specifically, most cells store data in DNA, receive chemical inputs in the form of ribonucleic acid (RNA), perform logic operations using complex RNA molecules called ribosomes, and produce output by synthesizing proteins. All of the elements required to build an artificial, organic computer therefore already exist in natural biological systems.

In 2013, a team at Stanford University led by Drew Endy used synthetic biology to create a 'biological transistor' or 'transcriptor' from DNA and RNA. Technically known as a 'boolean integrase logic gate', this three-terminal biological switch can control the flow of an enzyme called RNA polymerase along a strand of a DNA molecule. As part of their work, Endy and his team succeeded in creating biological equivalents of the AND, NAND, OR, XOR, NOR, and XNOR gates on which silicon chip microprocessors are based. Or in other words, at the component level they laid the foundations for building an organic computer.

Other research teams have managed to use DNA as a digital storage technology. For example, in 2012 a team led by George Church at Boston's Harvard Medical School encoded a 55,000 word genetics textbook into DNA. In the natural world, every DNA 'nucleotide pairing' or 'base pair' stores one of the four chemical letters C, C, G or T. This means that, in theory, each DNA base pair should be able to store two binary bits of information. Due to rare DNA writing errors, the actual figure is 1.8 bits of data per DNA base. But this still packs an awful lot of data into a very tiny biological space.

Demonstrating the potential, in March 2017 Yaniv Erlich from Columbia University, and Dina Zielinski from the

New York Genome Center, reported a method for storing 215 petabytes of information (or 215 million gigabytes) in a single gram of DNA. This is the highest density storage solution ever invented (or evolved), and could become a common means for artificial data retention in the second half of this century.

Yet other cutting-edge scientists have attempted to create 'artificial brains' by taking neurons from existing species and linking them together. Most famously, in 1999 at the Georgia Institute of Technology, Professor William Ditto created a computer in a Petri dish by using tiny electrodes to link together neurons obtained from leeches. The resulting system functioned via neural interaction, and was able to add two numbers together.

At the time Professor Ditto's intention was to create a robot brain by this method, as conventional supercomputers were 'too large for a robot to carry around'. Since then, computer hardware has of course got much smaller, with cloud AI emerging as a core technology for robot control. Hardly surprisingly, Professor Ditto has therefore moved on. But the principle behind his 'leechulator' may one day be employed to interface organic computing components.

## TOWARD DNA COMPUTING?

Outside of the lab, all modern computers are imperfect, practical manifestations of deterministic 'universal Turing machines' or 'UTMs'. Without getting bogged down in theory, this basically means that modern computers are able to execute a very wide range of programs, and apply rules that calculate outputs by considering each potential possibility in turn. As we saw when we looked at AI in chapter 3, when large numbers of potential possibilities are involved, this can prove problematic. The practical, computational limits of UTMs are therefore going to constrain the development of molecular modelling and future deep learning AIs.

As we have already seen, one solution may involve the construction of quantum computers that will rely on qubit superpositions to process a wide range of possible solutions simultaneously. Alternatively, 'non-deterministic universal Turing machines' (NUTMs) could be created by employing a form of massively parallel DNA computing. Here a very large number of DNA strands would function as individual processors, with each executing a different computational possibility. Any conventional approach that attempted such massive parallelism would be doomed by a lack of available space and system cost. But given that DNA molecules are so small, it is possible to use an extraordinarily large number of them as parallel processors in a very small space.

In March 2017, a team from Manchester University led by Ross King revealed the first physical design for a DNA NUTM. Their creation 'exploits DNA's ability to replicate to execute an exponential number of computational paths'. Within their wetware, computation thereby resembles 'an explosion', as DNA molecules (processors) that all start in the same state diverge to 'follow all computational paths in parallel'. To get your head around what this involves in practice, imagine a tank of computational soup that contains a large number of DNA strands, each of which is functioning as a biological processor, and each of which is working on a different potential solution to the problem posed.

The design of the Manchester NUTM is based on the premise that strands of DNA can be constantly re-arranged using gene editing techniques. By mixing a large number of DNA fragments with gene-editing molecules, it thereby becomes possible to run a large number of parallel random combinations – and all without resorting to supercooling a quantum computing processor down to 0.015 degrees Kelvin.

As the Manchester team argue in the paper that reports their work, 'DNA is an excellent medium for information processing and storage'. This is because it is very stable, can be reliably copied, and affords the opportunity to run a large number of processors in parallel. As they go on to note:

> These advantages mean that it is feasible that a DNA NUTM based computer could potentially utilize more processors than all the electronic computers in the world combined, and so outperform all standard computers on significant practical problems.

Right now, the inputs to and outputs from the Manchester NUTM are DNA sequences that have to be written with synthetic biology tools and read by genetic sequencing. The team hence have no means of programming or accessing their wetware using any traditional form of input or output peripheral. Moreover, they note that 'further experimentation is required to complete the physical construction of a fully working NUTM'.

Due to the fact that individual DNA strands process information relatively slowly, the team also concede that wetware able 'to compete effectively with existing electronic computer hardware . . . will require fabrication of a NUTM with appropriately $10^{12}$ processors executing in parallel'. This is 10,000,000,000,000 DNA processors, or 'an order of magnitude more processors than in all the computers in the rest of the world combined'. Given the size of a DNA molecule, this is actually a perfectly reasonable theoretical possibility. But there is a very long way to go before such a computer may usefully operate in practice.

## PRINTING OR HARVESTING BIOCOMPUTERS

The parallel operation of billions of individual, liquid-resident DNA strands is unlikely to provide a viable method for creating substitutes for most silicon-based computers. Our own organic brains are single, integrated pieces of wetware that form via a process of biologically-controlled self-assembly, and I strongly suspect that this is how most future biocomputers will be created. Granted, we may use gene-editing methods to piece together very tiny organic computers as a form of smart medicine. These could, for example, be injected into our bodies to detect and fight cancer and for other healthcare reasons. But when it comes to organic computing machines that are able to host an AI or control a robot, I imagine that we are far more likely to develop large-scale organic fabrication techniques.

In chapter 2 we saw how 3D printing pioneers like Organovo have already created the first bioprinters. These construct human tissues, and potentially other organic objects, by building them up from successive layers of living cells. As you may remember, the fine details in such objects do not have to be 3D printed, as most bioprinters lay down an aggregate of cells that then 'naturally' re-arranges and self-assembles into the required final tissue.

In the future, it is just possible that bioprinters will be able to be fed with artificially-programmed cells that will self-assemble into functional biocomputers. This idea is entirely hypothetical, if based on an understanding of where synthetic biology and bioprinting are potentially headed. Many times I have been asked whether or not it will be possible to bioprint a living brain, and decades from now this may just be possible. The resulting printout could be the DNA CPU of an android, and would come off the printer totally 'empty'. It would therefore need to learn via experience, be populated with a very large data upload, and probably both.

In the future I expect that we will routinely bioprint many replacement human organs and organic android components. Nevertheless, I imagine that organic brains/biochips are more likely to be grown. Such cultivation could perhaps occur in a nutrient tank in a lab, but is probably more likely to utilize a host animal. Already pigs are being 'humanized' with human DNA to allow them to grow organs that will be compatible for transplant into a person. It is therefore perfectly conceivable that pigs or other animals may one day be used to cultivate organic biocomputers.

Future donor animals may even grow bioprocessors in addition to their own brains. So, for example, in the future we may use synthetic biology to create a new species of goat or pig that will grow multiple bioprocessors along its spine, or perhaps in one or more artificial wombs. Or maybe synthetically modified chickens will lay smartphone biochips as regularly as they now output eggs. Some synthetic biologists do already now talk about the creation of future 'factories on legs'.

These really are crazy ideas – almost as crazy as a wireless pocket computer – and will not prove popular with animal rights protestors. But a few decades from now, it is conceivable that the digital assistant embodied in your Amazon Echo, or living in a remote cloud data centre, will have a biological central processing unit and DNA memory that were harvested from an animal.

Such future biochips would need to be sustained with chemical feedstocks rather than an electrical supply, and may mature and then degenerate with age. Your favourite digital assistant's neural network may hence end up suffering from dementia. Figure 5.2 illustrates a fanciful biological microprocessor living on its motherboard.

One day, even humans could be synthetically modified to internally or externally grow bioprocessors that would be safely harvested without damaging the host. After all, to date the human body has proved more effective than any other mechanism at growing the best biocomputers on the planet. In a world in which AIs and robots take many of the jobs, an alternative role for some people could therefore be the cultivation of the biochips on which the planet's dominant workforce may depend. In the 2050s, our descendants may

**Figure 5.2: A Future Biological Microprocessor?**
Image: Christopher Barnatt.

hence sit around cultivating biochips and boasting about their number of artificial wombs or synthetic spinal nodes.

Talking of AI, I suspect that no human being will ever design a functional biocomputer, let alone fully understand its operation. Rather, I would place a very strong bet that it will be future AIs – possibly running on quantum processors – that will innovate and manifest the kinds of hardware and production methods that I have just described. The ideas outlined in this section are indeed fantastical, and would require levels of genetic knowledge and DNA manipulation that are always likely to lie beyond the capabilities of a natural human brain.

※ ※ ※

## BACK TO REALITY

For many decades the end-user computing devices that populate most workplaces and homes will continue to be based on silicon chips. Yet, in around ten years time, these peripherals will begin to access AI and other cloud services that are delivered by new computing technologies. In the late 2020s and into the 2030s, these new forms of hardware are most likely to be based on those quantum technologies currently being pioneered by IBM, D-Wave Systems and others. Beyond that, organic hardware is also likely to come into play, and in the process will start to blur the boundaries between human beings and artificial computing machines.

In comparison to our other chapters, these 29 pages have covered a great deal of quite mind-boggling material that may have left you rather shell-shocked. However, it would have been inappropriate to have left this chapter out. Within most people's lifetimes, quantum and organic hardware could increase the power of computers by thousands or millions of times, as well as facilitating the evolution of beyond-human AI. Nobody should therefore remain entirely ignorant of quantum and organic computing and how it may change the world.

Sadly, it is impossible to predict exactly how computer hardware will develop in the next 50 years. Many radical innovations therefore lie ahead that I have not anticipated in this chapter. This said, we do know with certainty that all physical matter is quantum mechanical, and that the best computers on the planet – the ones in our own heads – are made from living matter. It is therefore logical to assume that some of our best future physical analysis tools will themselves be quantum mechanical, and that some of our best future computers ought to be built from living cells.

# 6
# CYBORG FUSION

The technology behind most of the future computing developments included so far in this book is already in the lab. We can therefore be fairly confident that the majority of these products, services and applications will come to market by 2030. This is not to suggest that absolutely *everything* described in the previous five chapters is inevitable. Not least, there will be a wide range of political and social challenges to some of the more controversial developments. But I would be amazed if AI, robots and associated mass automation do not dominate computing in the 2020s. By the 2030s, I suspect that quantum computing will also be a commercial technology, with organic hardware just starting to move beyond the research phase.

I mention the above because this chapter looks ahead to computing and other digital technologies in the 2040s and beyond. Specifically, we are going to focus on the period of 'Cyborg Fusion' that I believe will follow the Cognitive Computing Age. This inevitably takes us beyond the mainstream research pursuits of the current giants of computing, and out into the realm of conjecture and speculation. Where possible, I will still ground the discussion by including information on real innovations and experiments that may suggest a certain road ahead. But it is important to stress that this final chapter is inevitably based far more on my own opinion and insight and than it can be on hard fact.

My opening assumption is that, by 2040, the computers in most data centres will be at least 1,000 times more powerful than those we have today. This will simply have required computer power to have doubled every two years, which is what Moore's Law continues to predict. Granted, when it comes to classical, transistor-based hardware, I suspect that Moore's Law will have broken down before 2030. But I also anticipate new quantum variants of Moore's Law will have come into play. D-Wave Systems is already doubling the number of qubits in its adiabatic quantum processors every two years, and so by 2040 the company could have a 2 million qubit machine on the market. By this time, universal gate, topological or other variants of quantum hardware also ought to be operating with 10,000+ qubits, so delivering extraordinary new computing possibilities.

As just one consequence of a thousand-fold increase in data centre power, by 2040 I expect many AIs to have far greater scientific and engineering capabilities than any human. I also expect most forms of end-user hardware to rely on one or more cloud AI services that possess beyond-human mental capabilities.

In 2040, smartphones will probably still exist, as well as laptop and desktop PCs for those of us retro-geeks who really want them. But I imagine that, most of the time, the majority of people will converse with entirely unseen computers using natural spoken language. Visual output will then be effortlessly directed to the nearest large or small screen, or projected onto the most convenient flat or curved surface. Twenty years from now, it will probably be rare for most people to perceive that they are actually 'using a computer'.

Around two decades hence, almost all vehicles are going to be autonomous. In addition to these billion or more self-driving automobiles, by 2040 I predict that at least one billion mobile robots will be sharing the Earth with around nine billion human citizens. This means that there will be at least one mobile, AI-controlled machine for every five people, with the figure more like one-to-one in the richest parts of the most developed nations. In the future, when we access digital information, it will often be via a robot's speakers, projectors or screens.

Also by 2040, we should anticipate 3D printing, bioprinting, synthetic biology and molecular self-assembly to be everyday manufacturing technologies. Due to all of these digital transformations, the landscape of 2040 will be very different to the world of today. And it is against this future backdrop that I expect the new era of Cyborg Fusion to arrive.

## MERGING WITH MACHINES

In 1960, academics Manfred Clynes and Nathan Kline coined the term 'cyborg'. Their new word first appeared in the journal *Astronautics,* and referred to a human being who had decided 'to take an active part in his own biological evolution' by incorporating artificial parts. Clynes and Kline imagined such 'exogenous components' as technological enhancements that would allow a person to survive in the hostile environment of space. In digital evolutionary terms, this is a critical concept that we will return to later in this chapter. But right now, the key takeaway from Clynes and Kline is that they came up with the word 'cyborg' to refer to a living entity that has chosen to adopt some artificial parts in order to more comfortably survive in a new environment.

Already a lot of people depend on artificial mechanisms to allow them to live in new ways. Most of these prosthetics are digital technologies that have in the past few decades become critical additions to many lives. In this respect, some humans have already started to become cyborgs, as their effective functioning in the modern world depends on a close and near-constant interaction with computer technology. This said, today all computer users retain the option to move away from the screen, and to put down their smartphone and turn it off.

Cyborg fusion will remove our ability to separate from computer hardware, and refers to the physical convergence of human beings and digital technologies. Around 2040 this is likely to become a practical proposition, and will be achieved either by transplanting computer peripherals inside the body, or through genetic manipulations that will direct the human anatomy to grow additional, synthetic organs. Either way, the bestowed artificial enhancements will provide a person with new capabilities. These are most likely to include the capability to store and process information in new ways, to wirelessly connect to the global web, and to control cybernetic body parts.

## CYBORGS ARRIVE

Artificial additions to the human body are hardly anything new. For example, the Etruscans were fitting gold crowns and other dental prosthetics over 1,800 years ago. In the late 1950s, pacemakers then became the first electrical additions to the human body. Since 1982, over 300,000 people have also had their hearing restored with an electronic prosthesis called a cochlear implant.

Cochlear implants are particularly significant as they directly connect to the human nervous system. The implant itself is a surgically-inserted electrode array that delivers electrical impulses to its host's auditory nerves. This array is then connected to a surgically-inserted receiver-stimulator device, which receives wireless signals from an external sound processor connected to a microphone.

Some external sound processors can transmit audio from a computer, television or other electronic device directly to a cochlear implant's receiver-stimulator device. This means that over 300,000 people are already able to receive audio via a cybernetic prosthesis, and potentially directly from a computer. It is, for example, perfectly possible for a person with a cochlear implant to interface it with a digital assistant such as Amazon's Alexa or Google Assistant. In certain circumstances, an AI may therefore already transmit its voice straight into a human being's head.

Medical technology that is able to provide some level of vision via a surgical implant is also in development. Here the most significant pioneer is a Californian company called Second Sight, who market a retinal prosthesis called the Argus II. This can be used to restore very rudimentary vision to patients with retinitis pigmentosa. Those with this condition no longer have functional photoreceptors, which means that the retinas in the back of their eyes no longer convert light into electrical impulses.

Second Sight's Argus II is surgically implanted inside the eye where it is attached to a patient's retina. It is also attached to some electronics and an antenna that are surgically positioned on the outside of the eyeball. Special glasses and a visual processing unit are then worn externally. As Second Sight further explain:

> A miniature video camera housed in the patient's glasses captures a scene. The video is sent to a small patient-worn computer . . . where it is processed and transformed into instructions that are sent back to the glasses via a cable. These instructions are transmitted wirelessly to an antenna in the retinal implant. The signals are then sent to the electrode array, which emits small pulses of electricity. These pulses bypass the damaged photoreceptors and stimulate the retina's remaining cells, which transmit the visual information along the optic nerve to the brain, creating the perception of patterns of light.

The Argus II features an array of just 60 electrodes, which is a very small number compared to the retina's 100 million or more photoreceptors. Yet even the 60 electrode array allows those fitted with the implant to make out shapes, and sometimes even large letters.

The Argus II was only approved for implant into patients in 2011 in Europe, and 2013 in the United States, so these are still very early days. However, in July 2015, a three year study of the first 30 patients was published in the journal *Ophthalmology*. This concluded that the Argus II is safe, reliable, and 'significantly improves visual function and quality of life for people blinded by retinitis pigmentosa'. In turn, the Argus II also proves that it is possible to interface digital technology with a human being's natural visual hardware.

## CONNECTING TO THE BRAIN

In addition to its Argus II retinal prosthesis, Second Sight is working on a 'visual cortical prosthesis' called the Orion I. This is intended to connect directly to a patient's brain, so bypassing their eyeballs and optic nerves entirely. In October 2016, Second Sight reported that a 30 year old patient had been 'implanted with a wireless multichannel neurostimulation system on the visual cortex and was able to perceive and localize individual phosphenes or spots of light with no significant adverse side effects'. As they further explained in a press release:

> This first human test confirms that we are on the right track with our Orion I program to treat blind patients who cannot benefit from the Argus II Retinal Prosthesis (Argus II). This initial success in a patient is an exciting and important milestone even though it does not yet include a camera. By bypassing the optic nerve and directly stimulating the

visual cortex, the Orion I has the potential to restore useful vision to patients completely blinded due to virtually any reason, including glaucoma, cancer, diabetic retinopathy, or trauma.

In addition to Second Sight, several other research teams are developing brain-computer interfaces (BCIs). Some of these are based on electroencephalography (EEG) sensor headwear, and wirelessly read brainwave patterns that a computer then attempts to interpret. Already consumer EEG BCI heatsets are on the market, including the $79 Mindwave from NeuroSky. Such hardware is not good at reading specific brainwave patterns, but with practice can be used to control simple games and to enhance meditation.

In 2014, Researchers at the University of Washington used more sophisticated EEG BCIs, as well as 'transcranial magnetic stimulation' (TMS) headsets, to link pairs of volunteers over the Internet so that they could play the same computer game. Here, one subject watched a screen and concentrated on pushing a 'fire' button to shoot down a missile. This thought was picked up by their EEG headset, and transmitted over the Internet to the TMS headset worn by a second player. This caused the second player to experience visual stimuli, so signalling them to press a trigger and fire at the missile that only the first player could actually see. Amazingly, the brain-to-Internet-to-brain connection worked for three pairs of test subjects, although their accuracy in shooting down missiles varied from between 25 to 83 per cent.

The above experiment proved that human brains can be linked together over the Internet without the involvement of any natural sense organs or physically motive body parts. Nevertheless, accurately reading and interpreting brainwaves via hardware worn on the outside of the skull is unlikely to develop into a generally useful human-computer interface. The majority of future BCIs will therefore depend on hardware that is directly connected to the brain inside the human body.

A major, long-term project that is developing implantable BCIs is BrainGate. This describes itself as 'developing and testing practical, groundbreaking medical devices to restore communication, mobility and independence to people affected by neurologic disease, paralysis, or limb loss'.

The first 'BrainGate Neural Interface System' was created in 2002 by a Brown University spin-off company called Cyberkinetics. By 2008, the hardware had been upgraded to 'BrainGate2', and was being developed by academics from five universities supported by a score of institutions and foundations. This co-ordinated approach has also proved highly beneficial, as all researchers benefit from the same chain of hardware development and regulatory permissions.

The BrainGate2 system consists of a sensor, a decoder, and some kind of external hardware that the sensor and decoder allow a patient to control. Currently the sensor is a 4 x 4 mm array of 100 electrodes that, when surgically implanted, can read 'neuronal action potentials' and 'local field potentials' from the brain.

The BrainGate decoder is a set of computers and embedded software that turn the brain signals from the sensor into a useful command for an external device. In 2004, a team from the University of Pittsburgh implanted a BrainGate sensor into the motor cortex of a monkey, so allowing the primate to feed itself by using its mind to control a robot arm. In May 2012, a team from Brown University replicated this experiment with two paralyzed human subjects. One of these was a 58-year-old woman who learnt how to use a robot appendage to pick up a bottle, raise it to her mouth, take a drink, and put it back on the table.

Another pioneer is Battelle, who are developing a technology called 'NeuroLife Neural Bypass' to help patients with spinal cord damage. The system consists of a tiny chip for brain implantation, together with a 'high-definition electrode stimulation sleeve' that is worn on the appropriate limb. The idea is for patients with severed spinal cord connections to have their thoughts interpreted by a computer that will in turn artificially simulate the motion of part of their body.

In June 2014, a paralyzed man called Ian Burkhart was fitted with the NeuroLife system. He subsequently became the first quadriplegic to move a paralyzed extremity (his right hand and wrist) using his mind. By the end of 2016 he could grasp, control individual fingers, swipe a credit card, and even play *Sweet Child O' Mine* by Guns N' Roses on a modified *Guitar Hero* video game.

Another team researching neural interfaces is based at the John Hopkins Applied Physics Laboratory in Baltimore. Here, since 2006, they have been working on a DARPA project to allow amputees to control and even feel prosthetic limbs. Most notably, a 52 year old man called Johnny Matheny has learnt to precisely operate a robotic lower arm and hand. This has been achieved by implanting two 96-channel intracortical microelectrodes into the motor cortex of Matheny's brain. Like Ian Burkhart, Matheny required weeks of extensive training to master mind control. But once again, the potential of making viable digital connections to the human brain has been demonstrated.

The most recent organization to join the BCI party is a company called Neuralink. Based in San Francisco, this was quietly founded in 2016 by SpaceX and Tesla CEO Elon Musk. In April 2017, Neurolink then publicly announced its goal to develop 'ultra high bandwidth brain-machine interfaces to connect humans and computers'. As with other initiatives, the preliminary idea is to help people with medical problems. But, in the longer-term, Musk hopes that Neuralink will help to supercharge the human condition, so allowing people to compete with increasingly smart machines.

## ORGANIC AUGMENTATION

All of those developing BCIs are doing amazing work that in the medium-term will be highly beneficial for those who are blind, paralyzed, or inflicted with other disabilities. In the longer-term, today's BCI pioneers are in addition laying the foundations for the era of Cyborg Fusion in which many of those without a medical need will opt to have digital technology interfaced to their brain. This said, it remains unlikely in the extreme that mass market direct human-computer interfaces will rely on the surgical implantation of inorganic peripherals.

For a start, while the auditory nerves and retina generally tolerate an implanted electrode array, the brain is far more likely to reject this kind of foreign body. Given that the brain is a highly complex piece of electrochemical wetware, it is also fairly obvious that the best peripherals to directly connect to it should be similarly electrochemical and fabricated from biocompatible, living materials. By 2040, some of the computers that we want to directly interface ourselves with may also be biological.

For the above reasons, future BCIs are likely to be organic. Many such implants may in turn be wirelessly interfaced with inorganic cybernetic components – such as control interfaces and robot parts – that are grafted to the body or externally worn. Nevertheless, to achieve the best fidelity, comfort and operational resilience, the most fundamental BCI components will rely on wetware-to-wetware connections, rather than wetware-to-metal, wetware-to-plastic, or wetware-to-silicon.

As we have seen across this book, various technologies that may one day facilitate the fabrication of organic BCIs are already on the cards. By 2040, it is hence perfectly possible that some combination of synthetic biology, bioprinting and biocomputing will allow human brains to be directly fed high definition video and audio via internal organic peripherals. Further, our brains may be able to be upgraded with additional processing capacity, extra storage and wireless networking. Such innovations are, after all, the kind of thing that Elon Musk has already hypothesized as the ultimate goal of his Neuralink venture. By 2050, direct wireless access to the Internet may have become some people's sixth sense.

I further predict that even implantable, organic BCIs will be no more than an intermediate, minority technology. In part this is because they will require a surgical procedure to either implant them, or to bioprint them in situ. Having such an operation is bound to put many people off, even if it would result in an enhanced quality of life, augmented intelligence, and new or more secure employment opportunities. Once future AIs become clever enough to create organic BCIs, it is also reasonable to conclude that they will be able to reprogram people to grow their own organic brain interface hardware.

Human bodies are already very good at fabricating the highly sophisticated wetware of our own brains. To grow BCIs that will connect us to the Internet, to audio-visual feeds, and to future robotic systems, our natural anatomy may therefore just need to be provided with an appropriate digital blueprint and given a genetic helping hand.

Already synthetic biologists and genetic engineers are advancing methods that can introduce artificial genetic material into a living creature, and that will in turn reprogram its DNA to perform in a desired manner. Such techniques include the creation of artificial viruses called 'vectors' that are printed or otherwise self-assembled in the lab. These are then used to 'infect' patients with the desired genetic material, although at present it is hard to ensure that the vectors only manipulate the DNA of specific target cells.

Other methods for introducing new DNA sequences into a human include the injection of a 'naked' DNA plasmid. In the future, it is therefore possible that an injection will be available that will stimulate the brain to grow an organic BCI.

As yet another alternative, 'non-viral vectors' may be utilized. Known as lipoplexes and polyplexes, these are comprised of the required DNA strands coated with a fatty substance called a liposome, or some form of polymer gel. Both lipoplexes and polyplexes stick to the outside of target cells, thereby enabling some of their genetic material to enter and re-write its DNA. Once again lipoplexes or polyplexes can be introduced to the body via injection. Alternatively, they can be delivered via a nebulizer inhaler.

Right now, even 'simple' genetic treatments remain in the lab. A very few test patients, including some people with an eye condition known as Leber congenital amaurosis, have experienced functional improvements following a treatment with viral vectors. But we are a very long way indeed from being able to genetically reprogram brain or other cells to grow into entirely new organs that will constitute an internal human-computer interface. Even so, current cutting-edge science does at least suggest some specific mechanisms that future AIs may one day utilize to digitally alter and augment human biology.

## REPROGRAMMING THE HUMAN RACE

When people are equipped with wetware that can directly link their brain to a computer, so a great many things will change. For a start, those with such BCIs will be permanently online, with access to all of the information accessible over the Internet. People with a BCI may additionally have access to a 'brain co-processor' and other cloud computing resources that will significantly enhance their mental capabilities. In turn, this could allow BCI-enhanced humans to become at least as clever as the most sophisticated AIs.

Future BCI-enhanced humans should also have the ability to wirelessly communicate with any computing device without having to speak or type. Further, two people with a BCI should even be able to directly connect their brains to each other. In the era of Cyborg Fusion, digital telepathy is therefore likely to become a reality. This would significantly advance mass human connectivity, as there should be no reason to limit direct brain connections to a human network of two. Potentially hundreds, thousands or even millions of BCI-enhanced humans could connect their brains together, so bringing a whole new meaning to the term 'LAN party'. Such mass brain-to-brain networking could even allow the crowdsourcing of a 'hive mind'. As I argued earlier in this book, while computing developments are destined to give rise to new forms of superior intelligence, we should not assume that all of these will be artificial.

As and if brain-to-brain networking becomes a reality, so it may be necessary to install a 'brain firewall', as well as to password protect your thoughts and memory. This would ensure that you could guarantee individual privacy while you slept. Or when you were in a meeting. Or on a date. Or in court. Or in an examination.

This all raises the question of who will write the software that will run on wetware 2.0. It could be that we all just learn to use our new BCI organs to conduct web searches, think smarter, and to communicate without activating our external senses. Yet I suspect that most people will rely on some form of internal wetware operating system and applications to take most of the computational strain. In the future, we may hence have to trust the likes of Google, Apple and Microsoft to provide the code that runs in parts of our brains.

In turn, there may be a risk of our internal wetware being hacked and hijacked. In a few decades time, robot doctors and AIs may hence prescribe malware protection to prevent human beings from getting a computer virus.

Of course, you may argue that we will never allow digital developments to progress this far. Though I suspect that we will. The majority of people from 50 years ago would be staggered not just at current computing technology, but at how much we rely on it and already quite dangerously digitally share. Most people actually like or at least accept where computing is taking us, even when they express disgust at extreme digital futures. History indeed strongly indicates that, when presented with new digital technologies, most people are prepared to go along for the ride.

The above suggests that, in the second half of this century, at least some people will opt to have their heads reprogrammed by the kinds of corporations that others already despise. Once again many people may believe this to be a pretty ghastly and dangerous idea, and it may well be so. Yet, since our very early history, human brains have been programmed on-mass by religious leaders, zealots and dictators. So, in some respects, only the mechanism of consensual mass brainwashing will change.

Today people do not all upload the same operating system updates. Yet, even in democratic nations, they are taught what to think by religions, social media and the so-termed 'free' press. Very few people choose to live without a close mental association with a sect of others, and if only because the world of the free, independent thinker is seldom a comfortable place to call home. Humans naturally seek a safe cognitive harbour and to adopt a consensual viewpoint. I therefore suspect that many in the future will willingly opt-in to the Cyborg Fusion order of permanent digital interconnection, and in the process will sign up for its associated controls and risks. It is quite possible that some future AIs may be employed as real thought police.

A Cyborg Fusion future in which the human body is programmed to grow additional computing components would also raise other fundamental issues. Not least, the possibility may one day exist for this digital alteration to become a gene-line attribute of the human animal. This may mean that, at some point in the future, two reprogrammed, BCI-enhanced humans may mate and have a child that 'naturally' possesses 'artificial' computational add-ons. Future children may therefore be born online, and automatically announce their own arrival via social media.

If this kind of scenario ever happens, the ability to receive, process and transmit wireless information would have become as 'natural' as seeing, hearing and talking. Human beings would hence have fused with computing technology at the level of the species, in addition to that of the individual.

## THE TRANSHUMAN AGENDA

Talking of a new human species, there is a growing movement that advocates the technological upgrading of ourselves. This is known as 'transhumanism', and may become the prime social, political and cultural driver of Cyborg Fusion.

The words 'transhuman' and 'transhumanism' were invented by biologist Julian Huxley in 1927. In a book called *Religion without Revelation*, he noted that the human species may choose to 'transcend itself', and that a new name was needed for such a belief. As he went on to ponder, 'perhaps transhumanism will service: man remaining man, but transcending himself by realizing new possibilities'.

A far later founding father of transhumanism was Max More, who in 1990 wrote an essay entitled *Transhumanism: Toward a Futurist Philosophy*. This defines transhumanism as 'a class of philosophies of life that seek the continuation and acceleration of the evolution of intelligent life beyond its currently human form and human limitations by means of science and technology'. Already there are political parties seeking to take this agenda forward. These include the Transhumanist Party of the United States, which was formed by futurist Zoltan Istvan in 2014. The following year, John

McAfee – founder of the computer security giant McAfee – also created the Cyberparty of the USA, while in Britain in 2014 the UK Transhumanist Party was established.

A network called Transhuman Party Global loosely connects 'recognised Transhumanist Party organisations' in Australia, Austria, France, Germany, India, Korea, Poland, the United Kingdom and the United States. There is also an international organization called Humanity+ (formerly the World Transhumanist Association) which describes itself as 'an international nonprofit membership organization that advocates the ethical use of technology to expand human capacities'.

Over on its website, Humanity+ maintains a 'Transhumanist Declaration' that was initially drawn up by an international group of contributors in 1998. This notes that humanity stands on the brink of being able to overcome 'aging, cognitive shortcomings, involuntary suffering, and our confinement to planet Earth', with our potential 'still mostly unrealized'. As point 8 of the Transhumanist Declaration then makes explicit, in the future we may proactively progress toward our potential using 'human modification and enhancement technologies'.

All of the aforementioned parties and organizations are on the same page. For example, the constitution of the Transhumanist Party of the United States indicates that it 'supports significant life extension achieved through the progress of science and technology'. Or as its sister organization in the United Kingdom indicates in its principles:

> The Party shall support and advocate science and technology, and exists to improve the human and societal condition through the use of technological tools. TP shall strive to create and implement technologies including but not limited to anti-aging, rejuvenation medical technology, a policy of making people 'Better Than Well' if they want, artificial and

augmented intelligence, and other augmentations of human capabilities.

As this all demonstrates, already there are at least some people who back the notion of Cyborg Fusion as detailed earlier in this chapter. Absolutely, transhumanism is about far more than augmenting the human body with computer technology. For a start, extending the human lifespan and solving global problems are very high on the list. Yet most of the things that transhumanists want to achieve are contingent on developing higher levels of intelligence in either artificial machines or human bodies. Cyborg Fusion, and the advancement of AI, therefore inevitably underpin a great deal of transhumanist thought and aspiration.

In particular, some future transhumanists may seek to augment themselves into mentally superior 'post-humans' or 'Humanity 2.0'. This could potentially allow them to compete with and control the most sophisticated future AIs, not to mention 'normal' humans. As I argued back in chapter 3, those who worry about the development of AI ought really to fear the new, digitally-enhanced human species that future AIs will help to create, rather than future AIs themselves.

Right now, few people may have heard of transhumanism, let alone treat it as a serious political, cultural and social force. Yet only a few decades ago the same could be said of the green movement that has now successfully managed to influence mainstream political and economic thinking. In its growing bid for hearts and minds, the transhumanist movement also has the significant advantage of seeking to take technology in the same direction as the key players in the computing industry.

## CROSSING THE FOURTH DISCONTINUITY

The human species has always longed to be special. For most of our history we therefore conceptually positioned ourselves at the centre of creation. This all went rather well, until Nicolaus Copernicus demonstrated that the Earth rotated around the Sun and not the other way around. This somewhat upset the Spanish Inquisition, who did not like the role of our planet being relegated to that of a minor player.

A few centuries later, the cosy establishment of Victorian England was similarly thrown into a state of enraged turmoil by the exploits of one Charles Darwin. What this upstart naturalist proved was that humans had evolved from other animals, and that people are hence no more than biologically upgraded apes.

Yet another troublesome individual was Sigmund Freud, who queried any absolute divide between our conscious and subconscious selves. In his challenge to the status quo, Freud hence highlighted human beings as psychological as well as physiological creatures who may not always be in conscious control.

When Copernicus dispelled the myth that humanity was at the centre of the Solar System, Darwin demonstrated that there is no divide between human beings and the animal kingdom, and Freud linked our conscious and subconscious selves, so long-standing 'discontinuities' were challenged and fell. No longer was it 'humans' and the 'rest of creation', 'humans' and 'the rest of the animal kingdom', or our 'conscious' and 'subconscious', with an absolute divide down the middle. Rather, it became clear that a spectrum existed, with a somewhat grey area in the middle.

Why do I mention all of this? Well, in 1993 the late and great MIT historian Bruce Mazlish published a book called *The Fourth Discontinuity*. Within, he identified the three discontinuities that I have just described, and then added another to the list.

As you can probably guess, Mazlish defined the 'Fourth Discontinuity' as our perception that there is a fundamental divide between human beings and machines. He also suggested that there are two reasons to believe that the Fourth Discontinuity is starting to be crossed. Firstly, he stated that it is no longer realistic to think of humans without machines. And secondly, he suggested that the same concepts increasingly explain and govern the function of both human beings and artificial technologies.

To my mind at least, these are extremely reasonable propositions. In respect of the first, it is clear that many people's lives now depend on highly complex technological infrastructures – from the Internet to water, food and power supply networks – without which most city dwellers would not survive. In respect of Mazlish's second proposition, the development of computing, AI, robotics and synthetic biology is increasingly blurring any absolute divide between 'ourselves' and the 'artificial' tools on which we rely. This is not to suggest that a human being and a computer or an AI are exactly the same or will ever become so. But the idea that we humans are totally different and conceptually disconnected from our technologies is an increasingly difficult proposition to justify.

The closer 'human beings' and 'machines' become, so the more likely it is that we will converge, and hence that cyborg fusion will occur. In part, this mashup of 'natural' beings and 'artificial' technology will take place as transhumanists opt for digital augmentation. But the other way around, the more similar our technologies become to us, the greater the potential will be for machines to merge with people, in addition to people merging with machines.

To illustrate this point, imagine what will occur when synthetic biology becomes a mainstream manufacturing technology, and organic computing emerges from the lab. One of the many things this will facilitate is the creation of organic robots. Such bioprinted or synthetically grown wetware could be built from roughly the same material as ourselves, could possess 'intelligence' based on the same kind of biocomputers, and may even eat and sleep in a fairly similar manner.

Since Karel Capek coined the term 'robot' nearly a century ago, we have generally assumed that such machines would be materially and operationally different from ourselves. Yet this need not be the case. Some future 'robots' may one day even request and receive transplants of human blood or donor organs, which would clearly constitute cyborg fusion 'the other way around'.

Cyborg fusion may also occur if a human and a robot ever partner up to have a child. This could involve each party supplying a sample of genetic material to the lab that would grow or bioprint their kid. An AI doctor would probably also have to become involved so that it could tweak each parent's DNA to achieve biocompatibility, and so ensure viable reproduction across the species barrier.

Right now, this kind of musing is no more than science fiction. It is, however, one logical consequence of the development of the digital art of synthetic biology, and the creation of beyond human AI. Remember, as I noted at the start of this chapter, by 2040 computers can reasonably be expected to be 1,000 times more powerful than those we have today, and we are likely to use this new computational might for something. It may also be in all of our best interests for future human beings and smart, organic technology to mingle into a new, combined species.

## ACCESSING NEW REALMS

So far I have argued that cyborg fusion will occur for two fundamental reasons. Firstly, because of a growing transhuman desire to be augmented, and secondly due to a narrowing of the divide between 'humans' and 'machines'. However, in addition, I also expect our cybernetic augmentation to be driven by our basic instincts to explore and to survive.

In such pursuits, cyborg fusion will allow us to access and conquer new realms. This is hardly a new proposition, with lungs having helped us out of the oceans, and aeroplanes into the skies. Already the Internet has enabled the human race to spend some of its waking hours in cyberspace. By 2040, the fusion of computing technologies with the human body could also have accelerated this trend by expanding the possibilities for us to inhabit virtual realms.

Back in chapter 2, I noted how virtual reality (VR) remains handicapped by its hardware. Like it or not, however good we get at delivering a 3D experience via a head mounted display (HMD), this is always going to be a second best solution for immersing a person in a virtual world.

By 2040, it is possible that we will have VR contact lenses. These could be wirelessly networked and wirelessly powered, and would project images directly onto the retina. Such peripherals would almost certainly boost the adoption of augmented reality, and may be popular on public transport as you could watch a movie with your eyes closed. But even so, VR contact lenses will still not deliver a totally convincing and fully immersive VR experience.

The problem with all current VR hardware is that it targets the wrong sense organ. Or in other words, existing VR systems attempt to fool the eye rather than the brain. A strong driver for cyborg fusion may therefore be the development of BCI VR systems. These would stimulate every human sense via direct digital input to the brain, and could deliver totally 'real' immersive VR experiences.

Future BCI VR systems may in parallel enable us to control totally realistic virtual bodies. This would require our minds to be partially disconnected from our real bodies when we were in VR. Though fortunately, we already have an inbuilt muscle paralysis mechanism for achieving this (which we usually activate in our sleep while we dream). With enough processing power and biological know-how, by 2050 we may therefore be able to use a BCI to enjoy VR experiences that will be indistinguishable from reality. It also seems pretty inevitable that this would become a very powerful driver for cyborg fusion.

With BCI VR systems, we could travel anywhere we wanted, including anywhere in history as well as back into our own past lives. Old people could experience being young again, while the disabled could have all of their facilities restored in VR worlds. We could also hold virtual meetings in any location, take out-of-body holidays, and of course gaming would be transformed.

Once they had access to a BCI VR system, some people may even choose to spend most of their life in a virtual world, with their physical body tended by a robot carer. Quite what this may do to real society is difficult to imagine. It could indeed be argued that our social fabric would be totally destroyed if many people opted to spend a large proportion of their time online. Though in a sense, this is something that has already happened.

We should also remember that, in addition to allowing us to visit digital virtual worlds, future BCIs are likely to provide entry to the headspace of others. In the future, we may hence decide to spend more time visiting each other's minds than inhabiting artificially crafted synthetic realities. The possibilities really are intense, and again have to constitute a powerful driver for cyborg fusion.

In addition to allowing people to enter new digital and mental realms, cyborg fusion will also enable us to access new physical locations. Given that the resources of the Earth are finite, our requirement to access raw materials and energy sources that are currently out of reach may indeed become the greatest driver for the cybernetic augmentation of at least some members of the human race. In the relatively near future, robotic deep sea miners may extract cobalt, copper, nickel, gold, platinum, silver and zinc from the ocean beds.

But if future humans want or need to work with them many miles below the ocean surface, it is possible that they could be equipped with outer robotic shells. Alternatively, people in the future may remotely inhabit deep undersea robots over a BCI wireless link.

More fundamentally, cyborg fusion may one day allow our civilization to leave the Earth in search of extraterrestrial resources. We already know that the Moon and the asteroids contain trillions of dollars of pristine raw materials just waiting to be utilized. These locations are also just a small part of our solar system, and an extremely tiny fragment of the galaxy and universe beyond.

Life survives by evolving to conquer new realms. It would therefore be extraordinary if – at some point in the future – we do not evolve outwards into space. At present we are taking baby steps by sending robotic probes beyond our first planet, and by rocketing humans into orbit (and previously to the Moon) in pressurized cabins and spacesuits. This approach is, however, not a realistic, long-term proposition.

The current human form is about as suited to living and working in space as a fish is adapted to residing on dry land. In order to become an extraterrestrial civilization, we will therefore need to embrace cyborg fusion and develop one or more new physical forms. As Manfred Clynes and Nathan Line argued in *Astrophysics* way back in 1960, 'space travel challenges mankind . . . to take an active part in his own biological evolution'. Or as I similarly argued in my 2012 book *25 Things You Need to Know About the Future*:

> When our ancestors crawled out of the oceans they had to evolve to cope and then thrive in a new environment. We should therefore not necessarily believe that humans in their current form will become tomorrow's most successful space mariners. The evolutionary leap from our first planet to the

vacuum of space is, after all, at least as great as that from water to dry land.

The first Earthlings to go in search of extraterrestrial resources will almost certainly be robots with silicon brains. But in time, such entirely synthetic intelligent entities are likely to be joined on the final frontier by new versions of ourselves. Some of these beings may be entirely organic, but with a biology reprogrammed to be more suited to life in zero gravity and more tolerant of extraterrestrial radiation.

Alternatively, other future space pioneers could be a cybernetic mashup of natural biology and inorganic robot parts, with previously-human wetware residing in a very tough outer shell fuelled by solar power. Once again this paints a picture of an evolutionary future dependent on cyborg fusion. When computing's early pioneers built their first digital machines, they really did not know what they had started.

\* \* \*

## PRIMEVAL SOUP 2.0

This book has been about the future of computing, robots and AI. Within I have reported a great deal of information, and have also made quite a few predictions. Just one of these is that, in the next decade or so, we will witness the digital genesis of at least one new intelligent species. This new smart being will drag itself not out of an ancient ocean, but from the primeval soup of cyberspace. It also seems likely that this new thinking machine will develop cognitive abilities beyond human comprehension, and which will one day enable it to reprogram human biology.

The idea of our species being upgraded by a future AI may be an extraordinary proposition. Though to me at least, it seems far more likely than the earliest single-cell life form evolving into a modern human. The latter is, of course, a reality that did defy apparently impossible odds, and with no level of directing intelligence applied beyond the blind chance of natural selection.

Think back to where we started – and you can take this to mean a mental return to the history of computing covered in chapter 1 of this book, or an invitation to pontificate on early life in the ancient oceans. Either way, reflect for a second on the truly extraordinary progress that has taken place between then and now. Evolution, whether 'natural' or 'artificial', consistently delivers staggering results. And it is poised to repeat its best trick.

Today, it is easy to experiment with a digital assistant like Amazon's Alexa, to find fault, and to dismiss the dawning Cognitive Computing Age as fanciful. It is even easier to look at the current state of play in synthetic biology and brain-computer interface development, and to reject the notion of providing people with biological, digital augmentations as entirely insane. But look back and reflect, and it becomes clear that far more radical things have already occurred. The stage is now set for the next phase of digital genesis, and it is going to drive both the future of computing and the evolution of ourselves.

# REFERENCES

### Preface: Cyber Business
Christopher Barnatt *Cyber Business: Mindsets for a Wired Age* (Chichester: John Wiley & Sons, 1995).
Liat Clark 'Elon Musk Reveals More About His Plan To Merge Man And Machine With Neuralink', *Wired* (21 April 2017). Available from: http://www.wired.co.uk/article/elon-musk-neuralink
William Gibson *Neuromancer* (New York, Ace, 1984).
Alan McIntyre, Steve Westland & Schira Lillis *Accenture Banking Technology Vision 2017* (Accenture, 28 March 2017). Available via: https://www.accenture.com/us-en/insight-banking-technology-vision-2017
Neuralink website at: https://neuralink.com
James Randerson 'How Many Neurons Make A Human Brain? Billions Fewer Than We Thought', *The Guardian* (28 February 2012). Available from: https://www.theguardian.com/science/blog/2012/feb/28/how-many-neurons-human-brain

### Chapter 1: The Computing Machine
Randy Alfred 'April 4, 1975: Bill Gates, Paul Allen Form A Little Partnership', *Wired* (4 April 2011). Available from: https://www.wired.com/2011/04/0404bill-gates-paul-allen-form-microsoft/
Christopher Barnatt *Cyber Business: Mindsets for a Wired Age* (Chichester: John Wiley & Sons, 1995).
Peter J. Bird *LEO: The First Business Computer* (Wokingham: Hasler Publishing, 1994).
Bryan's Old Computers *Mark-8 Mini-Computer*. Available from: http://bytecollector.com/mark_8.htm
Centre for Computing History *First Network Email Sent by Ray Tomlinson*. Available from: http://www.computinghistory.org.uk/det/6116/first-e-mail-sent-by-ray-tomlinson/
Computer History Museum timeline at: http://www.computerhistory.org/timeline/
Federico Faggin 'After the 4004: the 8008 and 8080', *Electronics Weekly* (8 August 2008). Available from: https://www.electronicsweekly.com/blogs/mannerisms/yarns/after-the-4004-the-8008-and-80-2008-08/
Google *From the Garage to the Googleplex*. Available from: https://www.google.com/intl/en/about/our-story/
Harvard University *The Mark I Computer at Harvard University*, web page available at: http://sites.harvard.edu/~chsi/markone/about.html
History of Computers *Micral N of François Gernelle*. Available from: http://history-computer.com/ModernComputer/Personal/Micral.html

IBM *IBM 1401: The Mainframe*. Available from: http://www-03.ibm.com/ibm/history/ibm100/us/en/icons/mainframe/

IBM *System 360: From Computers to Computer Systems*. Available from: http://www-03.ibm.com/ibm/history/ibm100/us/en/icons/system360/

IBM *The Birth of the IBM PC*. Available from: https://www-03.ibm.com/ibm/history/exhibits/pc25/pc25_birth.html

ICANN website at: https://www.icann.org

IEEE Standards Association *The 40th Anniversary of Ethernet*. Available from: http://standards.ieee.org/events/ethernet/history.html

Internet Live Stats *Internet Users*. Available at: http://www.internetlivestats.com/internet-users/

Internet Society *Brief History of the Internet* (1997). Available from: http://www.internetsociety.org/internet/what-internet/history-internet/brief-history-internet

ITU *ITU Agrees On Key 5G Performance Requirements For IMT-2020*. (Press Release, 23 February 2017). Available from: http://www.itu.int/en/mediacentre/Pages/2017-PR04.aspx

Sean Kinney 'What is IMT-2020 and What Does it Mean for 5G?', *RCR Wireless News* (7 March 2017). Available from: http://www.rcrwireless.com/20160307/policy/what-is-imt-2020-tag17-tag99

National Museum of Computing website: http://www.tnmoc.org

Nik Rawlinson 'History of Apple: The Story of Steve Jobs and the Company He Founded' *MacWorld* (25 April 2017). Available from: http://www.macworld.co.uk/feature/apple/history-of-apple-steve-jobs-mac-3606104/

OldComputers.net *IBM 5150 Personal Computer*. Available from: http://oldcomputers.net/ibm5150.html

OldComputers.net *Radio Shack TRS-80 (Model 1)*. Available from http://oldcomputers.net/trs80i.html

Tim O'Reilly *What Is Web 2.0 Design Patterns and Business Models for the Next Generation of Software* (O'Reilly, 30 September 2005). Available from: http://www.oreilly.com/pub/a/web2/archive/what-is-web-20.html

Qualcomm *Qualcomm Unveils "pdQ" CDMA Digital Smartphone* (Press Release, 21 September 1998). Available from: https://www.qualcomm.com/news/releases/1998/09/21/qualcomm-unveils-pdq-cdma-digital-smartphone

Guy Swarbrick 'Windows 3.0', *Personal Computer World* (July 1990).

*The Economist* 'A Brief History of Wi-Fi' (10 June 2004). Available from: http://www.economist.com/node/2724397

Texas Instruments *The Chip That Jack Built*. Available from: http://www.ti.com/corp/docs/kilbyctr/jackbuilt.shtml

Toshiba T5100 web page at: http://www.toshiba-europe.com/computers/products/notebooks/t5100/index.shtm

World Wide Web Foundation *History of the Web*. Available from: http://webfoundation.org/about/vision/history-of-the-web/

**Chapter 2: Digital Transformation**

Apache Hadoop website at: http://hadoop.apache.org/

AWS IoT Platform website at: https://aws.amazon.com/iot-platform/

Azure IoT Suite website at: http://www.smithsonianmag.com/innovation/kevin-ashton-describes-the-internet-of-things-180953749/

Christopher Barnatt *3D Printing: Third Edition* (Nottingham, ExplainingTheFuture.com, 2016).

Christopher Barnatt *The Next Big Thing: From 3D Printing to Mining the Moon* (Nottingham, ExplainingTheFuture.com, 2015).

Bitcoin website at: https://bitcoin.org

Bixby web pages at: http://www.samsung.com/us/explore/bixby/

BlockGeeks *What is Blockchain Technology? A Step-by-Step Guide For Beginners.* Available from: https://blockgeeks.com/guides/what-is-blockchain-technology/

Matthew Carr 'How Dark Factories Are Changing Manufacturing (and How to Profit)', *Investment U* (2 March 2017). Available from: http://www.investmentu.com/article/detail/53769/dark-factories-changing-manufacturing-profit#.WXJERhXytpg

Cyber Physical Systems website at: http://cyberphysicalsystems.org/

European Commission Digital Transformation web pages at: https://ec.europa.eu/growth/industry/digital-transformation_en

EY Digital Transformation web pages at: http://www.ey.com/us/en/services/advisory/managing-it-to-accelerate-your-business-digital-transformation#

Feetz website at: https://feetz.com/

Conner Forrest 'Chinese Factory Replaces 90% Of Humans With Robots, Production Soars', *TechRepublic* (30 June 2015). Available from: http://www.techrepublic.com/article/chinese-factory-replaces-90-of-humans-with-robots-production-soars/

Arik Gabbai 'Kevin Ashton Describes "The Internet of Things"', *Smithsonian Magazine* (January 2015). Available from: http://www.smithsonianmag.com/innovation/kevin-ashton-describes-the-internet-of-things-180953749/

GE Additive *GE Agrees to Purchase Controlling Shares of Arcam AB* (Press Release, 15 November). Available from: http://www.geadditive.com/press-releases/ge-agrees-to-purchase-controlling-shares-arcam-ab

Gartner *Gartner Says 8.4 Billion Connected "Things" Will Be in Use in 2017, Up 31 Percent From 2016* (Press Release, 7 February 2017). Available from: http://www.gartner.com/newsroom/id/3598917

Gartner *Gartner Says Worldwide Public Cloud Services Market to Grow 18 Percent in 2017* (Press Release, 22 February 2017). Available from: http://www.gartner.com/newsroom/id/3616417

Gartner *Gartner Survey Shows 42 Percent of CEOs Have Begun Digital Business Transformation* (Press Release, 24 April 2017). Available from: http://www.gartner.com/newsroom/id/3689017

Kewyn George 'Five Constructive Ways To Transform Your Business Through Digital' *Forbes* (3 April 2017). Available from: http://www.forbesindia.com/blog/digital-navigator/five-constructive-ways-to-transform-your-business-through-digital/

IBM Blockchain website at: https://www.ibm.com/blockchain/

IBM Institute for Business Value *Digital Transformation* web pages at: https://www-935.ibm.com/services/us/gbs/thoughtleadership/ibv-digital-transformation.html

IDC *IDC Forecasts $1.2 Trillion in Worldwide Spending on Digital Transformation Technologies in 2017* (Press Release, 23 February 2017). Available from: http://www.idc.com/getdoc.jsp?containerId=prUS42327517

IDC *New IDC Research Highlights Impact of Blockchain on Data and Data Management* (Press Release, 7 March 2017). Available from: https://www.idc.com/getdoc.jsp?containerId=prUS42352517

Tomas Kellner 'GE is Building the World's Largest 'Additive' Machine For 3D Printing Metals', *GE Reports* (20 June 2017). Available from: http://www.ge.com/reports/ge-building-worlds-largest-additive-machine-3d-printing-metals/

Will Knight 'China Is Building a Robot Army of Model Workers', *MIT Technology Review* (26 April 2016). Available from: https://www.technologyreview.com/s/601215/china-is-building-a-robot-army-of-model-workers/

Doug Laney *3D Data Management: Controlling Data Volume, Velocity, and Variety*, (META Group, 6 February 2001). Now available from: http://blogs.gartner.com/doug-laney/files/2012/01/ad949-3D-Data-Management-Controlling-Data-Volume-Velocity-and-Variety.pdf

# REFERENCES

Doug Laney 'Deja VVVu: Others Claiming Gartner's Construct for Big Data', *Gartner Blog Network* (14 January 2014). Available from: http://blogs.gartner.com/doug-laney/deja-vvvue-others-claiming-gartners-volume-velocity-variety-construct-for-big-data/

James Macaulay & Markus Kückelhaus *Internet of Things in Logistics* (DHL Trend Research | Cisco Consulting Services, 2015). Available from: http://www.dhl.com/content/dam/Local_Images/g0/New_aboutus/innovation/DHLTrendReport_Internet_of_things.pdf

OMICtools GenoCAD website at: https://omictools.com/genocad-tool

Gil Press '6 Predictions For The $203 Billion Big Data Analytics Market', *Forbes* (20 January 2017). Available from: https://www.forbes.com/sites/gilpress/2017/01/20/6-predictions-for-the-203-billion-big-data-analytics-market/#ae8575f20838

Prevolve website at: https://www.pre-volve.com/biorunners

*RT News* 'Russian 3D-Bioprinted Thyroid Gland Implant Proves Functional In Mice' (26 November 2015). Available from: https://www.rt.com/news/323494-russian-3dprinted-thyroid/

SGI-DNA BioXp 3200 web page at: https://sgidna.com/bxp3200.html

Gregory Stock *Metaman: Humans, Machines, and the Birth of a Global Super-organism* (London: Transworld Publishers, 1993).

## Chapter 3: The Dawn of AI

AIY website at: https://aiyprojects.withgoogle.com/

AlanTuring.net website at: http://www.alanturing.net

Tom Brennan, 'Alipay Launches "Smile To Pay" For Commercial Use In China', *Aliza* (1 September 2017). Available from: http://www.alizila.com/alipay-launches-smile-to-pay-commercial-use/

Amazon AI web pages at: https://aws.amazon.com/amazon-ai/

Apple Siri web pages at: https://www.apple.com/uk/ios/siri/

Kate Baggaley 'There Are Two Kinds Of Ai, And The Difference Is Important', *Popular Science* (23 February 2017). Available from: http://www.popsci.com/narrow-and-general-ai#page-6

Nick Bostrum *Superintelligence: Paths, Dangers, Strategies* (Oxford: Oxford University Press, 2014).

Marshall Brain *Robotic Nation*. Available from http://marshallbrain.com/robotic-nation.htm

Ashley Carman 'Xiaomi's New Smart Speaker Costs $130 Less Than an Amazon Echo', *The Verge* (26 July 2017). Available from: https://www.theverge.com/circuitbreaker/2017/7/26/16034726/xiaomi-mi-ai-speaker-home-assistant

Case IH *Case IH Reveals New Tagline, New Focus and a New Autonomous Concept Vehicle*, (Press Release, 30 August 2016). Available from: https://www.caseih.com/northamerica/en-us/News/Pages/Case_IH_News_Release_Case_IH_Reveals_New_Tagline_New_Focus_and_a_New_Autonomous_Concept_Vehicle.aspx

Rory Cellan-Jones 'Stephen Hawking Warns Artificial Intelligence Could End Mankind', *BBC News* (2 December 2015). Available from: http://www.bbc.co.uk/news/technology-30290540

CNN Money *Could This Computer Save Your Life?* (12 March 2015): Available from: http://money.cnn.com/2015/03/12/technology/enlitic-technology/

Jillian D'Onfro 'Why Google's Smart Assistant Doesn't Have a Name Like Siri, Alexa, or Cortana', *Business Insider* (20 May 2016). Available from: http://uk.businessinsider.com/why-doesnt-googles-smart-assistant-doesnt-have-a-name-like-siri-cortana-alexa-2016-5

Thomas H. Davenport & Julia Kirby 'Just How Smart Are Smart Machines?', *MIT Sloan Management Review* (Spring 2016).

Thomas H. Davenport & Julia Kirby "Beyond Automation" *Harvard Business Review* (June 2015).

Jeff Dean & Urs Hölzle 'Build and Train Machine Learning Models On Our New Google Cloud TPUs' *Google Blog* (17 May 2017). Available from: https://www.blog.google/topics/google-cloud/google-cloud-offer-tpus-machine-learning/

Deep Learning for Java website at: https://deeplearning4j.org/

DeepMind *AlphaGo at The Future of Go Summit*, 23-27 May 2017. Available from: https://deepmind.com/research/alphago/alphago-china/

Daimler Freightliner *Inspiration Truck World Premiere on Hoover Dam* (Press Release, 5 May 2015). Available from: http://www.daimler.com/dccom/0-5-1809607-1-1809608-1-0-0-0-0-0-0-0-0-0-0-0-0.html

Enlitic website at: https://www.enlitic.com/

Facebook AI Research website at: https://research.fb.com/category/facebook-ai-research-fair/

Forrester *2017 Customer Service Trends: Operations Become Smarter and More Strategic* (27 January 2017). Report available for purchase via: https://www.forrester.com/report/2017+Customer+Service+Trends+Operations+Become+Smarter+And+More+Strategic/-/E-RES135929

Donna Fuscaldo 'Samsung: Soft Launch for Bixby Voice Interface', *Investopedia* (20 June 2017). Available from: http://www.investopedia.com/news/samsung-soft-launch-bixby-voice-interface/

Elizabeth Gibney 'Google AI Algorithm Masters Ancient Game of Go', *Nature* (27 January 2016). Available from: http://www.nature.com/news/google-ai-algorithm-masters-ancient-game-of-go-1.19234

Google Assistant web pages at: https://assistant.google.com/

Google Cloud AI web pages at: https://cloud.google.com/products/machine-learning/

Google Cloud Platform web pages at: https://cloud.google.com/

Omed Habib 'Conversational Technology: Siri, Alexa, Cortana, and the Google Assistant', *AppDynamics* (1 March 2017). Available from: https://blog.appdynamics.com/engineering/conversational-technology-siri-alexa-cortana-and-the-google-assistant/

Andrew J. Hawkins 'Uber's Self-driving Truck Company Just Completed Its First Shipment: 50,000 Cans Of Budweiser', *The Verge* (25 October 2016). Available from: https://www.theverge.com/2016/10/25/13381246/otto-self-driving-truck-budweiser-first-shipment-uber

Jessi Hempel 'Facebook Launches M, Its Bold Answer To Siri And Cortana', *Wired* (26 August 2015). Available from: https://www.wired.com/2015/08/facebook-launches-m-new-kind-virtual-assistant/

IBM *IBM Forms New Watson Group to Meet Growing Demand for Cognitive Innovations* (News Release, 9 January 2014). Available from: https://www-03.ibm.com/press/us/en/pressrelease/42867.wss

IBM *Staples Inc.: Revolutionizing Customer Service With Ibm Watson And The Push Of An Easy Button* (Watson Case Study, 2016). Available from: http://ecc.ibm.com/case-study/us-en/ECCF-WUC12550USEN

IBM Watson website: https://www.ibm.com/watson/

Intel Mobileye *Intel Acquisition of Mobileye* (Announcement, 2017). Available from: http://intelandmobileye.transactionannouncement.com/

Juniper Research *Chatbots, A Game Changer For Banking & Healthcare, Saving $8 Billion Annually By 2022* (Press Release, 9 May 2017). Available from: https://www.juniperresearch.com/press/press-releases/chatbots-a-game-changer-for-banking-healthcare

Leo Kelion 'Amazon's Race to Make Alexa Smarter', *BBC News* (28 July 2017). Available from: http://www.bbc.co.uk/news/technology-40739709

# REFERENCES

Julia Kirby & Thomas H. Davenport "The Knowledge Jobs Most Likely to Be Automated", *Harvard Business Review* (June 23 2016).

Will 'Knight Paying with Your Face', *MIT Technology Review* (March/April 2017). Available from: https://www.technologyreview.com/s/603494/10-breakthrough-technologies-2017-paying-with-your-face/

Mary C. Lacity & Leslie P. Willcocks "A New Approach to Automating Services", *MIT Sloan Management Review* (Fall 2016).

Brad Linder 'Tmall Genie is Alibaba's Amazon Echo Clone (for China)', *Liliputing* (5 July 2017). Available from: https://liliputing.com/2017/07/tmall-genie-alibabas-amazon-echo-clone-china.html

Jack Loechner 'AI-Driven Personal Assistant Apps Shaping Digital Consumer Habits', *MediaPost* (24 July 2017). Available from: https://www.mediapost.com/publications/article/304750/

James Manyika, Michael Chui, Brad Brown, Jacques Bughin, Richard Dobbs, Charles Roxburgh & Angela Hung Byers *Big Data: The Next Frontier for Innovation, Competition, and Productivity*, (McKinsey Global Institute, May 2011). Available via: http://www.mckinsey.com/business-functions/digital-mckinsey/our-insights/big-data-the-next-frontier-for-innovation

John Markoff 'Computer Wins on "Jeopardy!": Trivial, It's Not', *New York Times* (16 February 2011). Available from: http://www.nytimes.com/2011/02/17/science/17jeopardy-watson.html

Matt McFarland 'Elon Musk: "With Artificial Intelligence We Are Summoning The Demon"', *Washington Post* (24 October 2014). Available from: https://www.washingtonpost.com/news/innovations/wp/2014/10/24/elon-musk-with-artificial-intelligence-we-are-summoning-the-demon/?utm_term=.9853955d9a4f

Rich Haridy 'AI Predicts Patients' Lifespans As Well As A Doctor' *New Atlas* (7 June 2017). Available from: http://newatlas.com/ai-predicts-lifespan-patients/49930/

Lucas Matney 'Facebook Improves Its AI Messenger Assistant 'M' With New Wits' *Tech Crunch* (27 June 2017). Available from: https://techcrunch.com/2017/06/27/facebook-improves-its-ai-messenger-assistant-m-with-new-wits/

Christina Mercer '12 Companies Working On Driverless Cars: What Companies Are Making Driverless Cars?', *TechWorld* (14 June 22017). Available from: http://www.techworld.com/picture-gallery/data/-companies-working-on-driverless-cars-3641537/

Cade Metz 'AI's Factions Get Feisty. But Really, They're All On The Same Team', *Wired* (14 February 2017). Available from: https://www.wired.com/2017/02/ais-factions-get-feisty-really-theyre-team/

Cade Metz 'Google Rattles The Tech World With A New AI Chip For All' *Wired* (17 May 2017). Available from: https://www.wired.com/2017/05/google-rattles-tech-world-new-ai-chip/

MI AI Speaker website at: https://www.mi.com/aispeaker/

Microsoft Cortana web page at: https://support.microsoft.com/en-gb/help/17214/windows-10-what-is

Danielle Muoio 'Ranked: The 18 Companies Most Likely To Get Self-driving Cars On The Road First', *Business Insider* (3 April 2017). Available from: http://uk.businessinsider.com/the-companies-most-likely-to-get-driverless-cars-on-the-road-first-2017-4

Navigant Research *Navigant Research Leaderboard Report: Automated Driving* (2Q, 2017). Available from: https://www.navigantresearch.com/research/navigant-research-leaderboard-report-automated-driving

Michael A. Nielsen *Neural Networks and Deep Learning* (2015). Online book available from: http://neuralnetworksanddeeplearning.com/

OK Google web pages at: http://ok-google.io/

Partnership on AI website at: https://www.partnershiponai.org/

Antony Peyton 'AI at RBS for TLC', *Banking Technology* (6 October 2016). Available from: http://www.bankingtech.com/450662/ai-at-rbs-for-tlc/

PwC *Up To 30% Of Existing UK Jobs Could Be Impacted By Automation By Early 2030s, But This Should Be Offset By Job Gains Elsewhere In Economy* (Press Release, 24 March 2017). Available from: http://pwc.blogs.com/press_room/2017/03/up-to-30-of-existing-uk-jobs-could-be-impacted-by-automation-by-early-2030s-but-this-should-be-offse.html

Matt Reynolds 'DeepMind's AI Beats World's Best Go Player In Latest Face-off', *New Scientist* (23 May 2017). Available from: https://www.newscientist.com/article/2132086-deepminds-ai-beats-worlds-best-go-player-in-latest-face-off/

Microsoft AI Platform website at: https://www.microsoft.com/en-us/AI/ai-platform

Microsoft Azure Cognitive Services website at: https://azure.microsoft.com/en-gb/services/cognitive-services/

Margaret Rhodes 'All The New Google Hardware? It's a Trojan Horse for AI', *Wired* (5 October 2016). Available from: https://www.wired.com/2016/10/new-google-hardware-trojan-horse-ai/

Robert Rosenblatt *The Perceptron: A Perceiving and Recognizing Automation* (Cornell Aeronautical Laboratory, 1957). Available from: https://blogs.umass.edu/brain-wars/files/2016/03/rosenblatt-1957.pdf

Salesforce Einstein cloud AI website: https://www.salesforce.com/uk/products/einstein/overview/

Kaz Seto 'An In-depth Look at Google's First Tensor Processing Unit (TPU)', *Google Cloud Big Data And Machine Learning Blog* (12 May 2017). Available from: https://cloud.google.com/blog/big-data/2017/05/an-in-depth-look-at-googles-first-tensor-processing-unit-tpu

Christie Schneider *10 Reasons Why AI-Powered, Automated Customer Service Is The Future* (Watson Conversational Services Blog, 25 April 2017). Available from: https://www.ibm.com/blogs/watson/2017/04/10-reasons-ai-powered-automated-customer-service-future/

Simon Sharwood 'Driverless Trucks Roam Australian Mines', *The Register* (26 November 2012). Available from: https://www.theregister.co.uk/2012/11/26/autonomous_mining_trucks/

Sam Shead 'Google's DeepMind Wants to Cut 10% Off The Entire UK's Energy Bill', *Business Insider* (13 March 2017). Available from: http://uk.businessinsider.com/google-deepmind-wants-to-cut-ten-percent-off-entire-uk-energy-bill-using-artificial-intelligence-2017-3

Alexandra Simon-Lewis 'Ford is the Leading Self-driving Car Manufacturer – Ahead Of Waymo, Tesla and Uber', *Wired* (4 April 2017). Available from: http://www.wired.co.uk/article/ford-autonomous-cars-navigant-leader

Brett Smith 'Sensor Technology in Driverless Cars', *AZO Sensors* (18 May 2016). Available from: https://www.azosensors.com/article.aspx?ArticleID=688

Mustafa Suleyman 'A Milestone for DeepMind Health and Streams', *DeepMind* (17 February 2017). Available from: https://deepmind.com/blog/milestone-deepmind-health-and-streams/

TeslaFlow website at: https://www.tensorflow.org/

Alan M. Turing 'Computing Machinery and Intelligence'. *Mind*, (Volume LIX, Number 236, October 1950). Now available from: http://loebner.net/Prizef/TuringArticle.html

Kurt Wagner 'Elon Musk Just Told A Group Of America's Governors That We Need To Regulate AI Before It's Too Late', *Recode* (15 July 2017). Available from: https://www.recode.net/2017/7/15/15976744/elon-musk-artificial-intelligence-regulations-ai

Oscar Williams-Grut 'Robots Will Steal Your Job: How AI Could Increase Unemployment and Inequality', *Business Insider* (15 February 2016). Available from: http://

uk.businessinsider.com/robots-will-steal-your-job-citi-ai-increase-unemployment-in-equality-2016-2

Windows Development Center Cortana Overview. Available from: https://developer.microsoft.com/en-us/windows/iot/docs/cortanaoniotcore

Wit.ai website at: https://wit.ai/

Mark Zastrow '"I'm in shock!' How an AI Beat the World's Best Human at Go', *New Scientist* (9 March 2016). Available from: https://www.newscientist.com/article/2079871-im-in-shock-how-an-ai-beat-the-worlds-best-human-at-go/

### Chapter 4: Robot Horizons

Evan Ackerman 'Fetch Robotics Introduces Fetch and Freight: Your Warehouse Is Now Automated', *IEEE Spectrum* (29 April 2015). Available from: http://spectrum.ieee.org/automaton/robotics/industrial-robots/fetch-robotics-introduces-fetch-and-freight-your-warehouse-is-now-automated

AgriBot website at: http://agribot.eu/?lang=en

Amazon Robotics website at: https://www.amazonrobotics.com/

Aethon website at: http://www.aethon.com

Blue Frog Robotics website at: http://www.bluefrogrobotics.com/en/

Boston Dynamics Atlas robot web page at: https://www.bostondynamics.com/atlas

Morgan Brasfield 'How The Rise Of The Robots Will Change Future Jobs' *CNBC* (17 April 2017). Available from: https://www.cnbc.com/2017/04/07/jobs-report-robots-will-make-future-reports-even-more-dire.html

Jeff Daniels 'Future of Farming: Driverless Tractors, Ag Robots', *CNBC* (16 September 2016). Available from: https://www.cnbc.com/2016/09/16/future-of-farming-driverless-tractors-ag-robots.html

Deepfield Robotics BoniRob web pages at: https://www.deepfield-connect.com/en/BoniRob.html#

Travis Deyle 'Why Indoor Robots for Commercial Spaces Are the Next Big Thing in Robotics', *IEEE Spectrum* (1 March 2017). Available from: http://spectrum.ieee.org/automaton/robotics/robotics-hardware/indoor-robots-for-commercial-spaces

DHL Trend Research Logistics Trend Radar (2016). Available from: http://www.dhl.com/content/dam/downloads/g0/about_us/logistics_insights/dhl_logistics_trend_radar_2016.pdf

Epson *Epson to Unveil New Autonomous Dual-Arm Robot* (News Release, 5 November 2013). Available from: http://global.epson.com/newsroom/2013/news_20131105.html

European Parliament *European Civil Law Rules in Robotics* (October 2016, PE 571.379). Available from: http://www.europarl.europa.eu/RegData/etudes/STUD/2016/571379/IPOL_STU(2016)571379_EN.pdf

Executive Office of the President *Artificial Intelligence, Automation, and the Economy* (US Government, December 2016). Available from: https://obamawhitehouse.archives.gov/sites/whitehouse.gov/files/documents/Artificial-Intelligence-Automation-Economy.pdf

Fetch Robotics website at: http://fetchrobotics.com/

Dyllan Furness 'Russia's Deputy Prime Minister Insists Gun-toting Robot Is Not A Terminator', *Digital Trends* (18 April 2017). Available from: https://www.digitaltrends.com/cool-tech/fedor-russia-space-robot/

Future of Life Institute *An Open Letter To The United Nations Convention On Certain Conventional Weapons* (20 August 2017). Available from: https://futureoflife.org/autonomous-weapons-open-letter-2017

Weio Gao et al 'Artificial Micromotors in the Mouse's Stomach' *ACS Nano* (Volume 9 No 1, 2015). Available from: http://pubs.acs.org/doi/ipdf/10.1021/nn507097k

J.P. Gownder *et al* 'The Future Of Jobs, 2027: Working Side By Side With Robots' *Forrester* (April 2017). Available for purchase via: https://www.forrester.com/report/The+Future+Of+Jobs+2027+Working+Side+By+Side+With+Robots/-/E-RES119861

GTI *GTI 5G & Cloud Robotics White Paper* (21 June 2017). Available from: http://www-file.huawei.com/-/media/CORPORATE/PDF/x-lab/Cloud-robotics-white-paper-final-0628.pdf?la=en

Alex Hern 'Amazon Claims First Successful Prime Air Drone Delivery', *The Guardian* (14 December 2016). Available from: https://www.theguardian.com/technology/2016/dec/14/amazon-claims-first-successful-prime-air-drone-delivery

Hitachi *EMIEW3 and Robotics IT Platform*. Web page at: http://www.hitachi.com/rd/portal/highlight/robotics/emiew3_01/index.html

Hitachi *Hitachi Begins Proof of Concept Tests of EMIEW3 Humanoid Robot at Haneda Airport* (News Release, 2 September 2016). Available from: http://www.hitachi.com/rd/news/2016/0902.html

Hitachi *Humanoid Dual Arm Industrial Robot NEXTAGE*. Web page (including video) available at: http://www.hitachi-hightech.com/eu/product_detail/?pn=ind-nextage&version=

Honda *Honda Unveils All-new ASIMO with Significant Advancements* (News Release, 8 November 2011). Available from: http://asimo.honda.com/news/honda-unveils-all-new-asimo-with-significant-advancements/newsarticle_0125/

iCub website at: http://www.icub.org/

InMoov website at: http://inmoov.fr/

International Federation of Robotics website at: https://ifr.org/

Cho Jin-young 'S. Korean Government to Make Legal Preparations Regarding Artificial Intelligence', *Business Korea* (17 February 2017). Available from: http://www.businesskorea.co.kr/english/news/ict/17331-legal-preparation-ai-era-s-korean-government-make-legal-preparations-regarding

Knightscope website at: http://www.knightscope.com/

Kawasaki Robotics *"duAro" Dual-Arm SCARA Robot Now Launched* (Press Release, 6 August 2015). Available from: https://robotics.kawasaki.com/en1/news-events/news/detail/index.html?f=20150806_4563&language_id=4

Adrienne LaFrance 'What Is A Robot?', *The Atlantic* (22 March 2016). Available from: https://www.theatlantic.com/technology/archive/2016/03/what-is-a-human/473166/

Barry Libert & Megan Beck 'AI May Soon Replace Even the Most Elite Consultants', *Harvard Business Review* (24 July 2017). Available from: https://hbr.org/2017/07/ai-may-soon-replace-even-the-most-elite-consultants

Tony Long 'Jan. 25, 1921: Robots First Czech In', *Wired* (25 January 2011). Available from: https://www.wired.com/2011/01/0125robot-cometh-capek-rur-debut/

NASA R5 web page at: https://www.nasa.gov/feature/r5

Tom O'Conner 'Russia Built A Robot That Can Shoot Guns And Travel To Space', *Newsweek* (19 April 2017). Available from: http://www.newsweek.com/russia-built-robot-can-shoot-guns-and-travel-space-586544

Poppy Project website at: https://www.poppy-project.org/en/

Georgina Prodhan 'Europe's Robots To Become 'Electronic Persons' Under Draft Plan', *Reuters* (2 June 2016). Available from: http://www.reuters.com/article/us-europe-robotics-lawmaking-idUSKCN0Z72AY

Jacopo Prisco 'Will Nanotechnology Soon Allow You To "Swallow The Doctor"?' *CNN* (20 January 2015). Available from: http://edition.cnn.com/2015/01/29/tech/mci-nanobots-eth/index.html

Realdoll website at: https://www.realdoll.com/

Robot Worx FAQ web pages, available from: https://www.robots.com/faq

# REFERENCES

Robotic Industries Association *UNIMATE // The First Industrial Robot*. Available from: https://www.robotics.org/joseph-engelberger/unimate.cfm

Robots of London *Pepper the Receptionist* web page. Available from: http://robotsoflondon.co.uk/pepper-the-receptionist/

Sam Shead 'Amazon Now Has 45,000 Robots in its Warehouses', *Business Insider* (3 January 2017). Available from: http://uk.businessinsider.com/amazons-robot-army-has-grown-by-50-2017-1

SoftBank *SoftBank Announces Agreement To Acquire Boston Dynamics* (Press Release, 9 June 2017). Available from: https://www.softbank.jp/en/corp/news/press/sb/2017/20170609_01/

SoftBank Robotics website at: https://www.ald.softbankrobotics.com

SoftBank Robotics Romeo website at: https://www.ald.softbankrobotics.com/en/robots/romeo

Symbiotic website at: http://www.symbotic.com/

Frank Tobe 'How is Pepper, SoftBank's Emotional Robot, Doing?', *The Robot Report* (27 May 2016). Available from: https://www.therobotreport.com/news/how-is-the-emotional-robot-pepper-doing

UNCTAD 'Robots and Industrialization in Developing Countries' (Policy Brief No.50, November 2016). Available from: http://unctad.org/en/PublicationsLibrary/presspb2016d6_en.pdf

Jane Wakefield 'A Sex Doll That Can Talk - But Is It Perfect Harmony?', *BBC News* (15 May 2017). Available from: http://www.bbc.co.uk/news/technology-39859939

Tom Watson 'When Robots Do All The Work, How Will People Live?' *The Guardian* (8 March 2016). Available from: https://www.theguardian.com/commentisfree/2016/mar/08/robots-technology-industrial-strategy

World Bank *World Development Report 2016: Digital Dividends* (Washington DC, 2016). Available from: http://documents.worldbank.org/curated/en/896971468194972881/pdf/102725-PUB-Replacement-PUBLIC.pdf

Zenbo website at: https://zenbo.asus.com/

## Chapter 5: Quantum & Organic Frontiers

Alibaba Group *Aliyun and Chinese Academy of Sciences Sign MoU for Quantum Computing Laboratory* (Press Release, 30 July 2015). Available from: http://www.alibabagroup.com/en/news/article?news=p150730

Christopher Barnatt *25 Things You Need to Know About the Future* (London: Constable, 2012).

Woodrow Bellamy III 'Quantum Computing for Aerospace, What are the Possibilities?', *Aviation Today* (15 August 2016). Available from: http://www.aviationtoday.com/2016/08/15/quantum-computing-for-aerospace-what-are-the-possibilities/

John Bohannon 'DNA: The Ultimate Hard Drive', *Science* (16 August 2012). Available from: http://www.sciencemag.org/news/2012/08/dna-ultimate-hard-drive

Jerome Bonnet, Peter Yin, Monica E. Ortiz, Pakpoom Subsoontorn & Drew Endy 'Amplifying Genetic Logic Gates', *Science* (Vol. 340, Issue 6132, 3 May 2013). Available via: http://science.sciencemag.org/content/340/6132/599

Mary Branscombe 'Why Microsoft Believes We're On The Threshold of Quantum Computing', *Tech Radar* (20 December 2016). Available from: http://www.techradar.com/news/why-microsoft-believes-were-on-the-threshold-of-quantum-computing

Jeffrey Burt 'China Making Swift, Competitive Quantum Computing Gains', *The Next Platform* (27 March 2017). Avialable from: https://www.nextplatform.com/2017/03/27/china-making-swift-quantum-computing-gains-u-s/

Jerry Chow 'The future of supercomputers? A Quantum Chip Colder than Outer Space', *TED Institute* (10 December 2015). Video available on Youtube at: https://www.youtube.com/watch?v=VsBuuwGj3zs

Rachel Courtland 'Intel Now Packs 100 Million Transistors in Each Square Millimeter', *IEEE Spectrum* (30 March 2017). Available from: http://spectrum.ieee.org/nanoclast/semiconductors/processors/intel-now-packs-100-million-transistors-in-each-square-millimeter

Andrew Currin, Konstantin Korovin, Maria Ababi, Katherine Roper, Douglas B. Kell, Philip J. Day, & Ross D. King Computing Exponentially Faster: 'Implementing a Non-deterministic Universal Turing Machine Using DNA', *Journal of the Royal Society Interface* (18 August 2017). Available from: http://rsif.royalsocietypublishing.org/content/royinterface/14/128/20160990.full.pdf

D-Wave Systems *Announcing the D-Wave 2X Quantum Computer* (Press Release, 15 August 2015). Available from: https://www.dwavesys.com/blog/2015/08/announcing-d-wave-2x-quantum-computer

D-Wave Systems *Brochure* (January 2017), available from: https://www.dwavesys.com/sites/default/files/D-Wave-Overview-Jan2017F2.pdf

D-Wave Systems *D-Wave Systems Breaks the 1000 Qubit Quantum Computing Barrier* (Press Release, 22 June 2015). Available from: https://www.dwavesys.com/press-releases/d-wave-systems-breaks-1000-qubit-quantum-computing-barrier

D-Wave Systems *Oak Ridge National Laboratory Acquires D-Wave 2000Q Cloud Services to Accelerate Hybrid Computing Applications* (Press Release, 25 June 2017). Available from: https://www.dwavesys.com/press-releases/oak-ridge-national-laboratory-acquires-d-wave-2000q-cloud-services-accelerate-hybrid

D-Wave Systems *Recruit Communications and D-Wave Collaborate to Apply Quantum Computing to Marketing, Advertising, and Communications Optimization* (Press Release, 12 May 2017). Available from: https://www.dwavesys.com/press-releases/recruit-communications-and-d-wave-collaborate-apply-quantum-computing-marketing

D-Wave Systems *What is Quantum Annealing?* (26 October 2015). Video available on YouTube at: https://www.youtube.com/watch?v=zvfkXjzzYOo

Vasil S. Denchev, Sergio Boixo, Sergei V. Isakov, Nan Ding, Ryan Babbush, Vadim Smelyanskiy, John Martinis & Hartmut Neven 'What is the Computational Value of Finite-Range Tunneling?', *Physical Review X* (6, 031015, 1 August 2016). Available from: https://journals.aps.org/prx/abstract/10.1103/PhysRevX.6.031015

Talia Gershon *A Beginner's Guide to Quantum Computing* (IBM Research, 31 May 2017). Video available on YouTube at: https://www.youtube.com/watch?v=S52rxZG-zi0

Dario Gil 'Paving the Path to Universal Quantum Computing' *IBM Think Blog* (6 May 2017). Available from: https://www.ibm.com/blogs/think/2017/03/ibm-quantum/

Google Quantum AI web page at: https://research.google.com/pubs/QuantumAI.html

William Herkewitz 'Google and NASA Say Their Quantum Computer Finally Works', *Popular Mechanics* (9 December 2015). Available from: http://www.popularmechanics.com/technology/gadgets/a18475/google-nasa-d-wave-quantum-computer/

IBM *IBM Builds Its Most Powerful Universal Quantum Computing Processors* (News Release, 17 May 2017). Available from: http://www-03.ibm.com/press/us/en/pressrelease/52403.wss

IBM *IBM Building First Universal Quantum Computers for Business and Science* (News Release, 6 March 2017). Available from: https://www-03.ibm.com/press/us/en/pressrelease/51740.wss

IBM *IBM Makes Quantum Computing Available on IBM Cloud to Accelerate Innovation* (News Release, 4 May 2016). Available from: https://www-03.ibm.com/press/us/en/pressrelease/49661.wss

IBM Q Experience Library at: https://quantumexperience.ng.bluemix.net/qx/user-guide

# REFERENCES

Brad Jones 'Intel Will Leverage Its Chip-making Expertise For Quantum Research', *Digital Trends* (22 December 2016). Available from: https://www.digitaltrends.com/computing/intel-silicon-qubits-quantum-computer/

Russ Juskalian 'Practical Quantum Computers', *MIT Technology Review* (March/April 2017). Available from: https://www.technologyreview.com/s/603495/10-breakthrough-technologies-2017-practical-quantum-computers/

Allison Linn 'Microsoft Doubles Down on Quantum Computing', *Microsoft Blog* (20 November 2016). Available from: https://blogs.microsoft.com/ai/2016/11/20/microsoft-doubles-quantum-computing-bet/

Intel Moore's Law 40th Anniversary web pages at: https://www.intel.com/pressroom/kits/events/moores_law_40th/

Anastasia Marchenkova 'What's The Difference Between Quantum Annealing And Universal Gate Quantum Computers?', *Quantum Bits* (28 February 2016). Available from: https://medium.com/quantum-bits/what-s-the-difference-between-quantum-annealing-and-universal-gate-quantum-computers-c5e5099175a1

John Markoff 'Microsoft Makes Bet Quantum Computing Is Next Breakthrough', *New York Times* (23 June 2014). Available from: https://www.nytimes.com/2014/06/24/technology/microsoft-makes-a-bet-on-quantum-computing-research.html?_r=1

Masoud Mohseni, Peter Read & Hartmut Neven 'Commercialize Early Quantum Technologies', *Nature* (Vol 543, 9 March 2017). Available from: https://static.googleusercontent.com/media/research.google.com/en//pubs/archive/45919.pdf

Cade Metz 'The Race to Sell Quantum Computers Before They Really Exist', *Wired* (6 March 2017). Available from: https://www.wired.com/2017/03/race-sell-true-quantum-computers-begins-really-exist/

Microsoft Station Q website at: https://stationq.microsoft.com/

Microsoft *Building The Future: Microsoft And TU Delft Work On Creating A Quantum Computer* (News Release, 6 June 2017). Available from: https://news.microsoft.com/europe/2017/06/06/building-the-future-microsoft-and-tu-delft-work-on-creating-a-powerful-quantum-computer/

Gordon E. Moore 'Progress in Digital Integrated Electronics' *IEEE Technical Digest* (1975). Available from: http://www.eng.auburn.edu/~agrawvd/COURSE/E7770_Spr07/READ/Gordon_Moore_1975_Speech.pdf

Mark Papermaster 'How Computing Will Change Amid Challenges To Moore's Law', *Tech Crunch* (3 April 2017). Available from: https://techcrunch.com/2017/04/13/how-computing-will-change-amid-challenges-to-moores-law/

Gabriel Popkin 'Moore's Law Is About To Get Weird', *Nautilus* ( 12 February 12 2015). Available from: http://nautil.us/issue/21/information/moores-law-is-about-to-get-weird

V. Nvas Prabu & J. Gowtham Kumar 'Wetware Technology (Technology of the Future)', *IRD India* (Vol. 3, Issue 8, 2015). Available from: http://www.irdindia.in/journal_ijraet/pdf/vol3_iss8/7.pdf

QuTech website at: https://qutech.nl/

Matt Reynolds 'First Hint Of How DNA Calculators Could Supercharge Computing', *New Scientist* (2 March 2017). Available from: https://www.newscientist.com/article/2123322-first-hint-of-how-dna-calculators-could-supercharge-computing/

Matt Reynolds 'Google On Track For Quantum Computer Breakthrough By End Of 2017', *New Scientist* (26 June 2017). Available from: https://www.newscientist.com/article/2138373-google-on-track-for-quantum-computer-breakthrough-by-end-of-2017/

John Russell 'Quantum Bits: D-Wave and VW; Google Quantum Lab; IBM Expands Access', *HPC Wire* (21 March 2017). Available from: https://www.hpcwire.com/2017/03/21/quantum-bits-d-wave-vw-google-quantum-lab-ibm-expands-access/

Robert Service 'DNA Could Store All Of The World's Data In One Room', *Science* (2 March 2017). Available from: http://www.sciencemag.org/news/2017/03/dna-could-store-all-worlds-data-one-room

Agam Shah 'Intel Researches Quantum Computing And Neuromorphic Chips For Future PCs', *PC World* (11 February 2017). Available from: http://www.pcworld.com/article/3168753/components-processors/intel-researches-tech-to-prepare-for-a-future-beyond-todays-pcs.html

Tom Simonite 'Google's New Chip Is a Stepping Stone to Quantum Computing Supremacy', *MIT Technology Review* (21 April 2017). Available from: https://www.technologyreview.com/s/604242/googles-new-chip-is-a-stepping-stone-to-quantum-computing-supremacy/

Graham Templeton 'How MIT's New Biological 'Computer' Works, And What It Could Do In The Future', *Extreme Tech* (25 July 2016). Available from: https://www.extremetech.com/extreme/232190-how-mits-new-biological-computer-works-and-what-it-could-do-in-the-future

Patrick Tucker, 'What Quantum Computing Means for National Security', *The Futurist* (July–August 2010).

Volkswagen *The Beginnings of a Quantum Leap* (News Release, 20 March 2017). Available from: https://www.volkswagenag.com/en/news/stories/2017/03/the-beginnings-of-a-quantum-leap.html

Bob Yirka 'Google Combines Two Main Quantum Computing Ideas In One Computer', *Phys.org* (9 June 2016). Available from: https://phys.org/news/2016-06-google-combines-main-quantum-ideas.html

### Chapter 6: Cyborg Fusion

Christopher Barnatt *25 Things You Need to Know About the Future* (London: Constable, 2012).

Roland Benedikter & Katja Siepmann '"Transhumanism": A New Global Political Trend?', *Challenge* (Volume 59, No.1, 2016). Available via: http://www.tandfonline.com/doi/abs/10.1080/05775132.2015.1123574?journalCode=mcha20

BrainGate website at: https://www.braingate.org/

Liat Clark 'Elon Musk Reveals More About His Plan To Merge Man And Machine With Neuralink', *Wired* (27 April 2017). Available from: http://www.wired.co.uk/article/elon-musk-neuralink

Manfred E. Clynes & Nathan S. Kline 'Cyborgs and Space', *Astronautics* (September 1960). Now available from: http://www.medientheorie.com/doc/clynes_cyborgs.pdf

Jennifer L. Collinger et al, 'High-Performance Neuroprosthetic Control By An Individual With Tetraplegia', *The Lancet* (17 December 2012). Available from: http://www.thelancet.com/journals/lancet/article/PIIS0140-6736(12)61816-9/abstract

*Gizmag* 'Scientists Demonstrate A Mind-controlled Future' (4 November 2014). Available from: http://www.gizmag.com/go/3423/

Allen C. Ho et al 'Long-Term Results from an Epiretinal Prosthesis to Restore Sight to the Blind', *Ophthalmology* (Vol 122, No.8. August 2015). Early proof available from: http://www.aaojournal.org/pb/assets/raw/Health%20Advance/journals/ophtha/ophtha_8651.pdf

Julian Huxley *Religion without Revelation* (The New American Library, 1927. Revised 1956).

Tros de Ilarduya, Sun Y & Düzgünes N. 'Gene Delivery By Lipoplexes And Polyplexes', *European Journal of Pharmaceutical Science* (Volume 40 No 3, 14 June 2014). Available via: http://www.ncbi.nlm.nih.gov/pubmed/20359532

Kevin Loria 'Elon Musk Wants To Link Computers To Our Brains To Prevent An Existential Threat To Humanity', *Business Insider* (17 June 2017). http://www.businessinsider.com/elon-musks-neuralink-artificial-intelligence-2017-6?IR=T

Michelle Ma 'UW Study Shows Direct Brain Interface Between Humans' *UW Today* (5 November 2014). Available from: http://www.washington.edu/news/2014/11/05/uw-study-shows-direct-brain-interface-between-humans/

# REFERENCES

Alexis C. Madrigal 'The Man Who First Said "Cyborg," 50 Years Later', *The Atlantic* (30 September 2010). Available from: https://www.theatlantic.com/technology/archive/2010/09/the-man-who-first-said-cyborg-50-years-later/63821/

Mazlish, B. (1993) *The Fourth Discontinuity: The Co-evolution of Humans and Machines* (New Haven: Yale University Press).

Max More 'Transhumanism: A Futurist Philosophy', *Extropy* (1990, no.6).

Neuralink website at: https://www.neuralink.com/

NeuroSky website at: http://neurosky.com/

Eileen Scahill *He Thought He Could* (Ohio State University, News Release, September 2016). Available from: https://www.osu.edu/alumni/news/ohio-state-alumni-magazine/issues/september-october-2016/he-thought-he-could.html

Second Sight website at: http://www.secondsight.com

Second Sight *Second Sight Announces Successful Implantation and Activation of Wireless Visual Cortical Stimulator in First Human Subject* (Press Release, 25 October 2016). Available from: http://investors.secondsight.com/releasedetail.cfm?ReleaseID=995211

Maddie Stone 'DARPA's Mind-Controlled Arm Will Make You Wish You Were a Cyborg', *Gizmodo* (12 May 2016). Available from: http://gizmodo.com/darpas-mind-controlled-arm-will-make-you-wish-you-were-1776130193

Transhumanist Party Global website at: https://sites.google.com/site/transhumanistpartyglobal/

UK Transhumanist Party website at: http://www.transhumanistparty.org.uk/

United States Transhumanist Party website at: http://transhumanist-party.org/

# INDEX

1401 Data Processing System, 17
3D printing, 30, 52, 53, 75-83, 86, 87, 89, 167, 168–9, 201
3D Systems, 79
4004, 20
5G, 42, 56, 167
8008, 20
802.11, 40
802.3, 32
86-DOS, 28

abacus, 12
Abyss Creations, 147
Accenture, 2
additive manufacturing, 76
adiabatic quantum computing, 177, 200
Advanced Research Fund (Russian military), 160–2
Advanced Research Projects Agency Network, see ARPANET
Aethon, 142
AGI, 98, 100, 124, 131
Agribot, 143
agricultural robots, 142-4
AI, 2, 5, 9, 44, 46, 51–2, 53, 70, 71–2, 73, 89, 91–134, 148-9, 158, 166–7, 169, 190, 192
AI denial, 45, 52, 59, 129–30
AI XPRIZE, 134
Airbus, 80–1, 187
Aldebaran, 153, 160
Alexa, 2, 101, 103–4, 105, 106, 119, 203, 223
Alibaba, 105, 108, 184–5
Allen, Paul, 27–8

AlphaGO, 99
Altair 8800, 20, 27, 44
AM, see additive manufacturing
Amazon, 38, 54, 55, 57, 58, 62, 70, 100, 102, 103–4, 109-10, 112, 118–19, 133, 138, 145, 173
Amazon cloud AI, 118–19
Amazon Echo, 68-9, 103–4, 105, 107, 135, 196
Amazon Robotics, 138
Amazon web services, see AWS
Amiga, 22, 24
AMRs, 138–40, 200–1
Amyris, 84
Analytic Engine, 12–13
Android (operating system), 43, 102, 104
Android Technics, 160
ANNs, 94–7, 190
Apache Hadoop, see Hadoop
Apache Software Foundation, 60
Apache Spark, 61
APIs (for cloud AI), 112, 115, 116
Apple, 20–1, 24, 40, 42, 67, 100, 102, 105, 120, 133, 173, 211
Apple I, 21
Apple II, 21, 24, 28
Apple Macintosh, see Macintosh
Apple Newton, 26
application programming interfaces, see APIs
applied AI, 98
Arcam, 80
ARCNET, 32

# INDEX

Argus II, 203–4, 205
ARKit, 67
ARPANET, 31, 32–3
artificial general intelligence, *see* AGI
artificial intelligence, *see* AI
ASIMO, 149, 156–8, 169
Asimov, Issac, 164–5
assembly languages, 17
Associated Press, 129
Asus, 146
AT&T, 41
Atanasoff, John Vincent, 14
Atanasoff-Berry Computer, 14
Atari Portfolio, 26, 29
Atari, 24, 26, 29–30
Atlas, 158
attentive computing, 10, 44–5, 74, 105–8, 120
Audi, 121
augmentation, 129–30
augmented reality, 52, 53, 66–7, 89, 219
Augusta, Lady Ada, 12–13, 190
Automatic Sequence Controlled Calculator, 14
automation, 3, 128–31, 139–40, 162–4, 199
Autonomous Dual-Arm Robot, 151
autonomous mobile robots, *see* AMRs
autonomous vehicles, 3, 4, 44, 52, 53, 74, 76, 89, 96, 98, 100, 108, 120–3, 131, 137, 142–3, 166, 200–1
autonomous weapons, 144–5
AWS, 56, 70, 119
AWS Deep Learning AMI, 119
AWS IoT, 70
Azure, 55
Azure Cognitive Services, 115–16
Azure IoT Suite, 70

Babbage, Charles, 12–13, 190
Baidu, 120
Bartley, Ryan, 113
BASIC, 27–8
Battelle, 206–7
BCI VR, 219–20
BCI-enhanced humans, 210–13
BCIs, *see* brain-computer interfaces
Bell Labs, 16, 40

Bercow, Mark, 43
Berners-Lee, Tim, 36–7
Berry, Clifford, 14
Bexos, Jeff, 38
Bhor, Niels, 174, 183
Big Data, 52, 53, 57–62, 68, 70, 76, 89, 98, 100, 108, 112, 114, 124–5, 127
binder jetting, 78
bio-ink, 82, 83
bio-paper, 82, 83
biocomputer, 190, 194–7
biocomputing, *see* organic computing
Biofene, 84
biological computing, *see* organic computing
biological transistors, 191
Bioprinting Solutions, 81
bioprinting, 81–3, 149, 169, 190, 195, 201, 209, 217, 218
BioXp 3200, 85, 190–1
Bitcoin, 63–4
Bixby, 104
Blasé Pascal, 12
Bletchley Park, 7–8, 9, 14
Blockchain, 52, 53, 62–5, 89
BlockGeeks, 64
Blue Frog Robotics, 146
Boeing, 80–1
Bombe, 14
Bond, Stewart, 64–5
BoniRob, 143–4
Bosch, 144
Boston Dynamics, 158
Bostrum, Nick, 123–4
Brain, Marshall, 130
brain-computer interfaces, 4, 45–6, 88, 204–13, 223
brain-to-brain networking, *see* telepathy (digital)
BrainGate, 206
Breathing Air Revolution, 5–6
Brin, Sergey, 39
broad AI, 98, 100
broadband, 36, 41
Brown University, 206
Buddy, 146, 147, 169
Budweiser, 122
bulletin board systems, 36

Burke, Martin D., 87
Burkhart, Ian, 207
bytes, 19

C-3PO, 136
C++, 17
CAD, 76
Cambridge University Mathematical Laboratory, 15
cancer diagnosis, 126
Capek, Karel, 136, 218
care robots, 147
CAS - Alibaba Quantum Computing Laboratory, 184–5
Case IH, 122, 142
CCTV cameras, 108
cellular networks, 40, 41–2
CERN, 37, 38
Changying Precision Technology Company, 75
Chase Manhattan Bank, 32
chatbots, 2, 113, 114, 115, 137
checkers AI, 93–4, 98
Chen, Steven, 39
chess AI, 93, 98, 99
China Mobile, 167
Chinese Academy of Sciences, 185
Church, George, 191
Cisco, 68, 70
Clarizen, 55
CLI, *see* command line interface
climate change, 3, 133
cloud AI, 57, 109–19, 123, 137, 167 192, 200
cloud AI services matrix, 109–11
cloud computing, 52, 53, 54–7, 58, 61, 62, 68, 81, 89, 109–19, 173, 198, 210
cloud robotics, 156, 166, 167, 192
Cloud TPU, 117
Cluster Map Reduce, 61
Clynes, Manfred, 201, 221
Cobalt, 141
COBOL, 17
cochlear implants, 202–3
codebreaking, 7, 8, 14, 188
Cognitive Computing Age, 10, 11, 43–5, 52, 93, 100, 101, 131, 132–4, 199, 223

Colossus, 7, 14–15, 44, 47, 54
Columbia University, 191
command line interfaces, 28
Commodore 64, 22, 24
Commodore Business Machines, 21–2, 24
Compaq, 23–4, 25
Comptometer, 13
computer aided design, *see* CAD
computer mediated communication, 32
computing generations, 8-9
Concept Laser, 80
connectionists (AI), 97
convergence, 217–8
Copernicus, Nicolaus, 216
core storage, 189
Cornell Aeronautical Laboratory, 95
Cornell University, 137
Cortana, 2, 101–2, 105
CP/M, 28
cryptocurrencies, 63–4
customer interface, 2, 105–8, 123, 163
*Cyber Business*, 1, 2, 35, 47
cyber physical systems, 72–4
Cyberkinetics, 206
Cyberparty of America, 214
Cyberspace, 1, 219, 222
Cyborg Fusion, 5, 11, 43, 45–7, 66, 67, 131-2, 149, 199–223
cyborgs, 201–2

D-Wave 2000Q, 179, 180
D-Wave 2X, 179, 181
D-Wave One, 178
D-Wave Systems, 174, 175–81, 182, 183, 186, 187, 198, 200
D-Wave Two, 178
Daimler, 121, 122
dangers of AI, 123–4, 131-2
dark factories, 3, 52, 53, 74–5, 76, 89, 100, 164
DARPA, 31, 144, 207
Darwin, Charles, 216
data exhaust, 61, 125
Datapoint Corporation, 32
Davenport, Thomas, 128–9
Deep Blue, 98

# INDEX

deep learning, 59, 95–7, 112, 115, 119, 125, 127, 167, 174, 188, 190, 192
deep sea mining, 220–1
Deepfield Robotics, 144
DeepMind, 96, 99, 126, 133
Defence Advanced Research Projects Agency, *see* DARPA
Delft University of Technology, 183–4
developing nations, 164
Deyle, Travis, 141
DHL, 70, 139
dial-up Internet access, 34, 36
Difference Engine, 12
digital assistants, 2, 98, 101–7, 108, 127, 131, 135–6, 187, 196, 203
Digital Research, 29
digital transformation, 50–4, 89-90, 169, 201
Ditto, William, 192
DNA computing, *see* organic computing
DNA printer, 85
DNA storage, 191–2
domestic robots, 141, 145–6, 162
Domingos, Pedro, 97
DOS, 28, 30, 36
Dot Com bubble, 38
driverless vehicles, *see* autonomous vehicles
drones, 136, 143, 144, 145
duAro, 151

e-mail (first), 32
Early Computing Age, 10, 11, 12–19
Echo, *see* Amazon Echo
EDSAC, 15–16, 17
EDVAC, 15, 16
EEG brain interfaces, 205
Einstein (AI service), 118
electromechanical computers, 13–14
EMIEW3, 154–6, 169
employment, 3, 45, 128-131, 162–4, 196–7
Endy, Drew, 191
energy minimization problems, 179
Engelberger, Joseph, 165
Englebart, Douglas, 28
English, Bill, 28

ENIAC, 15, 54
Enlitic, 125–6, 127
entanglement, 174, 187
Epson, 150, 151–2
Erlich, Yaniv, 191–2
Ernst & Young, 51
ETH Zürich, 141
Ethernet, 32
European Commission, 51, 166
evolutionists (AI), 97
expert systems, 98
extraterrestrial resources, 221–2

Fabrisonic, 79
Face++, 107
Facebook, 39, 47, 104, 119, 133
facial payment, 108
FCC, 40
Federal Communications Commission, *see* FCC
Federal Networking Council, *see* FNC
FEDOR, 160–2, 169
Feetz, 81
Felt, Dor Eugene, 13
Ferranti Mark 1, 93
Fetch Robotics, 139, 140
Five Ages of Computing, 9–47
Flowers, Tommy, 7
FNC, 35
Force.com, 55
Ford, 104, 121
Forgacs, Gabor, 81–2
Forrester, 114, 163
*Fourth Discontinuity, The*, 215–7
Freightliner Inspiration truck, 122
Freud, Sigmund, 216

Gartner, 51, 68
Gates, Bill, 27–8
gateways, 34
GE, 80, 81
GEM, 29–30
gene editing, 193, 195, 209–10
gene therapies, 127
genetic algorithms, 94
GenoCAD, 85–6
Georgia Institute of Technology, 92
Gibson, William, 1, 65

global hardware platform, 33–5
GM, 121, 137
Go (game), 99
GO (Intel product), 123
Goldman Sachs, 142–3
Google, 4, 39, 43, 54, 57, 58, 60, 67, 99, 100, 102–3, 104, 106, 112, 116–18, 119, 120, 133, 158, 173, 175, 178, 181–2, 186, 187, 188, 211
Google AIY, 118
Google Assistant, 2, 101, 102–3, 105, 203
Google cloud AI, 116–8
Google Docs, 55, 57
Google Glass, 67
Google Home, 68–9, 103, 107, 135
Google Now, 102
Google Quantum AI Laboratory, 181–2
GPUs, 117
granular materials binding, 77–8
graphical user interface, 28–30
Grigoriev, Andrey, 160
GTI, 167
GUI, *see* graphical user interface

Hadoop, 59–61
Haneda Airport, 156
Hanson, Ronald, 184
Harvard Mark 1, 14
Harvard Medical School 191
Hawking, Steven, 123
HDFS, 60
healthcare (human), 69, 114, 124–7, 140–1, 142, 148–9, 202–5, 206–7, 211, 218
heuristics, 94, 96, 99
hidden layers, 95, 97
high-level languages, 17
history of computing, 8–43
Hitachi, 150, 151, 152, 154–6
hive mind, 132, 211
Hololens, 67
HomePod, 105
Honda, 121, 149, 156–8
horizontal AI, 98
Howard, Jeremy, 125–6
HP, 80

HPCC, 61
HTML, 37
HTTP, 37
Huawei, 167
Hui, Fan, 99
human brains, 4, 87, 95, 190
human upgrading, 5
Humanity 2.0, 215
Humanity+, 214
humanoid robots, 3, 74, 146–162
Hurley, Chad, 39
Huxley, Julian, 213
hybrid integrated circuits, 19
Hydra, 61
Hyundai, 121

IaaS, 55, 56, 57
IBM, 4, 13, 17, 19, 22–4, 26, 28, 50–1, 56, 57, 58, 62–3, 96, 99, 100, 112–14, 119, 126, 127, 133, 134, 173, 175–6, 177, 178, 181, 182, 183, 186, 198
IBM PC, 22–4, 29–30, 33, 36, 38, 42, 44, 47,
IBM Q, 165-6
IBM Watson AI XPRIZE, 134
ICAAN, 34
ICs, *see* integrated circuits
iCub, 162
IDC, 50, 62, 64–5
IEEE, 32, 40
IMT-2020, 42
industrial robots, 137–8
Industry 4.0, 72–3
Inmoov, 162
Institute for Electrical and Electronic Engineers, *see* IEEE
integrated circuits, 8, 18-19, 20, 170–2
Intel, 20, 120, 122, 133, 170–1, 184
intelligence, 91–3
International Federation of Robotics, 138
International Space Station, 160
International Telecommunications Union, *see* ITU
Internet, 2, 5–6, 8, 9, 33–5, 36, 37, 38, 47, 49, 54, 56, 89, 109, 167, 205, 209, 210, 217, 219
Internet of Everything, 70–1

# INDEX

Internet of Things, *see* IoT
Internet service providers, *see* ISPs
internetworking, 32
Interop, 34
IoE, *see* Internet of Everything
iOS, 43, 101, 102, 104
IoT, 52, 53, 58, 67–71, 73, 76, 89, 100, 101, 103, 104, 107, 111
IP addresses, 33, 34
iPad, 26
iPhone, 43, 101
IRC, 36
IREX, 151, 152
ISPs, 34
Istvan, Zoltan, 213
ITU, 42

J. Craig Venture Institute, *see* JCVI
Jacquard, Joseph-Marie, 12
JANET, 34
Japanese Ministry of Trade & Industry, 9
Jarvis, Jonathan, 103
JCVI, 84-5
*Jeopardy*, 112
Jie, Ke, 99
Jobs, Steve, 20–1
jobs (human), *see* employment
John Hopkins Applied Physics Laboratory, 207
Johnson Space Centre, 160
Juniper Research, 114

Karim, Jared, 39
Kasparov, Gary, 98
Kawasaki Robotics, 150–1, 152
Keen, Harold, 14
KFC, 108
Khan, Bob, 33–4
Kilby, Jack, 18
killer robots, 123, 136, 144–5
King, Ross, 193
Kirby, Julia, 128–9
Kiva Systems, 138
Kline, Nathan, 201, 221
Knightscope, 141–2, 143
Kress-Gazit, Hadas, 137
Krishna, Arvind, 176

Krzanich, Brian, 184

Lacity, Mary, 129
LaFrance, Adrienne, 126
Laney, Doug, 58
language translation, 109, 110, 113, 115, 116, 117
LANs, 32, 33
large scale integration, 18
laser sintering, 78
*Lawnmower Man, The*, 65
Laws of Robotics, 164–5
LDM, *see* local digital manufacturing
Lee, Peter, 183
leechulator, 192
legal issues, *see* robot laws
LEO, 16
Lewis, Randy, 84
LG, 104
LiDAR, 121, 168
Limp, Dave, 104
LinkedIn, 61
lipoplexes, 210
Lisa, 29
local area networks, *see* LANs
local digital manufacturing, 76, 87–8, 167
Local Motors, 81
Lockheed Martin, 178, 187
logistics, 58, 69–71, 76, 99, 111, 138–9, 174, 187
Luvo, 113
Lyons Electronic Office, *see* LEO

M digital assistant, 104
machine learning, 94, 95–7, 112, 116–17, 118–19, 189
Macintosh, 24, 26, 29
macOS, 29, 30, 101, 105
makers, 104, 118
management by knowing, 61, 62
MapReduce, 60–1
Mark-8 "Do-It_Yourself" kit, 20
Massachusetts Institute of Technology, *see* MIT
material extrusion, 76
material jetting, 77, 78
Matheny, Johnny, 207

Mazak, 80
Mazlish, Bruce, 216–7
McAffe, Jon, 213–4
McKinsey Global Institute, 124
mechanical computers, 12–13
medical robots, 140–1, 142
medical symbiosis, 149
Memorax, 19
META Group, 58
*Metaman*, 49
Metcalfe, Bob, 32
Mi AI Speaker, 105
Micral N, 20
microfabricators, 87–8
microprocessors, 9, 20, 87-8, 117, 170–2, 184, 188, 191, 196, 197
Microsoft, 4, 27–8, 54, 57, 58, 67, 70, 100, 101-2, 104, 105, 109, 112, 115–16, 119, 133, 173, 175, 182–4, 186, 211
Microsoft Tablet PCs, 26
military robots, 144–5, 158, 160
Mindwave, 205
MIT, 16, 216
mobile phones, 41–2
Mobileye, 120
modems, 34, 36
molecular 3D printer, 87
molecular self-assembly, 52, 53, 82, 86–8, 89, 100, 169, 195, 201
Moore, Gordon E., 170–1
Moore's Law, 170–2, 173, 185, 188, 200
More, Max, 213
Mori, Masahiro, 148
mouse (first), 28
MS DOS, 28
Musk, Elon, 4, 123, 207–8, 209
Myralene, 84

nanobots, 140–1
nanotechnology, 86–8, 171
narrow AI, 98–100
NASA, 160, 161, 178, 180, 182
National Museum of Computing, 7, 16
Nature, 182, 186–7
Navigant Research Leaderboard Report, 121
NCR Corporation, 40

Nestlé, 154
Netflix, 55
Netsuite, 55
Networked Computing Age, 10, 11, 30–43, 102
networks, 31–6, 40–2
neural networks, 94–7, 117
Neuralink, 4, 207–8, 209
NeuroLife Neural Bypass, 206–7
*Neuromancer*, 1, 65
NeuroSky, 205
Neven, Harmut, 186
New York Genome Center, 192
newpdQ Smartphone, 43
*Next Big Thing, The*, 71, 148
Next Platform, The, 185
NEXTAGE, 151, 152-3
Nissan, 121
Nokia, 42–3
non-deterministic universal Turing machine, 193–4
NORSAIR, 31
Novogen MMX, 82
Noyce, Robert, 170
NSFNET, 34
NTT, 41
NUTM, *see* non-deterministic universal Turing machine

O'Reilly, Tim, 38, 39
Oak Ridge National Laboratory, 180
Oan, Jianwei, 185
OMICtools, 85–6
omnipresent computing, 107–8
oN-Line System, 28
open architecture networking, 33
open source robots, 162
operating systems, 22, 28–30
organic augmentation, 208–13
organic computing, 4, 46, 52, 53, 88, 89, 149, 188–97, 208–13, 217
organic robots, 4, 149, 169, 195, 217–8
Organovo, 82-1, 195
Orion 1, 204
Osborne 1, 25, 26
Oxford University, 123
Ozbolat, Ibrahim, 83

# INDEX    **245**

PaaS, 55, 57
pace makers, 202
packet switching networks, 33–4
Page, Larry, 39
Partnership on AI, 133
PC DOS, 28
Penn State University, 83
Pepper, 153–4, 155, 156, 169
Perceptron, 94–5
Personal Computing Age, 10, 11, 20–30, 35
Personal Electronic Transactor, see PET
personal robots, 145–6
PET, 21, 22
photopolymerization, 77
pocket calculators, 18
polyplexes, 210
Poppy Project, 162
post-humans, 132, 215
powder bed fusion, 78
Prevolve, 81
Prinz, Dietrich, 93–4
punched cards, 12, 13
PwC, 128

QPU, see quantum processor
QuAIL, 178, 179, 180
Qualcomm, 43
quantum annealing, 177, 179–80
Quantum Artificial Intelligence Lab, see QuAIL
quantum coherence, 178
quantum computing, 4, 52, 53, 88, 89, 173-88, 189, 193, 198, 200
quantum processors, 175–6, 179–80, 182, 197
quantum supremacy, 176
qubits, 173–4, 175–6, 178–9, 182, 183, 184, 185, 187, 193, 200
QuTech, 183–4

*R.U.R.*, 136
R2D2, 146
R2E Corp, 20
R5, 160, 161
Radio Shack, 21
Radio-Electronics, 20
RAM, 18

rapid prototyping, 79
Raspberry Pi, 172
RBS, 113
RealDoll, 147
recommendations engine, 109–10, 111, 115, 187
Recruit Communications Co, 180
*Religion without Revelation*, 213
Renault, 121
resource depletion/savings, 3, 71, 99, 133, 220–1
Rio Tinto Zinc, 122
robot laws, 164–7
robot personhood, 166
RobotCub, 162
robots, 3, 4, 44, 52, 53, 72–4, 75, 76, 89, 98, 100, 135–69, 192, 199, 201, 206, 209, 211, 217, 218, 220–2
Robots of London, 154
Rogozin, Dmitry, 162
Romeo, 158–9
Rosenblatt, Frank, 94–5
routers, 34, 68
Royal Bank of Scotland, see RBS
Royal Free Hospital, 126

SaaS, 55, 56, 113
SAGE, 31
Salesforce, 55, 119, 133
Samsung, 104
Samuel, Arthur, 94, 98
Saverin, Eduardo, 39
SBOL, 85
SCARA, 150-1
Sears-Burroughs, William, 13
Seattle Computer Products, 28
Second Sight, 203–5
security robots, 141–2, 143, 146
Sedol, Lee, 99
self-assembly, 82, 86–8, 194, 195
sensors, 121, 167, 168
servers, 54, 60
sex robots, 147
SGI-DNA, 85, 190
Shannon, Claude, 93
sheet lamination, 78–9
silicon chips, *see* integrated circuits
Simon Personal Communicator, 42

Sinclair, 24–5
Singularity, the, 71–2, 73, 90
Siri, 2, 101, 105
smart homes, 68–9
smart speakers, 68–9, 103–5, 107, 109, 111, 120
smartphones, 42–3, 45, 68, 101, 102, 106–7, 196, 200, 202
smartwatches, 69
social networking, 39
Sodick, 80
SoftBank, 153–4, 158, 159, 167
solid logic technology, 19
Sony, 133
South Korea, 166
space travel, 201, 221–2
Spanish Inquisition, 215
spider goats, 84
spreadsheets, 24
SRI International, 101
Stanford Research Institute, 28
Stanford University, 191
Staples, 113
*Star Trek*, 65
*Star Wars*, 136, 146
StationQ, 182–4
Stock, Gregory, 49
Strachley, Christopher, 93–4
Stratasys, 79
structured data, 59
Superintelligence, 123–4
superpositions, 173–4, 193
Swarbrick, Guy, 30
Symbiotic, 138–9
symbolists (AI), 97
synthetic biology, 4, 5, 52, 53, 84–6, 87, 89, 100, 148, 169, 190, 195–6, 201, 209, 217, 218, 223
synthetic biology open language, *see* SBOL
synthetic cell, 84–5
System/360, 19

Tandy Corporation, 21
TCP/IP, 33, 34, 35
telepathy (digital), 46, 211, 220
Telex, 19
Temporal Defence Systems, 180
tensor processing units, *see* TPUs
TensorFlow, 117
*Terminator II*, 26
Tesco, 61
Tesla Motors, 121, 123
Texas Instruments, 18
text message (first), 41
Thinkpad, 26
tiered storage systems, 58
Timex, 24
Titus, John, 20
Tmall Genie, 105
TMS headsets, 205
Tomlinson, Ray, 32
topological quantum computing, 183, 200
Toshiba T5100, 25, 27
Toyota, 121
TPUs, 117–8
Tranhumanist Party, 213–4
transcriptors, 191
Transhuman Party Global, 214
transhumanism, 132, 213–15, 217, 218
*Tranhumanism: Toward a Futurist Philosophy*, 213
transhumanists, *see* transhumanism
transistors, 8, 16–18, 171–2, 174, 183, 188, 191, 200
Trojan horses, 120, 123
TRS-80, 21, 24, 28
Tucker, Patrick, 188
TUG, 142
Turing test, 91–2
Turing, Alan, 14, 91–2, 93–4
TX-0, 16

UAVs, 144, 145
Uber, 122
UBS Wealth Management, 104
UGVs, 144
UK Transhumanist Party, 214–5
Ultimaker 3D printer, 76, 77
ultrasonic additive manufacturing, 79
uncanny valley, 148
UNCTAD, 164
unemployment, *see* employment
Unimate, 137, 165
United Nations, 144, 164

# INDEX

UNIVAC1, 16
universal gate quantum computing, 176, 178, 200
universal Turing machine, 192, 196–7, 198, 199, 200–1, 209, 210, 211, 215, 217, 219
University College London, 31
University of Adelaide, 126–7
University of California, 141, 183
University of Illinois, 87
University of Manchester, 93, 193
University of Pennsylvania, 15
University of Pittsburgh, 206
University of Washington, 97, 205
University of Wyoming, 84
unstructured data, 59, 96, 109, 110
unstructured environments, 141, 146
US military, 14, 15, 144, 145, 188
UTM, *see* universal Turing machine, 192

vacuum tubes, 9, 15, 16
Valkyrie, 160, 161
valves, *see* vacuum tubes
vectors (gene editing), 209–10
Venter, J. Craig, 85
Verkasalo, Hannu, 106
vertical AI, 98
Verto Analytics, 106
very large scale integration, 20
VIC-20, 21–2, 24
virtual reality, 1, 52, 53, 65–6, 67, 89, 219–20
VisiCalc, 24
vision recognition, 94–5, 104,107–8, 110, 111, 113, 115, 116
Volkswagen, 121, 180
Volvo, 122
von Neuman, John, 15
VR, *see* virtual reality

Walking Assist Device, 149
Walmart, 61
WANs, 32

warehouse robots, 138–40, 146
Watson, 96, 112–14, 116, 126, 127
Watson, Thomas John, 13
Watson, Tom, 164
WaveLAN, 40
Waymo, 120
weak AI, 98
wearable computing, 69, 127
Web 2.0, 38–9
web browser (first), 37
wetware, *see* organic computing
Wi-Fi, 40-1, 46
wide area networks, *see* WANs
Willcocks, Leslie, 129
WIMP, 29
Windows, 30, 31, 36, 67, 101, 105
WinSun Decoration Design Engineering, 81
*Wired*, 120
wireless networking, 40–2
Wit.ai, 119
World Bank, 128, 164
world-wide web, 2–3, 36–9, 60
Wozniak, Steve, 20–1

Xchanging, 129
Xerox Alto, 29
Xerox PARC, 29, 32
Xiaomi, 105
Yang-hee, Choi, 166
YouTube, 39, 89, 153, 156

Z3, 13
Z4, 13
Z80, 21, 24
Zenbo, 146, 169
Zenith Data Systems, 26
Zielinski, Dina, 191–2
Zoho, 55
Zuckerberg, Mark, 39
Zuse, Konrad, 13–14
ZX Spectrum, 24
ZX80, 24
ZX81, 24–5

Printed in Poland
by Amazon Fulfillment
Poland Sp. z o.o., Wrocław